PRAISE FOR *AN INCO...*

'This book takes us back to those weeks when New Labour 'spin' seemed to generate its darkest, most frantic moments... Goslett argues convincingly that potentially important witnesses were not called and inconsistencies in evidence were left unexplored.'
Mail on Sunday

'Masterful... Goslett's forensic skills put the highly paid lawyer James Dingemans to shame.' **Daily Mail**

'This searing excavation of the mysterious death of Dr David Kelly is investigative journalism at its best. It is brave, relentless, dazzlingly revealing.' **Peter Oborne**

'Everyone, from Tony Blair downwards, was insistent that Dr Kelly had committed suicide yet the evidence, which Goslett examines in scrupulous detail in this ripping narrative, suggests otherwise.' **Richard Ingrams**

'A notable contribution to contemporary political history.' **Open Democracy**

'Goslett confines himself to the demand for an inquest, and his fine book eloquently spells out why all of us, including Dr Kelly's family, friends and colleagues,

deserve one', The Lobster

AN INCONVENIENT DEATH

MILES GOSLETT is an award-winning journalist. He has written for the *Sunday Telegraph*, *Sunday Times*, *Mail on Sunday*, *Daily Mail*, *Sun*, *The Oldie* and *Spectator*.

AN INCONVENIENT DEATH

HOW THE ESTABLISHMENT COVERED UP
THE DAVID KELLY AFFAIR

MILES GOSLETT

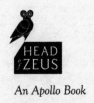

An Apollo Book

AN
INCONVENIENT
DEATH

This is an Apollo book, first published in the UK in 2018
by Head of Zeus Ltd
This paperback edition published in the UK in 2019
by Head of Zeus Ltd

9 7 5 3 1 2 4 6 8

A catalogue record for this book is available from
the British Library.

ISBN (PB): 9781788543118
ISBN (E): 9781788543088

Typeset by Adrian McLaughlin

Printed and bound in Great Britain by
CPI Group (UK) Ltd, Croydon CRO 4YY

Head of Zeus Ltd
First Floor East
5–8 Hardwick Street
London EC1R 4RG

WWW.HEADOFZEUS.COM

CONTENTS

INTRODUCTION

Shortly after 3 p.m. on Thursday, 17 July 2003, Dr David Kelly left his house in the Oxfordshire village of Southmoor to go for one of his regular short walks. He had changed into a pair of jeans, put his house key in his pocket, and tucked his mobile telephone into a pouch on his belt – the routine actions of a man preparing to do something he had done many times before.

His wife, Janice, had retired to bed two hours earlier because she felt unwell. He didn't say goodbye to her or leave a note.

Within fifteen minutes of setting off, he bumped into a neighbour who was walking her dog. They exchanged a few pleasant, unremarkable words. She then saw him stroll down the road as she turned for home. She was the last person known to have seen Dr Kelly alive.

Back at the house, Mrs Kelly had recovered sufficiently to go downstairs. When her husband failed to return after a couple of hours she began to feel some unease, but she did not try to ring his mobile phone. Instead, she waited until she was able to share her growing concerns regarding his whereabouts with her youngest daughter, Rachel, who had arranged to meet her father that evening so that they could go for a walk together.

On hearing the news, Rachel decided the situation warranted some kind of action. First on foot and then in her car, she began tracing the routes that she knew Dr Kelly habitually took. She also contacted her sisters, one of whom was prompted by Rachel's call to drive seventy miles from her house in Hampshire to join in what was still just a family search. Despite hours of looking, neither daughter found him.

At 11 p.m. the two women went back to their parents' house and, with their mother, debated what to do next. Shortly before midnight, they decided they must contact the police to report him missing. By this point, Dr Kelly had not been seen for almost nine hours.

This was the relatively low-key start to an overnight hunt that would involve more than forty police officers, a police dog, a police helicopter, plus some volunteer searchers, with a mounted police unit and an underwater police search team also being called upon. In the early hours, Metropolitan Police officers from Special Branch were told to search Dr Kelly's London office, and senior figures in Whitehall were alerted to his disappearance.

Such an operation, launched so quickly, might have been expected for a top public figure, but Dr Kelly was – officially, at least – a mere civil servant.

Just after 9 a.m. on Friday, 18 July, two volunteer searchers helping the police found a body matching the description of David Kelly in a wood at Harrowdown Hill, about two miles from his house.

At the time the Prime Minister, Tony Blair, was on a plane travelling between Washington DC and Tokyo. The Lord Chancellor, Charles Falconer, who was in London, rang Blair on the aircraft's phone within minutes of the body being found and in a surprisingly brief call was instructed to set in motion a full-blown public inquiry into Dr Kelly's death.

Falconer established this inquiry several hours before any exact cause of Dr Kelly's death had been determined officially – and, indeed, before the body found that morning had even been formally identified.

What could possibly have led Falconer and Blair, the two most senior political figures of the day, to take this unusual step on the basis of what, according to contemporaneous police reports, appeared to be a tragic case of a professional man ending his own life? Why were they even involved at such an early stage in what was essentially an incident that was local to Oxfordshire?

What was it about the death of David Kelly that had disturbed Falconer and Blair so much that they went on to interrupt and ultimately to derail the coroner's inquest, which had been opened routinely? And why were they content to replace that inquest with a less rigorous form of investigation into Dr Kelly's death?

These questions preoccupied me, as a journalist, for years. They pointed to powerful forces working against the proper investigation of an unexpected event – in this case, a death mired in mystery.

Then, on 5 November 2014, I heard that a senior civil servant working in the Ministry of Justice had written an extraordinary letter to a man called Gerrard Jonas, a garage owner from Oxfordshire, urging him to stay away from Dr Kelly's grave. The letter noted that Mr Jonas had been visiting the grave at St Mary's churchyard in the nearby village of Longworth and, in a thinly veiled threat, advised him to 'carefully consider' whether this 'programme is appropriate and lawful'. It went on to say that a surveillance 'watch' had been put on the grave as a result of Mr Jonas's visits, though this point was worded ambiguously enough for it to remain unclear who had ordered the watch and how it was being policed. The letter was signed Barrie Thurlow, of the Ministry of Justice Coroners, Burial, Cremation and Inquiries Policy Team.

The tone of the letter certainly supported the idea that a Whitehall department and, maybe, others in officialdom still felt great sensitivity about Dr Kelly's death, which had occurred more than eleven years previously. Its clear inference was that Dr Kelly's grave was being monitored, perhaps by an arm of the State.

Mr Jonas – whom I did not know – sent me a copy of it and, being aware of my interest in the Kelly case, later rang me to explain the background to it. He said he had never met or spoken to Dr Kelly or his family; he had simply believed for many years that for reasons of public interest there should be a full coroner's inquest into Dr Kelly's death to establish how, where and when he had died – something which successive governments have refused to allow.

To that end he had set up a group, Justice For Kelly, and on behalf of its members had written to the then Home Secretary, Theresa May, asking her to consider ordering an inquest. Mrs May had passed Mr Jonas's letter on to the Ministry of Justice. Its representative, Barrie Thurlow, had replied to Mr Jonas because it was felt that the matter in question fell under his department's remit.

In his original letter to the Home Secretary, Mr Jonas had mentioned his self-appointed role as the maintainer of Dr Kelly's grave, which he believed had fallen into rather a sorry condition. In mid-2014 he had begun to weed it and to leave flowers on it occasionally. The result of Mr Jonas's declaration to the Home Secretary about his grave-tending activities was the Ministry of Justice's faintly menacing reply.

The ministry's letter also claimed that Dr Kelly's family had complained of 'interference' at the grave. Mr Jonas told me that he had erected a placard near it to mark the eleventh anniversary of Dr Kelly's death in July 2014. If Dr Kelly's family found out about this particular incident at the time, presumably it had upset them, for understandable reasons: most people would not be happy for a relative's resting place to become a site of protest. At about the same time, some flowers Mr Jonas had left on Dr Kelly's grave were removed. In their place was an anonymous note requesting that Mr Jonas stop tending it. He replied to the individual who left him the note in what he now admits was an inappropriately flippant way – by leaving a bottle of champagne on the grave and telling whoever had left the note that he hoped they might 'choke' on it for having removed the flowers. In his defence, Mr Jonas made no attempt to conceal his identity: he left his name and telephone number on his note and was deliberately provocative, precisely because he wanted to speak to whom-ever had objected to his grave-tending. Needless to say, the champagne disappeared, but nobody ever rang him.

And so Mr Jonas continued at intervals to look after the grave as an act of, in his words, 'civic duty' – even though officers from Thames Valley Police have made their presence felt in his life periodically, once calling on him at home unannounced late at night and also pulling him over to check his van when he was driving in Oxfordshire.

Regardless of Mr Jonas's actions, it seemed odd that the Ministry of Justice should have involved itself in what was little more than a local squabble. It also seemed surprising that Dr Kelly's grave was in a bad way. Having seen it several years earlier, in 2010, I know that it appeared rather neglected at that time. Mourning being an entirely private matter, Dr Kelly's family may have stopped visiting the grave, if indeed they were ever in the habit of doing so. But why would an official from the Ministry of Justice go to the trouble of, effectively, intimidating Mr Jonas by letter, especially when he had been so open about his activities?

When I read the letter, in one sense I was greatly surprised. Is it really the job of a government department to scare off a member of the public and talk about Dr Kelly's grave being monitored without explaining why this was necessary? And yet at the same time it came as no surprise at all. In sending the letter, another barbed-wire fence had effectively been erected around the topic of the Dr Kelly affair in order to keep the public away.

This had plenty of precedents. Minimizing the risk of anybody scrutinizing anything to do with Dr Kelly seems to have been a preoccupation of the State ever since he left his house on 17 July 2003 and was never seen alive again.

Since 2003, contradictions and peculiarities connected to Dr Kelly's death have emerged at every other turn, pointing to the idea that for some reason this hugely significant – and tragic – event was never investigated exhaustively, and certain details about it were simply withheld from the public.

In January 2010 I learned that, shortly after Dr Kelly's death six and a half years earlier, Lord Hutton, the Law Lord who had chaired the public inquiry into Dr Kelly's death, had secretly recommended that all medical and scientific records relating to him, plus photographs of his body, should be classified for seventy years. Hutton also advised the classification for thirty years of witness statements provided to his inquiry which were not disclosed at the time of his hearings.

It is highly unusual that these records should have been locked up by the State for so long, but somehow even more suspicious that the embargo had itself been carried out without anyone knowing. The burial of this key information, never aired in public, had itself been buried. It is thanks only to an accidental revelation by a local government official that anybody knows about it. That fact made me reflect on what else about Dr Kelly's death the public might be unaware of since it occurred. Plenty of new material has surfaced.

Thanks to Freedom of Information responses provided by Thames Valley Police to various people over a prolonged period of time, it is known that there were no fingerprints on the knife he allegedly used to kill himself or on some of the items found beside his body: a water bottle; some empty pill packets; a watch; a pair of glasses and a mobile phone. And yet when his body was discovered he wore no gloves. This lack of prints was never even mentioned at the Hutton Inquiry. Then there is the startling matter of the apparent theft of Dr Kelly's dental records from his dentist's surgery in Abingdon. Who took the records; when did they do so; why did they want them; and why did a senior police officer give inaccurate details about this to the Hutton Inquiry?

Among other urgent questions that remain unaddressed are why a factually contentious death certificate for Dr Kelly has been produced; why incomplete evidence concerning his whereabouts during the last week of his life was given to the Hutton Inquiry; why certain key witnesses were not called to give evidence to the Hutton Inquiry; and why a police search helicopter with thermal imagining equipment which flew over the wood where his body was found did not detect his body – despite the fact that his body temperature was warm enough at the time to register on the helicopter's search system.

It is clear that the Hutton Inquiry was an inadequate substitute for a coroner's inquest into Dr Kelly's death. It raised more questions than it answered. This book sets out to examine those questions, which have never been dealt with satisfactorily.

PART 1

LIFE AND DEATH

THE £4.15 SCOOP

At teatime on 22 May 2003, a quietly spoken government scientist with virtually no public profile walked into the Charing Cross Hotel in central London for a meeting that would lead to his death exactly eight weeks later. His name was Dr David Kelly and his rendezvous was with Andrew Gilligan, the defence correspondent of BBC Radio 4's *Today* programme.

Gilligan was regarded as a faintly unorthodox journalist not afraid to ask awkward questions of those in power. He was also a bit of a loner, known for keeping strange hours, who was rarely seen in his office at BBC Television Centre in west London. He had read History at Cambridge and his reporting skills were sufficiently highly prized for him to have been poached by the BBC from *The Sunday Telegraph* a few years earlier. Although only thirty-four, he looked older thanks to being prematurely bald.

Gilligan and Dr Kelly had known each other since 2001. They had met twice previously, but they were not close. Their third – and what turned out to be final – encounter was initiated by Gilligan and was intended as nothing more than a routine chat between a journalist and his contact, on this occasion about Iraq. American and British forces had invaded the country two months earlier and by that stage occupied much of it.

Dr Kelly had risen from relatively humble origins in Wales, where he was born in 1944, and was brought up by his mother and grandmother after his parents divorced to become one of the world's pre-eminent experts in the field of chemical and biological weapons. This meant he had spent long periods during the previous decade working for UNSCOM – the United Nations Special Commission – as a weapons inspector in Iraq. He had visited the country thirty-seven times.

His career route to this dangerous world began in 1973, when, aged twenty-nine, he became a senior scientific officer at the Unit of Invertebrate Virology at the National Environment Research Establishment. From 1984 he worked at Porton Down, the secretive Ministry of Defence chemical research unit near Salisbury, where he led experiments in how to defend troops in battle against biological warfare. In 1989 he became a technical expert in assessing germ warfare data coming out of the Soviet Union. From the early 1990s he had taken part in foreign weapons inspection programmes, working for both the Ministry of Defence and the Foreign Office, as well as briefing MI6. He had been a senior adviser to the United Nations Special Commission since 1995 and is also believed to have worked undercover for the intelligence services.

Among Dr Kelly's most significant achievements was his lead role in an inspection mission in Iraq in the mid-1990s which forced the country to admit to having a biological warfare programme. For this, in the Queen's birthday honours list in 1996, he was awarded the Companion of the Most Distinguished Order of St Michael and St George (CMG), which ranks just below a knighthood. The citation referred to his contribution to the UK's biological warfare defence programme and the success of his inspection duties in Iraq.

As well as being one of the leading chemical and biological experts in the world, he was also the husband of thirty-five years of Janice, a retired teacher, and father of three grown-up daughters, one of whom, Rachel, was about to get married. Bearded, avuncular, hard-working, with a sense of humour and varied interests, he had many friends and had clearly made a success of his professional life.

Given the defence brief Gilligan covered, Dr Kelly was

certainly a very useful source, but in no way did he 'belong' to the reporter exclusively: Dr Kelly was working for the Ministry of Defence and often spoke to journalists from all over the world who were interested in his area of expertise. Indeed, his name and telephone number had been in the BBC's central database of contacts since 1988 and it was not unusual for him to be quoted in news reports.

Gilligan had recently returned from Iraq, from where he had filed reports for the BBC about the West's invasion of the country, and Dr Kelly was curious to hear what he had learned while there.

If the meeting had a specific purpose as far as Gilligan was concerned, it was to establish from Dr Kelly why he thought no weapons of mass destruction had been found in Iraq. The ability of the Iraqi dictator, Saddam Hussein, to deploy such an arsenal at forty-five minutes' notice had for months been cited by Tony Blair's government as the chief reason for the invasion on 20 March, but no weapons store had ever been found.

They sat down shortly after 4 p.m. Having ordered a Coca-Cola and an Appletise, the two men spoke on an unattributable basis for about an hour, with Gilligan taking notes on his electronic personal organizer after Dr Kelly agreed that he was happy for him to do so.

According to Gilligan, as the conversation progressed Dr Kelly told him that, in his opinion, Iraq continued to pose a potential threat to the West and might still possess weapons of mass destruction. Gilligan's notes recorded that Dr Kelly was even prepared to speculate on this possibility in percentage terms, with the likelihood of the existence of weapons being, apparently, up to '30 per cent'.

However, Dr Kelly allegedly then went on to tell Gilligan that there was considerable unease within the intelligence services about the accuracy of a dossier which had been published by the British government on 24 September 2002. Titled *Iraq's Weapons of Mass Destruction, the Assessment of the British Government*, it had been used to sell the case of the need for military action in Iraq. It was in this document that the infamous 'forty-five-minute' claim was first made.

Dr Kelly told Gilligan that he had had some involvement in the production of this dossier, writing the sections on the history of UN inspections and about Iraq's weapons programmes over the previous three decades, from 1971 to 1998. But he had had nothing to do with the dossier's central claim – clearly stated four times, including in the Foreword written by the Prime Minister, Tony Blair – that Iraq could deploy chemical and nuclear weapons within 'forty-five minutes'. This terrifying 'fact' had been duly splashed on the front pages of some newspapers. For example, the day after publication, 25 September 2002, *The Sun* informed its three million readers:

'BRITS 45 MINS FROM DOOM'

From a public relations perspective, the dossier was a success for the British government. There could not have been a more effective way of ratcheting up the tension and, by extension, increasing the likelihood of gaining public support for military action in Iraq. And yet here was Dr Kelly, a man who commanded worldwide respect in biological weapons matters, apparently suggesting to Gilligan that the 'forty-five-minute' claim had been included against the wishes of the experts who drew up the dossier.

Among Gilligan's contemporaneous electronic notes from the now-infamous Charing Cross Hotel meeting are the following: '[Dossier] transformed week before publication to make it sexier... The classic was the forty-five minutes... Most people in intelligence weren't happy with it because it didn't reflect the considered view they were putting forward.' There is also a reference to 'Campbell', and then 'not in original draft – dull, he asked if anything else could go in'. The 'Campbell' referred to was Alastair Campbell, Tony Blair's spin doctor. According to Gilligan, Dr Kelly apparently told him that Campbell had been personally involved in the transformation of the September dossier.

Without question, Dr Kelly had handed Gilligan a potential scoop, and one that had cost just £4.15, the price of the two soft drinks they had ordered. If it was true, it was extraordinary to think that Downing Street officials

– including Campbell, a former *Daily Mirror* journalist with no military or intelligence background whatsoever – had deliberately exaggerated the threat posed by Iraq to the West in order to justify going to war.

It was also a fascinating insight into how Tony Blair's government operated that fell squarely within the public interest.

After they parted company, an understandably excited Gilligan immediately carried out some checks in an attempt to corroborate what he had been told. These included analysing the September 2002 dossier itself. Officially, it had been produced by the Joint Intelligence Committee (JIC), the arm of the Cabinet Office which oversees intelligence and security matters. Gilligan knew his way around some of the earlier JIC assessments on weapons of mass destruction and in his view the language used in the September dossier did indeed appear to be far more definite than usual.

He also spoke to other contacts and went through a series of newspaper cuttings, discovering that references to the much-vaunted forty-five-minute claim had virtually disappeared from government speeches made in the months after publication of the September dossier and before the outbreak of war. Indeed, it had not been mentioned specifically by Blair during his eve-of-war speech to MPs in the House of Commons on 18 March 2003. It looked as though the government might well have had second thoughts about the wisdom of committing itself so firmly to the idea and quietly dropped it.

Despite encouragement from people who worked in and around intelligence that he was on to something, Gilligan has said he was unable to find a second source to back up exactly what Dr Kelly told him that day. Everything which Gilligan could find out independently indicated that Dr Kelly was right to doubt the forty-five-minute claim, however, and the reporter was able to satisfy his Radio 4 *Today* programme editor, Kevin Marsh, of this. In fact Marsh himself had heard from two separate sources – Cabinet Minister Clare Short and a senior intelligence contact of his own – opinions which clearly echoed what Dr Kelly had said.

Also at the front of the BBC journalists' minds would have been the dramatic resignation of Labour MP Robin Cook, the Leader of the House and former Foreign Secretary. He had quit the government immediately before the Iraq invasion because he did not believe, as the administration of which he had been a member had claimed, that the country had a stock of weapons of mass destruction.

With Marsh's backing, Gilligan was given clearance to run his report on the *Today* programme on 29 May, exactly one week after the Charing Cross Hotel meeting. That morning at 6.07, in a live, unscripted preview 'teaser' summary aired eighty minutes before his main *Today* report, Gilligan unwittingly fired the starting gun on the series of events which ultimately culminated in Dr Kelly's death. Most memorably, Gilligan said on air:

> What we've been told by one of the senior officials in charge of drawing up that [September 2002] dossier was that actually the government probably knew that that forty-five-minute figure was wrong even before it decided to put it in. What this person says is that a week before the publication date of the dossier it was actually rather a bland production. It didn't – the draft prepared for Mr Blair by the intelligence agencies – actually didn't say very much more than was public knowledge already and Downing Street, our source says, ordered it to be sexed up, to be made more exciting, and ordered more facts to be discovered.

For some reason, in this live, unscripted broadcast Gilligan had changed the story agreed the night before between himself and his team of editors and producers at *Today* by inserting the allegation that 'the government probably knew that that forty-five-minute figure was wrong even before it decided to put it in'. This was a significant upgrade from the original assertion he had been expected by his BBC bosses to make, which was simply that 'the intelligence agencies... didn't necessarily believe the claim'.

Furthermore, originally Gilligan had been expected by his bosses to say that the official to whom he had spoken had merely been 'involved' in the dossier. In the unscripted broadcast, this assertion was elevated to the official having been one of those 'in charge of drawing [it] up'.

Neither of these claims was ever repeated again in any BBC bulletin, either on radio or television, but the damage was done: these words became central to the ensuing scandal and their consequences are likely to be associated with Gilligan for the rest of his life.

CAMPBELL COUNTERATTACKS

Perhaps surprisingly, given its content, Gilligan's 6.07 a.m. broadcast caused little more than a ripple in the first instance. A Downing Street press officer called Anne Shevas made a written complaint to the *Today* programme on the day of the broadcast, grumbling that it had not reported sufficiently the government's denial of Gilligan's allegations. That was the only official reaction it generated at the time.

Three days later, on 1 June, *The Mail on Sunday* published an article written by Gilligan which was based on his BBC report. This newspaper piece differed in one significant respect from that report because it claimed that Gilligan's source had specifically named Alastair

Campbell as the person who had ordered the September dossier to be 'sexed up'. Indeed, the name 'Campbell' was written in capital letters in the newspaper's headline. When Gilligan had spoken on the *Today* programme, he had not mentioned Campbell by name.

It was well known among journalists that Campbell did not like the cut of Gilligan's jib and considered him a trouble-maker. On that basis alone, Campbell was unlikely to let this accusation pass. But what Gilligan had suggested first on the BBC and then in greater detail in *The Mail on Sunday* was of major international significance. It was career-threatening for all concerned if substantiated.

On 6 June, eight days after Gilligan's original broadcast, Campbell sent the BBC a four-page letter complaining that Gilligan had broken the Corporation's own guidelines by relying on a single source – as opposed to multiple sources – for his 6.07 a.m. broadcast. Campbell also claimed that Gilligan did not understand the role of the JIC. The BBC's lawyers batted this away in a written response on 11 June, but the next day Campbell returned to the attack, essentially repeating his earlier complaint. Correspondence continued until 16 June, at which point the row seemed to have faded away.

A few days later things changed for Campbell, however, and the dispute over Gilligan's broadcast was reignited. This was because two weeks earlier, on 3 June, Campbell had been asked to give evidence to the Foreign Affairs select committee (FAC), which had recently begun an inquiry into the decision to go to war with Iraq. He had refused the invitation.

Part of the committee's inquiry concerned a second Iraq dossier, which had appeared a few months after the notorious September dossier containing the dubious forty-five-minute claim. This second dossier, published under the direction of Campbell in February 2003, was seen by some as a further attempt to strengthen the government's case for going to war.

But the second dossier quickly became known as the 'dodgy dossier' after it emerged that Campbell's staff had lifted much of the material it contained from the internet – complete with grammatical errors – and presented it as their own careful research and analysis.

This largely plagiarized piece of work was an adaptation of an essay written by a Dr Ibrahim al-Marashi and had originally been published in the *Middle East Review of International Affairs* in 2002. Dr al-Marashi was a research associate at the Center for Nonproliferation Studies in Monterey, California. Without his knowledge, his text was turned into the February dossier overseen by Campbell and titled, somewhat ironically under the circumstances in which it was produced, 'Iraq: Its Infrastructure of Concealment, Deception and Intimidation'.

Channel 4 News had broken the plagiarism story on 6 February 2003; Campbell was utterly humiliated.

Criticism of Campbell was mounting over this incredible blunder, and a second invitation was issued to him by the FAC. Snubbing the FAC twice in the space of a few weeks was considered a serious breach of parliamentary etiquette, and he was forced to accept, agreeing to give evidence on 25 June.

Gilligan had already given evidence to the FAC the week before, on 19 June. When he had been asked by the committee about his single source, all he would reveal was that the person was 'one of the senior officials in charge of drawing up the dossier'. He added: 'I can tell you that he is a source of long standing, well known to me, closely connected with the question of Iraq's weapons of mass destruction, easily sufficiently senior and credible to be worth reporting.'

During his evidence session the following week Campbell put in what was widely seen as a rather hysterical performance. He used the three hours available to him largely for his own ends, admitting the central charge that February's 'dodgy dossier' was indeed unreliable, but devoting most of the session to lambasting the BBC for what he saw as its false reporting of the Iraq issue. Campbell also claimed, on thin evidence, that the BBC had suggested Tony Blair was a liar.

In his 2004 book *Inside Story*, ex-BBC Director-General Greg Dyke wrote: 'It is clear that the whole attack on the BBC from Campbell [at the FAC hearing] was a means of diverting attention away from the "dodgy dossier" and the disgraceful way he and his team had produced it.' Dyke added that Campbell 'wanted a public bust-up for political reasons'.

Campbell had apparently calculated that the reporters watching him give evidence to the FAC would be far more likely to latch onto the distracting new row he was advancing – that the BBC had it in for Downing Street and the Prime Minister – and far less likely to spend time picking over the bones of the older argument relating to the 'dodgy dossier'. His instinct was right.

Raising his voice theatrically, Campbell told the FAC: 'I simply say, in relation to the BBC story, it is a lie... that is continually repeated, and until we get an apology for it I will keep making sure that Parliament and people like yourselves know that it was a lie.'

Campbell's private diary entry for that day recorded his satisfaction at what he had said at the FAC hearing. He wrote: 'I felt a lot better. Flank opened on the BBC.' Little did he know that the fight for which he was spoiling would end with the death of Dr Kelly only three weeks later.

THE UNMASKING OF DR KELLY

On 26 June, the day after the FAC hearing, Campbell stepped up his campaign against the BBC with another long letter to its Director of News, Richard Sambrook, this time demanding immediate answers to twelve questions. Question three was: 'Does [the BBC] still stand by the allegation made on that day [29 May by Gilligan] that both we and the intelligence agencies knew the forty-five-minute claim to be wrong and inserted it despite knowing that? Yes or no?'

Provocatively, Campbell shared his letter with the press as a way of forcing the BBC's hand. The BBC responded rapidly, standing by Gilligan and the story, but Campbell was so aggravated by the BBC's refusal to apologize for its general coverage of the Iraq issue that he carried on with his war of attrition. His diary entry for 26 June even notes that he wanted to 'nail Gilligan completely'.

The next day, Friday, 27 June, Campbell took his adolescent son Calum, plus a friend of Calum's, to watch the tennis at Wimbledon, but his mind was clearly on other matters. This explains why in the late afternoon he left them to make their own way home while he went unexpectedly to the studios of Channel 4 News in central London shortly before its evening bulletin began at 7 to give an interview to the programme's presenter, Jon Snow. Such was Campbell's status as Blair's spin doctor at the time, he was able to secure this right of audience at short notice.

He was in an excitable state, and insisted live on air to Snow that the BBC 'just accept for once they have got it wrong' [about Gilligan's claim on the *Today* programme].

During the ten-minute interview he also said the BBC had 'not a shred of evidence to substantiate the allegation' [made in Gilligan's *Today* broadcast]. Again, he demanded an apology.

This hastily arranged encounter bore all the hallmarks of a man obsessed. Even Campbell's long-term girlfriend, Fiona Millar, privately criticized his Channel 4 News performance afterwards. But he would still not let the matter drop.

Parallel arguments were developing: the BBC's interest was moving in the direction of asking whether there really were any weapons of mass destruction in Iraq; Campbell's interest seemed to lie in painting Gilligan as an unreliable young journalist and the BBC as a partial broadcaster.

Campbell's Friday-night showdown with Jon Snow guaranteed further coverage of the row in the weekend papers, and by Monday, 30 June pressure surrounding the story was still intensifying. Now, though, the media's attention was turning to the identity of Gilligan's source.

Realizing that the temperature was rising, on 30 June Dr Kelly volunteered his involvement in the row in a private letter to Dr Bryan Wells, his line manager at the Ministry of Defence. With the benefit of hindsight this was, at best, ill advised. Dr Kelly cannot have realized that by doing so he was entering a lion's den.

Dr Kelly revealed to Wells that he had met Gilligan the previous month and discussed the forty-five-minute claim.

His letter said that he had told Gilligan the claim was there for 'impact'. But he did not endorse the suggestion about Campbell's involvement, saying that Gilligan had mentioned Campbell's name first, rather than him feeding it to the reporter. In his written clarification, Dr Kelly also categorically denied having alleged that Campbell had exaggerated the September dossier. He said his conversation with Gilligan about Campbell was 'essentially an aside'. Dr Kelly wrote:

> I did not even consider that I was the 'source' of Gilligan's information until a friend in RUSI [the Royal United Services Institute think-tank] said that I should look at [Gilligan's] oral evidence provided to the Foreign Affairs Committee on 19th June because she recognised that some comments were the sort that I would make about Iraq's chemical and biological capacity. The description of that meeting in small part matches my interaction with him, especially my personal evaluation of Iraq's capability, but the overall character is quite different. I can only conclude one of three things. Gilligan has considerably embellished my meeting with him; he has met with other individuals who truly were intimately associated with the dossier; or he has assembled comments from both multiple direct and indirect sources for his articles.

Dr Kelly's letter was passed to Sir Kevin Tebbit, the MoD's most senior civil servant and Dr Kelly's ultimate boss. He requested that Dr Kelly be interviewed by Bryan Wells and Richard Hatfield, the MoD's Personnel Director.

On 3 July, after a two-hour conversation with Dr Kelly, Wells and Hatfield decided that he was not the source of the most serious allegations advanced by Gilligan relating to Campbell and the forty-five-minute claim. They also decided he would face no penalty despite, as they saw it, his having broken departmental guidelines by speaking to a journalist without seeking the necessary authorization. (In fact, Dr Kelly's terms of employment did not forbid him from having discussions with reporters.) Bolted onto the MoD's conclusion, however, was the condition that a fuller inquiry into Dr Kelly's conduct could be launched if new information came to light.

Tony Blair and his Defence Secretary, Geoff Hoon, were both told that day that an official had come forward to admit having spoken to Gilligan. Blair and Hoon were apparently not given Dr Kelly's name at this stage but John Scarlett, the Chairman of the JIC and the government's chief intelligence adviser, was told it.

Inevitably, newspaper reporters were still on the case. On 5 July Tom Baldwin, then a reporter on *The Times*, wrote a story which dropped heavy hints as to the identity of Gilligan's source. Who can say where his information came from? It remains unclear who knew Dr Kelly's identity at this point.

With what seem to be good intentions, Sir Kevin Tebbit warned Downing Street that Dr Kelly was in danger of being compromised, so on Monday, 7 July Scarlett suggested that Dr Kelly should take part in 'a proper security-style interview' to find out if he really was Gilligan's only source. It was agreed at a meeting chaired by Tony Blair that day that the interview of Dr Kelly would go ahead.

Far from receding, after his admission to Bryan Wells a week earlier the seriousness of the situation was growing for Dr Kelly. On 7 July he was at RAF Honington in Suffolk on a training course in preparation for a forthcoming trip to Iraq where, ironically, he was intending to carry on searching for weapons of mass destruction. He was told to be in the London office of Richard Hatfield by 4 p.m.

During this interview, Dr Kelly reportedly said that he 'might have been led on' by Gilligan. Four days after initially clearing him, the MoD then decided that Dr Kelly probably had been Gilligan's source, but that Gilligan might have exaggerated what he had been told. In effect, Dr Kelly was found half guilty, but again the official decision was that no action would be taken against him.

Dr Kelly was also advised that it was likely that the press would persist in wanting to know who had briefed Gilligan ahead of his BBC broadcast, however, and therefore that his name might come out.

Alastair Campbell was clearly rampantly keen on the idea of Gilligan's source being identified as is evidenced by his diary entry for 4 July – three days before Dr Kelly was re-interviewed. It noted that Geoff Hoon told him that day that a possible source had come forward. Campbell did not name Dr Kelly in his diary and, officially, he did not know his identity, but he appears to have known what he did for a living because he described the source as 'an expert rather than a spy or full-time MoD official'. The source's comparatively lowly status as a mere expert and not a spy would, Campbell believed, reflect badly on the credibility of Gilligan's story. Campbell's perception was that Gilligan's source was simply not high up enough to know exactly what he was talking about. Indeed, with what seems considerable force, the spin doctor wrote that he and Hoon 'agreed that it would fuck Gilligan if that was his source.'

It is also possible that he wrote this sentence in his diary with a sense of triumph or relief, for it would have been disastrous for the government if Gilligan's real source had turned out to be someone very senior such as, say, Robin Cook, the former Foreign Secretary.

Campbell's personal animosity towards Gilligan seemed to have infected his professional judgement to such a degree that he would be happy to use Gilligan's source in whatever way necessary for victory in his clash with the BBC. And his diary entry for 6 July confirmed that he did view the situation in combative terms, in that he wrote that he was lusting after 'a clear win not a messy draw'.

On 8 July another news story about the affair appeared in *The Times*, again written by Tom Baldwin, revealing more details about Dr Kelly's identity but still falling short of naming him. His perceived status as just an 'expert' was being held up as a reason to cast doubt on Gilligan's claim.

That morning's papers also carried the news that the FAC had cleared Campbell of exerting 'improper influence' in the drafting of the September 2002 dossier, which claimed that Iraq's chemical and biological weapons could be launched at forty-five minutes' notice. Campbell was off the hook, though many in Westminster found the committee's decision convenient because Labour MP and committee Chairman Donald Anderson had had the casting vote in clearing him.

On the afternoon of 8 July the Ministry of Defence published a press release, with Dr Kelly's agreement, confirming only that an individual had come forward and admitted to being Gilligan's source. It did not name Dr Kelly, and Dr Kelly never sanctioned the release of his name. A short time afterwards, however, the MoD press office was instructed by officials to confirm Dr Kelly's identity to any journalist who guessed it correctly. Dr Kelly was unaware of this astonishing breach of the agreement he had understood he and the MoD had reached.

The meeting at which the decision was taken for this 'name game' to go ahead was chaired by Tony Blair in Downing Street on 8 July. Dr Kelly had no idea that he was at risk of identification, but the rules of the game allowed journalists an unlimited number of guesses, and a crib sheet with biographical information about Dr Kelly was even prepared for the MoD press office to assist any reporter who rang in with a question.

The government was helping reporters hungry for the hottest story in Westminster at the time but, crucially, in such a way as to allow anyone involved at an official level to claim that, technically, the government had not actively provided Dr Kelly's name to the press.

At 5.30 p.m. on 9 July James Blitz, a *Financial Times* reporter, was the first to guess Dr Kelly's name correctly. Not long after, *The Times* followed suit.

AN EARLY VISITOR

As Fleet Street's political correspondents were trying to work out what Gilligan's source was called, *Sunday Times* reporter Nick Rufford set off from London by car for the village of Southmoor, near Abingdon, to call on Dr Kelly at home.

At this point in his career Rufford, a respected journalist who has worked on the newspaper since 1987, mainly wrote stories about the world of intelligence. Dr Kelly was a trusted contact and source who had been furnishing him with reliable information since 1997. The pair had met by arrangement at least twenty times previously, either for lunch in Dr Kelly's local pub, or at Dr Kelly's house, or at restaurants in London. They had also spoken by telephone fairly frequently and exchanged emails. Their professional relationship was nothing if not friendly.

On this occasion, however, the purpose of Rufford's visit was entirely different to previous encounters. Not only was it unannounced, but the story on which he was working was about Dr Kelly himself – specifically whether he was the source of Gilligan's recent Radio 4 broadcast alleging that the British government had taken the country to war with Iraq on the basis of a lie.

No doubt having read the reports in *The Times* written by Tom Baldwin, Rufford speculated that Dr Kelly might be at the centre of the political skirmish by being Gilligan's source. To his mind, the seventy-mile trip to the Oxfordshire countryside which he made that afternoon was by no means a fishing expedition.

In fact, earlier in the day Rufford had tried to test his theory via the less awkward method of contacting Dr Kelly at home by telephone, to no avail. When he rang, the phone was answered by Dr Kelly's wife, Janice, who told him her husband was working in London. So, having discussed it with his news editor, Charles Hymas, Rufford decided to turn up in person unannounced at Dr Kelly's house, estimating that by the time he got there Dr Kelly would have returned.

On arrival in Southmoor at about 7.30 p.m. he parked in the Waggon and Horses pub car park. It was directly opposite Dr Kelly's house, an attractive five-bedroom Victorian property set in half an acre which reflected Dr Kelly's steady but financially unremarkable three-decade civil service career. Between 1997 and 2000, the Ministry of Defence failed to give Dr Kelly an annual salary rise, meaning he remained on only £51,071 – hardly the sort of money befitting a man of his stature and reputation. In 2003, months before he died, his pay was finally increased to £63,496 – but only because Dr Kelly had complained more than once.

As he got out of his car Rufford saw Dr Kelly standing in his driveway. He waved. Dr Kelly acknowledged him and waited while Rufford crossed the A-road that separated them. They began to chat while Janice Kelly was some distance away watering flowers. She was aware of Rufford's arrival but played no part in their ensuing conversation and was, by her own admission, unable to hear much of it.

Dr Kelly volunteered to Rufford that he had just been updated on the consequences of the 'name game' that MoD officials had decided to play. He said he had been contacted by the MoD and told that he would be named as Gilligan's source in national newspapers the following day. This put Rufford in a frustrating position familiar to many Sunday newspapermen: he was a reporter who couldn't report. He had some rights to the scoop but, as it was only Wednesday, he was going to be beaten to the punch by the daily papers.

The MoD – acting under orders from Downing Street – had taken the very unusual step of throwing Dr Kelly to the wolves by thrusting him into the limelight against his will. His name would be plastered all over Thursday's papers as the man at the centre of the row, likely leaving the Sunday titles no more than some scraps three days later.

This was bad news for Rufford professionally but, showing some genuine concern for Dr Kelly, and calculating that he could perhaps persuade him to write about the row in the next edition of *The Sunday Times*, he kept the conversation going.

He asked Dr Kelly whether the MoD had offered him advice and support, or whether they had volunteered to send anybody to be with him. He also asked whether the department had advised him to leave home and stay with friends or in a hotel. On hearing that no such advice had been given, Rufford told Dr Kelly that *The Sunday Times* could help by finding him a hotel if need be.

Dr Kelly asked Rufford what, in his experienced opinion, might happen next. The unpalatable answer Rufford supplied was that he was likely to be besieged by reporters. Unsurprisingly, Dr Kelly looked perplexed at the prospect.

Rufford then took the opportunity to ask Dr Kelly about his contact with Gilligan. Dr Kelly confirmed he had met the BBC journalist at the Charing Cross Hotel in May and, when Rufford asked him whether their conversation had been reported accurately in subsequent media coverage up to that point, replied: 'I talked to him about factual stuff, the rest is bullshit.'

Rufford was surprised by this uncharacteristic choice of language. It surely indicated the anger and stress which Dr Kelly felt – and prompted questions about the accuracy of Gilligan's reporting. The scientist then confided in Rufford that the twists and turns of the preceding few weeks meant that he felt he had been 'through the wringer'. Now, having been told just half an hour earlier by the MoD that his name was about to be published, he seemed genuinely shocked. More positively, though, he did volunteer to Rufford that he was looking forward to returning to Iraq the following week to carry on with his work there as a weapons inspector for the British government.

Realizing that time was running out for this impromptu chat and keen not to return to London empty-handed, Rufford asked Dr Kelly whether he would write an article for *The Sunday Times*. Dr Kelly said he would happily do so – but would need the blessing of the MoD press office. A quarter of an hour had passed, and Rufford sensed that since he was not going to be invited into Dr Kelly's house, the conversation had reached its natural conclusion. They parted perfectly amicably, he felt.

He returned to his car and immediately rang his news editor, Hymas, to let him know that the next day's papers were going to name Dr Kelly as Gilligan's source. Next, he made detailed contemporaneous notes of his conversation with Dr Kelly – everything which he considered had been said to him on or off the record – and included his own observation that the scientist had appeared 'pale and tired.' It would have been second nature for him to record the encounter as thoroughly as he could, knowing that *The Sunday Times* would probably want to include in its next edition at least part of what had been said to its man by Dr Kelly. Within half an hour Rufford also rang the MoD press office and spoke to a senior member of staff, Pam Teare, asking whether Dr Kelly might be allowed to write a piece for his newspaper putting across his side of the story about the row. He was told that this was unlikely, but that if the situation changed he would be the first to know. Rufford then began to drive home, unaware that he would never see Dr Kelly alive again.

What happened next is the subject of some debate, as shall become clear. The official story is that, immediately after Rufford left the Kellys' house, Dr Kelly was again rung by the MoD and advised to leave home straight away in order to avoid having to speak to any other reporters.

Mrs Kelly is then said to have told her husband about a friend's house in the West Country which they could use as a hiding place. They quickly packed a bag each and at about 8 p.m. Dr Kelly went over the road to the Waggon and Horses pub. There he asked Leigh Potter, a barmaid, to pass on a message to the publican, Graham Atkins, that he was going away for a few days because the 'press were going to pounce'. Bemused, Miss Potter agreed to do so and within thirty seconds Dr Kelly had gone.

The Kellys then apparently got into their car and headed for the motorway. They are said to have broken the journey that night in a hotel in the Somerset seaside town of Weston-Super-Mare, about eighty-five miles away, and the next morning, Thursday, 10 July, continued driving south, arriving in the Cornish fishing village of Mevagissey at about midday.

Supposedly, they passed the weekend quietly, visiting a couple of tourist attractions – the Lost Gardens of Heligan and the Eden Project – in between dealing with the fallout from Dr Kelly having been named by the MoD as Gilligan's source. This included Dr Kelly being told by his boss, Bryan Wells, over the phone that the following week he would be required to go to Westminster to give evidence to the FAC, which was still conducting its inquiry into Britain's invasion of Iraq. He would also be required to appear before the Intelligence and Security Committee (ISC).

It was Geoff Hoon, the Defence Secretary, who ultimately decided these appearances must take place, even though senior MoD staff including Sir Kevin Tebbit opposed the idea. Bryan Wells was merely the bearer of the bad news.

The FAC inquiry was to be televised, a fact which apparently upset Dr Kelly greatly while he was in his Cornish bolthole. He was powerless, however, to argue with the Defence Secretary. The Kellys agreed it would be best if Dr Kelly returned to Oxfordshire to stay with his soon-to-be-married daughter Rachel, who lived in Oxford, using her house as a secret base in order to dodge prying reporters. From there, he could reach London easily.

PALE AND TIRED

On Sunday, 13 July Dr Kelly awoke keen to begin the 230-mile car journey from Cornwall to Oxfordshire as soon as possible. Mrs Kelly tried to delay him from setting off too early because he seemed extremely tense and she was worried about him driving on the motorway in such a state. It had already been agreed between the couple that she would remain alone in Cornwall until the committee hearings in Westminster had concluded, three days later.

Before Dr Kelly set off, he and Mrs Kelly went into Mevagissey that morning to buy some newspapers, including a copy of *The Sunday Times*. Dr Kelly wanted to see what, if anything, Rufford had written about him as a result of their doorstep chat in Southmoor four nights previously.

The 600-word story Dr Kelly read, positioned unhelpfully on the front page, is said to have made him fume. The second sentence contained the words: 'In his first public comments since the row blew up, Dr David Kelly said the government's position on Iraq was credible and factual.' This was a piece of journalese which to the untrained eye would leave readers with the idea that Dr Kelly had entered into a formal conversation with *The Sunday Times*, when in fact he had given no such interview. His off-the-cuff comments were simply plucked from the chat he and Rufford had had in Dr Kelly's garden a few evenings previously. Such are the tricks of the trade.

Rufford had also made use of his observation that his long-standing contact had been 'looking pale and tired', words which were hardly likely to improve relations between the two men. The piece then added: 'Kelly admitted the affair had played heavily on his mind since it broke six weeks ago.' This arguably suggested guilt or wrongdoing. And Dr Kelly was also alleged to have told Rufford: 'It has been a very difficult time, as you can imagine.'

Dr Kelly clearly believed he deserved better from someone he had considered a friend, and was again apparently upset and angry. He was also no doubt worried that his bosses at the MoD would take a dim view of his having spoken to a newspaper reporter without their knowledge.

Rufford, however, was even-handed in that he did emphasize in his copy the crucial point that Dr Kelly did not believe he was the source of the BBC report which had led to this situation. Rufford's article quoted Dr Kelly as saying: 'I know Gilligan. But I did not talk to him about [Alastair] Campbell's role because I didn't know anything about it.'

Dr Kelly left Cornwall late that morning and by 5 p.m. rang his wife to let her know that he had arrived safely at Rachel's house in Oxford. Rachel had been working that day but returned home at about 7 p.m. to find her father waiting for her. He was visibly tired but, having been driving most of the day, this was perhaps unsurprising.

While they relaxed in the garden Dr Kelly confided that he felt concerned about appearing in front of TV cameras at the forthcoming FAC meeting. There was also unhappy talk about the MoD and the circumstances in which his name had been leaked, but Dr Kelly said friends and colleagues were showing him support. During their chat he also told Rachel that he was hoping to go out to Baghdad to carry on with his work and would fly there either on Monday, 21 July or Friday, 25 July.

Supper that evening, at which they were joined by Rachel's fiancé, David Wilkins, was not perhaps the strained affair Rachel might have feared, with her father apparently having started to unwind. He went to bed at about 10 p.m. after making some further phone calls but it was Rachel, not Dr Kelly, who spoke to Mrs Kelly again that evening.

PREPARATIONS

On Monday, 14 July Dr Kelly left his daughter's house after breakfast and walked the short distance to Oxford Station, where he caught the 9.15 train to Paddington. His business in London that day was focused exclusively on preparing for the two select committee hearings.

His boss, Bryan Wells, had cancelled an important trip to Washington so that he could see Dr Kelly to discuss the hearings with him. They met in Wells's office at about 11 a.m., with Dr Kelly appearing composed. Their conversation consisted of Wells advising Dr Kelly which areas he believed the FAC would wish to cover with him the following day. After lunch they met with Martin Howard, Deputy Chief of Defence Intelligence at the MoD. Howard had been asked by Sir Kevin Tebbit, Dr Kelly's ultimate boss, to talk Dr Kelly through the likely lines of questioning from both the FAC and the ISC and to satisfy himself that Dr Kelly was sufficiently prepared for these meetings. It was certainly ironic that the MoD was helping Dr Kelly to prepare for these two committee appearances given that it was the Defence Secretary, Geoff Hoon, who had pushed for them to take place.

Minutes taken that afternoon show that there was no question of the MoD seeking to impose on Dr Kelly the line he should take when he faced MPs. He was advised that he was free to tell his own story. Howard outlined to Dr Kelly the different bases on which the FAC and ISC were constituted, and their interests in the government's policy towards Iraq and weapons of mass destruction. He then listed the areas on which the two committees might want to question Dr Kelly. These were his role in government and relationship with the media; his role in drawing up the government's September 2002 dossier; and his meeting with Andrew Gilligan.

For the ISC meeting he was also told to expect questions on his access to intelligence in general, and specifically to intelligence on the 'forty-five-minute' claim. It was explained to him that other general topics might come up, including what Dr Kelly thought of government policy on Iraq; whether he believed he was Gilligan's source; and what disciplinary action was being taken against Dr Kelly for his contact with the media, which most people incorrectly seemed to think was unauthorized.

Following this meeting Dr Kelly sought and was granted a conversation with Patrick Lamb, Deputy Head of the Counter-proliferation Department in the Foreign Office, and a man who considered himself a friend and admirer of the weapons inspector. During their chat, which took place by telephone, Dr Kelly was asked whether he thought his pension rights might be in peril. He told Lamb that he understood they were not at risk. Relieved on behalf of Dr Kelly, Lamb tried to reassure him that he believed the worst was already over.

Dr Kelly then asked Lamb if he would also attend the FAC hearing, but was told that this would be impossible. Although, in the complicated world of Dr Kelly, the MoD paid his salary, he was effectively on loan to that department from the Foreign Office, meaning that the MoD reimbursed its sister department this expense. Dr Kelly would be appearing at the FAC as an MoD official, however. The FAC meeting had been sanctioned by Geoff Hoon, so Lamb had no professional locus in the matter.

Dr Kelly returned to his daughter Rachel's house in Oxford late that afternoon, letting himself in with a key she had given him. On her return, Rachel found him to be relaxed, if a little contemplative, and in better form than he had been the previous evening. Nonetheless, she remained concerned for him.

Supper followed, after which Dr Kelly took several phone calls from friends. He was overheard by his daughter telling one caller that he was 'depressed' by the media coverage he had attracted and received and unhappy that he was essentially living in exile. Sadly for him, things were about to become even more disagreeable.

FALL GUY?

Tuesday, 15 July was the Kellys' thirty-sixth wedding anniversary. Dr Kelly caught his usual 9.15 train to Paddington.

As he journeyed to London, his understanding was that he would be giving evidence that day first to the ISC in a private session, and then to the FAC in what was being talked of in the confines of the Westminster media bubble as a show trial complete with TV cameras. This was an unappetizing prospect for a reserved man like Dr Kelly, but in the event his luck turned from bad to worse.

It was one of the hottest days of the year, with temperatures in London touching the 90s Fahrenheit. On top of this, Dr Kelly's expectation of the day's agenda was about to disintegrate. He was originally advised that he would be seen by the ISC in the Cabinet Office building in Whitehall at midday. The televised FAC hearing was scheduled to follow, down the road in a House of Commons committee room, at 2.30 p.m.

Dr Kelly, accompanied by his line manager Bryan Wells and Wing Commander John Clark, who was a friend and colleague of Dr Kelly in the MoD, went to the Cabinet Office for the ISC meeting. They sat down and drank coffee while they waited for the committee members to arrive.

Earlier that morning, however, and unbeknown to Dr Kelly, the clerk to the ISC had informed Geoff Hoon's office that Dr Kelly's appearance before the committee had been postponed until the following day. It seems that Dr Kelly and his colleagues were the last to be told about this change of plan. This would have been a small but significant humiliation.

Having been advised that a car had been arranged to take them the short distance from the Old War Office building to the Commons for the FAC hearing, the trio returned to the MoD to wait. Dr Kelly was understandably anxious about having to give evidence in front of TV cameras anyway, but this extra time spent hanging around no doubt forced him to reflect upon the fact that his ordeal was to be staggered over two days.

Then, to compound matters, there was a bomb scare in Whitehall as they were walking to the Old War Office building to meet the car. Dr Kelly, Bryan Wells, Wing Commander Clark and Kate Wilson, the Chief Press Officer of the MoD who had joined them, were therefore forced to begin walking up to Trafalgar Square and then down Pall Mall to get to the FAC, a fair distance on a blisteringly hot day when late for an important meeting. The car did eventually manage to pick them up en route, and then dropped them off at the Commons as planned. But on his way into the Commons, Dr Kelly also had to run the gauntlet of the photographers waiting for him outside.

As he entered the stuffy, carpeted committee room, where electric fans buzzed instead of quiet air conditioning, he would have been forgiven for thinking that some malign force had conspired not only to prolong his humiliation but to force him to hurry to the televised meeting which he had been dreading. Rows of reporters and other observers were waiting for him, not just the group of MPs who had been instructed by Defence Secretary Geoff Hoon to interrogate him.

And yet, despite all the hurdles which were placed in his way, Dr Kelly appeared composed and performed remarkably well in front of the FAC. A view has gained credibility that this committee hearing was the event which perhaps tipped Dr Kelly over the edge and led directly to his death, but close analysis tells another story.

The hearing is very well known for one short piece of parliamentary pantomime provided by the then Labour MP Andrew Mackinlay, in which he seemed to accuse Dr Kelly in an aggressive way of being 'chaff'. The brief exchange between the two men, about five minutes before the end of the fifty-one-minute session, went as follows:

> ANDREW MACKINLAY: 'I reckon you are chaff; you have been thrown up to divert our probing. Have you ever felt like a fall guy? You have been set up, have you not?'
>
> DR KELLY: 'That is not a question I can answer.'
>
> ANDREW MACKINLAY: 'But you feel that?'
>
> DR KELLY: 'No, not at all. I accept the process that is going on.'

Undoubtedly, Dr Kelly appeared to buckle slightly at this point in the proceedings, wearied no doubt by the heat and the sheer relentlessness of the occasion. After all, Mackinlay's questions were logged in the official record of the occasion produced by Hansard as numbers 167 and 168 out of a total of 179 points raised, showing just how much information had been discussed with Dr Kelly in a relatively short space of time.

Ironically, however, anyone who watches a recording of the hearing in full might see things differently. It is true that Mackinlay's general manner can at times appear abrupt, but those who know him understand that his personality is the very opposite. In a professional sense he cared greatly about what was going on at the time, and was keen to try to help Dr Kelly out of the hole into which he thought he had been thrown by the MoD and the government spin machine. In fact, Mackinlay was trying to sympathize with Dr Kelly by telling him that he believed the scientist had been served up to the FAC on a plate by the government and/or the MoD as a diversion, to prevent them from reaching the truth. Mackinlay thought – and still believes – that Dr Kelly was being used to prevent the FAC from confirming the identity of Gilligan's *principal* source, whom Mackinlay did not believe Dr Kelly to be. Mackinlay later felt such remorse over the way his words were interpreted that, after Dr Kelly's death, he apologized publicly for his remarks. Understandably, Dr Kelly saw things differently at the time.

On that day, though – and perhaps even still now – Mackinlay's true intention was lost on the vast majority of people, who will have never watched the hearing in full, nor read the Hansard account of it, but instead will have seen this brief exchange on out-of-context television news clips. Viewers would have watched the tetchy MP raise his voice to a quietly spoken, bespectacled scientist, and assumed the former was haranguing the latter. The impression of Dr Kelly formed by thousands, possibly millions, via the news that evening would have been that he was a pathetic punchbag being bullied by a grandstanding Labour MP. Indeed, Dr Kelly himself told his daughter, Rachel, afterwards that he thought Mackinlay had been an 'utter bastard'.

All eleven members of the cross-party committee attended that day's hearing. They were ranged in the traditional horseshoe formation while Dr Kelly sat alone at a table facing them, with nothing but a large bottle of water and a glass for company. In the row of seats immediately behind him were Bryan Wells, Wing Commander Clark and Kate Wilson. Many of the committee members took off their jackets. Dr Kelly, dressed in a pale suit, did not because, he later told his half-sister, Sarah Pape, he was sweating so much.

But the session was not the free-for-all in which Dr Kelly

was savaged that most people might assume. It was for the most part a good-humoured affair. Within four minutes Dr Kelly was smiling broadly at Labour MP Bill Olner who, when Dr Kelly was asked to speak up because the noise of the electric fans was drowning out his voice, said: 'I am sure members of the public at the back cannot hear you.'

The fans were so loud that they were switched off after about ten minutes, allowing Dr Kelly to be heard more easily. It is fair to say that he did not seem like a man who ever spoke in a loud voice or forceful manner, but judging from a recording of his performance that day, and bearing in mind the many difficult circumstances of the hearing, he certainly did not come across as a pushover either. Indeed, in a lengthy TV interview he gave in the privacy of his own home to an Australian broadcaster the month before he was found dead, Dr Kelly spoke in exactly the same quiet and thoughtful manner as he did in front of the FAC.

During the hearing, there were eight times when Dr Kelly laughed or smiled in genuine amusement. Perhaps his heartiest laugh came when he was asked by the committee Chairman, Donald Anderson, 'What lessons have you learned from this episode?' Dr Kelly's quick-witted reply was: 'Never to talk to a journalist again, I think.' He spoke fluently and steadily. He was not struck dumb at any point. He barely stuttered and seemed confident for the most part. He did not fidget too much. This was impressive for someone who was asked so many questions in less than an hour.

Anybody who watches Peter Kosminsky's TV drama about Dr Kelly, *The Government Inspector*, first screened on Channel 4 in 2005, will find that the actor Mark Rylance portrayed him as a rather feeble, submissive man who seemed to live in a world of his own. On the strength of this hearing, held in an excessively hot, packed room in the glare of TV cameras, Rylance's depiction was not accurate. Dr Kelly was a leader in his chosen field of biological weapons. He had even been on an Iraqi hit list as recently as 1997, according to one of his former UN colleagues, Dick Spertzel, who was also, like Dr Kelly, a biological weapons expert and had met Dr Kelly in Iraq. To do the complicated and pressurized work which Dr Kelly had done, he simply could not have been a shrinking violet, even if he was quietly spoken.

The trickiest point of the FAC session came when he was questioned about his contact not with Gilligan, but with another BBC journalist, Susan Watts, the science correspondent of the BBC Two programme *Newsnight*.

Having established that Dr Kelly had only ever met Watts once, in November 2002, the following long quote, attributed to Dr Kelly, was put to him by committee member David Chidgey, a Liberal Democrat MP. Chidgey claimed that these words were taken from notes made by Watts during or after their meeting:

In the run-up to the dossier the Government was obsessed with finding intelligence to justify an immediate Iraqi threat. While we were agreed on the potential Iraqi threat in the future there was less agreement about the threat the Iraqis posed at the moment. That was the real concern, not so much what they had now but what they would have in the future, but that unfortunately was not expressed strongly in the dossier because that takes the case away for war to a certain extent... The 45 minutes was a statement that was made and it got out of all proportion. They were desperate for information. They were pushing hard for information that could be released. That was one that popped up and it was seized on and it is unfortunate that it was. That is why there is an argument between the intelligence services and Number 10, because they had picked up on it and once they had picked up on it you cannot pull back from it, so many people will say 'Well, we are not sure about that' because the wordsmithing is actually quite important.

Chidgey asked Dr Kelly if he agreed with the comments. As Dr Kelly believed that he had said nothing of the sort to Watts during their only meeting the previous November, he was able to deny having said those words 'on that occasion'. He said he did not recognize the words.

Tory MP Richard Ottaway then pursued the same line of questioning. He read the same quote from Watts's notes again, asking Dr Kelly if they were his words, to which Dr Kelly replied: 'It does not sound like my expression of words. It does not sound like a quote from me.' Ottaway then asked directly if Dr Kelly denied that those were his words. Committing himself to a position, he said simply: 'Yes.'

Why were these two MPs suddenly so interested in what Dr Kelly had – or hadn't – said to Susan Watts? Her name had never been mentioned in relation to Dr Kelly before, yet these politicians appeared to have done a considerable amount of research into her recent BBC broadcasts. The answer, it later emerged, was that Andrew Gilligan had sent this information to Chidgey. Gilligan did so, apparently, having studied one of Watts's *Newsnight* reports from June 2003 and allegedly guessed that Dr Kelly had spoken to her. This was certainly extremely unhelpful to Dr Kelly – whom Gilligan had previously been only too happy to use as a source – given that Dr Kelly's contact with Watts had never been of concern to anybody up until then. If this was an attempt by Gilligan to take some of the heat off himself by showing that he wasn't the only BBC journalist who had spoken to Dr Kelly in recent weeks, it gave no thought to the position in which it might put Dr Kelly.

Technically, Dr Kelly was telling the truth to the committee about Watts. He had said no such thing to her when they met. And yet it could be argued that he had been economical with the truth. It subsequently came to light that he *had* made those comments to Watts, but he had done so during a telephone conversation in June – the month before he died. Unbeknown to him, Watts had recorded their twenty-minute chat. Significantly, though, Dr Kelly died before his contact with Watts was known publicly.

After the questions had come to an end, the *Guardian*'s parliamentary sketch writer, Simon Hoggart, noted in his published account that 'as he [Dr Kelly] pushed past me at the end to leave… he was smiling'. Was this a smile triggered by tension, or was it one of relief? Whichever it was, Bryan Wells congratulated Dr Kelly afterwards and the pair went to Wells's office with Wing Commander Clark. After a brief discussion, Dr Kelly said he wanted to return to his daughter's house in Oxford immediately. He did so having been told that he wouldn't be required in London for the next day's ISC hearing before midday.

When he reached Oxford, he spoke for twenty minutes by phone to Sarah Pape, during which he said that he had been 'overwhelmed' by the number of friends and colleagues who had rung him to offer their support. He also mentioned that an offer of setting up a fighting fund had been made, should one be required in the event of legal action being taken against him by the MoD. Ms Pape, a plastic surgeon, later remembered: 'It really was a very normal conversation. Believe me, I have lain awake many nights since, going over in my mind whether I missed anything significant. In my line of work I do deal with people who may have suicidal thoughts and I ought to be able to spot those, even in a telephone conversation… He certainly did not convey to me that he was feeling depressed; and absolutely nothing that would have alerted me to the fact that he might have been considering suicide.'

In the meantime, the main point that the FAC took away from the hearing focused on Dr Kelly's assertion that he could not be the 'main source' of Andrew Gilligan's story. Within a couple of hours of the hearing's conclusion, Donald Anderson had written a short letter to the Foreign Secretary, Jack Straw, saying that the committee's view was that it was 'most unlikely that Dr Kelly was Andrew Gilligan's prime source'. He added, witheringly, that the committee believed Dr Kelly had been 'poorly treated by the government' since admitting on 30 June in his letter to the MoD to having met Gilligan. The letter was released to the press at 7 that evening.

QUESTIONS, QUESTIONS

By 16 July Dr Kelly seemed in better form than he had been for days. He and his daughter ate breakfast together with her fiancé, David, and they then spoke to Mrs Kelly to finalize the arrangements for her return by train from Cornwall that evening.

Arriving in London later that morning, his good mood did not go unnoticed at the ISC hearing, which lasted less than an hour. Although it was held in private it is known that Dr Kelly was again accompanied by Bryan Wells and their Ministry of Defence colleague, Wing Commander Clark. Wells said later that Dr Kelly seemed more comfortable than during his appearance before the FAC and was in good spirits afterwards, even going so far as to discuss when he would return to Iraq. A tentative date of 25 July was agreed on, which apparently cheered Dr Kelly.

During the hearing Dr Kelly again said that he believed the forty-five-minute claim had been included in the September dossier for 'impact', but he was unaware of the intelligence behind it. He said the dossier was a 'fair reflection of the intelligence that was available and it's presented in a very sober and factual way'. He added that he didn't think it had been 'transformed', saying that because he had not seen the earlier drafts of it, he 'wouldn't know whether it had been transformed or not'.

At some time approaching 5 p.m. Dr Kelly made his way back to Oxford. Rachel met him at the station about an hour later. Although he was anxious to return to his own house in order to have access to his computer so that he could do some work, Rachel persuaded her father to stay with her for supper. Janice Kelly arrived at about

8.30 p.m. after her train journey from Cornwall. Again, Rachel dutifully walked to the station to meet her mother and to carry her bag, knowing she was anxious for news of her husband. Rachel, plus her parents and David, then ate supper together during which Dr Kelly was, according to Rachel, apparently quiet but cheerful and looking forward to going home.

By 10 p.m. the Kellys had decided to return to their house in Southmoor. Before leaving, Dr Kelly arranged with Rachel that they would meet the following evening, Thursday, 17 July, to walk down to a field near his house to look at a foal together, something they had done several times since the animal's birth in May. Rachel was working the next day, and no set time was agreed upon for their walk at that point. David helped the Kellys to load some luggage into their car and then he and Rachel waved her parents goodbye, obviously unaware that they would never see Dr Kelly again.

Dr Kelly drove home. When he got there he switched on his computer and read some emails, knowing that he had an urgent task to complete by the following morning before he could fully draw a line under his business with the FAC. Shortly before his appearance in front of the FAC on 15 July, Andrew Mackinlay, the MP whose intentions towards him had seemingly been misunderstood by Dr Kelly, had tabled two Parliamentary Questions about Dr Kelly for answer by Geoff Hoon. For Hoon to provide these answers, Dr Kelly would have to supply him with the relevant information, via the MoD.

The first question asked when, over the previous two years, Dr Kelly had met Andrew Gilligan; the second requested a list of all journalists other than Gilligan whom Dr Kelly had met over the previous two years, plus the purpose of each meeting and when it took place.

This would have been an onerous job at the best of times, but having to revisit the very ground which he had left the previous day must have made it even tougher. Despite his tiredness, it seems that Dr Kelly tried to make inroads into the task that night in order to be able to send the necessary details to the MoD before the agreed time of 10 a.m. the following day, so that answers could be prepared for Parliament by officials in the department. Half an hour after arriving at home, Dr Kelly went to bed.

'MANY DARK ACTORS PLAYING GAMES'

The next morning, Thursday, 17 July, the Kellys woke up at their house at 8.30 a.m. For them, this was quite a bit later than usual and a probable result of the strain they had been under during the previous two weeks.

Dr Kelly was in his study working by 9 a.m. and at 9.28 a.m. James Harrison, Bryan Wells's deputy at the MoD, sent Dr Kelly four further Parliamentary Questions tabled by the Conservative MP Bernard Jenkin. These related to Dr Kelly's contact with Gilligan and whether he would face disciplinary action as a result of it.

Harrison's hurriedly written email to Dr Kelly was friendly in tone. It read: 'David, More PQs! But plenty of time for reply. I expect that Bryan will deal tomorrow, James.' As it was the last day on which the House of Commons was sitting before breaking for the long summer recess, there was no doubt a collective desire to square off the situation as soon as possible.

At about 10 a.m. Dr Kelly spoke to his colleague Wing Commander Clark by phone, who found him to be tired but in good spirits. Significantly, Dr Kelly confided in Clark that Mrs Kelly had taken recent events badly and had been very upset that morning.

Work may have been piling up but, proving that Dr Kelly was looking ahead, that morning Clark and Dr Kelly again discussed his imminent return to the Middle East. Clark booked a plane ticket to Iraq for Dr Kelly, scheduled for eight days later, on 25 July. He knew how keen Dr Kelly was to carry on with his duties supporting the Iraq Survey Group, the multinational fact-finding mission sent to find weapons of mass destruction there.

At about 10.45 a.m. Dr Kelly spoke to his friend Olivia Bosch, like him someone with international experience as a weapons inspector, whom he knew via his work for the UN, and at 11 a.m. he took a coffee break. Next, he sent eight short, individual emails to friends and professional contacts. He had typed these messages earlier, but records show they left his email account simultaneously at 11.18 a.m. Six of the messages spoke of his expectation of flying to Baghdad on 25 July. The seventh email, to a Philippe Michel, did not mention Baghdad but was also positive in that Dr Kelly wrote: 'I know that I have a lot of good friends who are providing support at a difficult time.'

The eighth email was in reply to Judith Miller, a reporter on *The New York Times* whom he had known for several years. She had written to him the previous day offering kind words over the political spat in which he had been caught and to congratulate him on his performance in front of the FAC. Miller's message read: 'David, I heard from another member of your fan club that things went well for you today. Hope it's true. J.'

In view of the fact that his body was found on Harrowdown Hill less than twenty-four hours later, Dr Kelly's response was darkly ominous. He wrote: 'Judy, I will wait until the end of the week before judging – many dark actors playing games. Thanks for your support. I appreciate your friendship at this time. Best, David.'

While her husband worked, Mrs Kelly left the house for about half an hour to meet a friend and collect some photographs relating to the local history society, of which she was an active member. When she returned she tried to show these pictures to Dr Kelly to lighten the atmosphere at home. She went into his study at about 12.15 p.m. but her gesture was gently rebuffed. He apparently smiled, stood up, and said he hadn't quite finished what he was doing. A little later, at about 12.30, he went to the sitting room where he sat alone in silence.

Her husband's low mood distressed Mrs Kelly. She was suddenly struck by a headache and nausea, and vomited, but within a few minutes had recovered enough to be able to make him some sandwiches and give him some water. He ate in silence as his wife, with him at the kitchen table, looked on.

At about 1.30 p.m., after he had eaten, Mrs Kelly went upstairs to lie down – something she did often to combat her arthritis. Dr Kelly apparently returned to his study for a while and then went upstairs to check on her. He also changed into a pair of jeans in preparation for a walk.

Mrs Kelly assumed that her husband then went for his walk at that point but, shortly before 3 p.m., she heard the telephone ringing downstairs. Believing that it could be an important call for her husband from the MoD, she got up to answer it. By the time she was downstairs, the ringing had stopped and she found Dr Kelly talking quietly on the phone in his study.

Mrs Kelly didn't know who had rung her husband but, by process of elimination, it is thought to have been Wing Commander Clark, whose phone records show that he called Dr Kelly at 2.54 p.m. for a further chat about the letter to be sent to the FAC. Clark told Dr Kelly that the letter needed to be tweaked so that the BBC reporter Susan Watts's name could be taken out of the general list of journalists to whom Dr Kelly had spoken and put into a different paragraph which referred to the specific contacts that he had had with journalists. Dr Kelly agreed to this.

Mrs Kelly returned to her bedroom without addressing another word to her husband. Similarly, he did not say goodbye to her. When she went downstairs at 3.20 p.m., he had gone. She never saw him again.

GILLIGAN RE-GRILLED

Just as Dr Kelly left for his walk, Andrew Gilligan was in Westminster sitting down for a private grilling in front of the FAC. This was the second time in the space of a few weeks that the BBC reporter had been required to give evidence to the committee, which was still investigating suggestions that Tony Blair's government had exaggerated the case for Britain's recent invasion of Iraq. The occasion was apparently a bad-tempered affair which did not go well for Gilligan. According to contemporaneous newspaper reports, it even resulted in the committee Chairman, Donald Anderson, holding an impromptu press conference in a corridor outside the committee room in which he accused Gilligan of changing his story about his meeting with Dr Kelly two months previously.

Even more significant, though, is the curious choice of words Gilligan used at one point near the end of this highly charged meeting. When asked again about the identity of the source for his now infamous *Today* programme report Gilligan said: 'I have tried to persuade my source to go on the record, for obvious career reasons he is unable to, and I must respect that confidence.'

In response, Conservative MP Sir John Stanley shot back: 'The fact you have just said that is clearly absolute confirmation from you that your source is not Dr Kelly.' Sir John's point was based on pure logic, for the identity of Gilligan's alleged source was, of course, already known to all and sundry. There was no honour, merit or reason in Gilligan continuing to protect the name of Dr Kelly given that the MoD had unmasked him so brutally the previous week. Gilligan, however, said: 'I simply cannot add anything at all to the evidence I gave [during my previous appearance] about my source.'

Had Gilligan slipped up by inadvertently suggesting that Dr Kelly was not the source primarily responsible for tipping him off about the claims of 'sexing up' the case for war? Sir John Stanley certainly appeared to think so. From this, the question follows: did Gilligan in fact have another source – a principal source – to whom he had spoken before or after his meeting with Dr Kelly? If so, it is not far-fetched to consider that this man (Gilligan had referred to him as 'he') was well known, or the current or past occupant of an elevated post in public life. Indeed, based on Gilligan's response, might he even have been a household political name? This would certainly explain Gilligan's unnecessarily reticent reply.

RUTH ABSALOM: LAST WITNESS

It is not known exactly what route Dr Kelly took from his house because nobody saw him leave, but it is most likely that he turned left and walked for a few hundred yards before turning right and heading north along a bridleway which eventually took him over the A420 bypass to the village of Longworth. This was the first part of a walk lasting about half an hour which he often did with his family, and sometimes alone, to aid a back condition from which he suffered.

By 3.20 p.m., when Mrs Kelly got up, Dr Kelly was about half a mile from his front door chatting to Ruth Absalom, their seventy-five-year-old neighbour.

Dr Kelly and Mrs Absalom bumped into each other at the top of Harris's Lane in Longworth. She found him to be just as he was whenever she saw him – friendly and polite. Her recollection is that he wasn't carrying anything and she thought he had been wearing a jacket. Dr Kelly asked her how she was and they spoke for a few minutes until Mrs Absalom's dog, Buster, started pulling at its lead. Mrs Absalom then told Dr Kelly she must go. He apparently replied: 'See you again then, Ruth,' and they parted with him saying 'Cheerio, Ruth,' and her replying 'Bye, David.' As she recounted the day after he was found dead, it couldn't have been a more normal, natural exchange of words. 'He wasn't edgy or anything like that,' she said.

Mrs Absalom said Dr Kelly walked to her right – in other words, east – towards the Appleton Road, which led ultimately to another neighbouring village, Kingston Bagpuize. Walking along the Appleton Road represented one of two possible routes home for Dr Kelly. It is a long, straight road with few houses on it and no pavement for the most part. One of the few turnings off it is Draycott Road, which leads back to the A420 bypass and then to Southmoor, where Dr Kelly lived. On this basis, the Appleton Road would have been the logical route for Dr Kelly to take had he been returning home. It would not be the natural route to take if he was heading to Harrowdown Hill, the place where his body was found the following morning, because it leads in the wrong direction altogether.

While Mrs Absalom was the last person known to have seen Dr Kelly alive, it is equally interesting to consider the number of people who did *not* see him that afternoon, despite being in the immediate area at the same time as he would have been on his walk. When the police carried out house-to-house inquiries in the weeks after his death, they visited a total of 167 local properties. Each was carefully selected to include any 'premise which overlooked the possible routes taken [by Dr Kelly on 17 July 2003]'. Furthermore, a checkpoint was established by the police on the public footpaths that cross Harrowdown Hill woods in an effort to identify potential witnesses to the movements of Dr Kelly. And yet not a single positive sighting is known to have been logged. It is as though Dr Kelly simply vanished.

THE DISAPPEARANCE

Back at Dr Kelly's house, Mrs Kelly's condition had not improved. She went to the sitting room and switched on the television to try to take her mind off the way she was feeling. Yet she was soon disturbed more than once by what she has described as some 'callers' at the front door, whom she spoke to momentarily. Who were these callers? Publicly, at least, nothing is known about them. Their identities, the times they called, whether Mrs Kelly had ever met them before, how many separate callers there were, what they wanted, or for how long they engaged Mrs Kelly in conversation, all remain a mystery.

Wing Commander Clark rang Dr Kelly's house for a second time at about 3.20 p.m. He spoke to Mrs Kelly, who explained that her husband had gone for a walk. Clark later said he asked whether Dr Kelly had his mobile phone with him and Mrs Kelly said she didn't know. Clark then rang Dr Kelly's mobile phone. It was switched off. Apparently an electronic voice said the number was unavailable at that time. Clark said he was 'very surprised' by this because Dr Kelly prided himself on being contactable at all times. He had once even taken a call from Clark while driving his noisy motorized lawn mower. Next, Clark rang Dr Kelly's landline again because the response to the FAC letter needed to be finalized that afternoon with Dr Kelly's help. Clark later said: 'I spoke to her [Mrs Kelly] and said I had not been able to contact Dr Kelly on his mobile and I thought she might say something but she was quite matter of fact… I then said: "Could you ask Dr Kelly when he returns, could he give me a ring." That is how the message was left with his wife.'

Demonstrating his need to speak to Dr Kelly urgently, Clark rang his mobile every fifteen minutes until 4.50 p.m. without success: his phone was always switched off. Clark then left work to attend an optician's appointment and handed over his duties to his colleague James Harrison, the Deputy Director for Counter-proliferation and Arms Control at the MoD.

It wasn't just work colleagues who were looking for Dr Kelly. Between 5 p.m. and 5.30 Rachel rang her parents' house to ask her father what time that evening they were going to see the foal together, as they had loosely arranged to do the previous evening. She and her mother spoke twice, and Mrs Kelly explained that Dr Kelly had not returned. Rachel rang her father's mobile phone but couldn't get through. Her reaction was the same as Wing Commander Clark's: this was odd. Her father's phone was always on.

She then drove to her parents' house, arriving at around 6 p.m., and spoke to her two sisters en route to tell them about Dr Kelly's apparent disappearance. Sian, the eldest, lived in Hampshire; Ellen, Rachel's twin, lived in Scotland.

At 5.50 p.m., James Harrison of the MoD rang Dr Kelly's mobile. Whereas before, when his colleague Wing Commander Clark had rung it, the phone appeared to have been switched off and a generic electronic message was played, on this occasion the phone rang and rang. Harrison made a contemporaneous note of this. He also discussed it with colleagues the next morning after it was announced by police that Dr Kelly was missing. Either Dr Kelly's phone had been switched off previously when Clark had tried to ring him and had then been switched on again when Harrison rang it; or the phone had been in an area with no reception when Clark had tried it but could receive a signal when Harrison rang it. Whichever explanation is true, nobody who rang Dr Kelly's mobile phone that afternoon managed to speak to him on it.

Having failed to get through on the mobile, Harrison then rang Dr Kelly's home number and spoke to his wife.

She told him that Dr Kelly had gone for a walk by the river because of a bad headache – a location and an ailment which she has at no point mentioned since. Harrison's notes then say that, according to Mrs Kelly, Dr Kelly had intended to go for a walk at 2 p.m. but had been delayed and that he sometimes took a long route. The notes also show that Harrison rang two colleagues to update them on the situation, one being Bryan Wells, who also tried to ring Dr Kelly's mobile phone without success.

By this point, Dr Kelly hadn't been seen by his wife for about three hours, having gone for a walk which would have apparently taken about thirty minutes at the most, assuming he had followed his normal route.

When Rachel arrived she told her mother she was going to search for her father. She realized that her mother was unwell, but decided that Dr Kelly's whereabouts took priority. She returned at about 6.30 p.m., having walked the footpath which she had assumed her father, a creature of habit, would have taken, but there was no sign of him.

She then got into her car to see if she could find Dr Kelly in a different area and searched various local routes including one close to Harrowdown Hill, a few miles from her parents' house, to no avail. It was an overcast evening and the light was fading earlier than expected for high summer. From the Harrowdown Hill area, Rachel drove to the nearby village of Hinton and then down to neighbouring Duxford. By the time she reached Duxford it was starting to get dark. She got out and walked around, feeling increasingly panicked and upset. She thought about looking in some barns but decided against doing so because she felt scared. She rang her sisters again as she made her way back to her mother. Where was her father?

At about this point Sian Kelly, who at thirty-four was the eldest of the Kellys' three daughters, rang and told her mother that she and her partner, Richard, would drive over immediately from their house in Fordingbridge, Hampshire to help look for her father. The journey, roughly seventy miles, would have taken at least ninety minutes – perhaps two hours on a Friday night.

At 6.40 p.m. James Harrison rang Mrs Kelly again to say that he was leaving work for the evening and that there was no need for anyone to ring him back that night. He wrote in his notes: 'Mrs K sounded okay.'

At about 7.45 p.m. Dr Kelly's friend, Olivia Bosch, rang Dr Kelly's landline number. Her call went unanswered, which seems strange. Assuming Mrs Kelly was at home, she might have been expected to answer the phone in case it was her husband ringing in, or one of her daughters with news. Bosch then tried to ring Dr Kelly's mobile number. She heard a message which said that the phone could not be connected at that time. Whether it was an answerphone is unclear. Certainly, she said, it did not ring.

As soon as Sian Kelly and her partner arrived in Southmoor they drove up and down nearby lanes looking in churches, bus shelters, and anywhere else they thought Dr Kelly might conceivably have taken himself. They, too, drew a blank.

Two neighbours, John Melling and Paul Weaving, a farmer, were recruited to assist in the hunt for Dr Kelly. Weaving had known Dr Kelly for twenty years and, fascinatingly, during the afternoon he was last seen alive had been supervising a young apprentice who was cutting the grass in a field beside Harrowdown Hill. Despite being in such close proximity to the place where his friend was found, he didn't see him.

On the one hand, it was logical for the Kelly family to presume that Dr Kelly had remained in the immediate area. His car was still parked in the driveway of his house and he had left his wallet at home, as Mrs Kelly had discovered. And yet on the other hand, there was nothing to indicate at that stage that he had not decided perhaps to visit a friend, however out of character this might have seemed.

With Rachel and Sian Kelly, and Sian's boyfriend, Richard, having exhausted all immediate options, they returned to the Kellys' house at about 11 p.m. feeling understandably perplexed. Some forty minutes later a member of the family rang Thames Valley Police to explain that Dr Kelly had gone for a walk at about 3 p.m. and, almost nine hours later, had not returned.

Within fifteen minutes of the call being made to report Dr Kelly missing, three officers from Abingdon Police

Station arrived at their house. Those familiar with the way Thames Valley Police operated at the time say this was not standard practice: usually only two officers were sent out in such a situation. Standing on the Kellys' doorstep on that cloudy and humid night, the trio had a missing persons' form with them.

TURBULENCE FOR BLAIR

At exactly the same time, 3,500 miles away in Washington DC, Tony Blair and his wife Cherie were having an early supper with President George W. Bush and his wife, Laura.

Blair was in the American capital to receive the Congressional Gold Medal and that afternoon he had addressed the US Congress. He was in an ecstatic mood and would later boast that he received a total of thirty-five standing ovations during his speech, in which he cemented his commitment to helping the US rid the world of terror. He was about to embark on a short visit to Japan and South Korea before taking a summer holiday at the Barbados house of the singer Cliff Richard.

Having said goodbye to the Bushes, the Blairs were driven to Andrews Air Force base on the outskirts of Washington and at about 8 p.m. local time – 1 a.m. in the UK – boarded British Airways flight 9127C, a Boeing 777 bound for Tokyo which had been specially chartered.

Accompanying the Prime Minister, but seated at the other end of the plane, was a pack of national newspaper and broadcast journalists.

The Blairs changed into BA sleeper suits in preparation for the journey over the Pacific Ocean, which was scheduled to take about fourteen hours, and were soon airborne.

Those on the flight remember it being hit by severe air turbulence at frequent intervals, bouncing the plane around in a most alarming way even for experienced flyers. One BA air stewardess was mentioned in a newspaper report as having said it was the worst bout of turbulence she had ever endured. For Blair, that sort of temporary discomfort was soon to be the least of his worries.

Roughly six hours into the flight, an emergency message came through from Downing Street to the travelling duty clerk via an on-board phone which had a satellite signal. Blair was woken up and told that Dr Kelly was missing – proof, if it were needed, of the importance of Dr Kelly to the government at the time. Needless to say, not a word of this was passed on to the group of reporters sleeping at the other end of the plane.

SEARCHING AND FINDING

In Britain it was 7 a.m., and over the previous seven hours there had been a frenzy of activity in the normally quiet corner of south Oxfordshire where Dr Kelly had last been seen.

Sgt Simon Morris was on duty at Abingdon Police Station on the night of 17 July and into the morning of 18 July. Of the three officers who turned up at the Kellys' house that night, Morris took the lead. He spent the first three hours of his inquiries establishing Dr Kelly's previous whereabouts, co-ordinating a search of the Kellys' house and its outbuildings and half-acre of garden by torchlight and liaising with the Kelly family. Having done so, he judged Dr Kelly to be a 'medium-risk' missing person, indicating the possibility that Dr Kelly might be a danger or threat to himself. This status would have been given after considering whether his disappearance was out of character and whether he was known to have problems in his personal or professional life.

Proving that Thames Valley Police took Dr Kelly's disappearance extremely seriously from the start, however – and perhaps reacting more vigorously than his 'medium-risk' status warranted – Morris then organized for a police search helicopter to be scrambled. At the time its crew was in the St Albans area of Hertfordshire responding to a fatal road accident. After finishing this task at 2.50 a.m. they flew across to south Oxfordshire, briefed to scour the fields and woods from the air with the aid of specialist thermal-imaging equipment.

As a further result of Morris's 'medium-risk' assessment,

a senior officer – Chief Superintendent Katherine Govier, the area Commander – was informed of the situation, as protocol demanded. Govier knew of Dr Kelly via the previous ten days' media coverage and quickly rang Assistant Chief Constable (ACC) Michael Page, who was told just after 3 a.m. about Dr Kelly's puzzling disappearance. Both senior officers went to Abingdon Police Station immediately.

Events certainly moved quickly and dramatically considering there was no direct evidence – such as a note of intent written by Dr Kelly – to lead any police officer of any rank to believe that something fatal, tragic or conclusive had occurred or was about to occur. Indeed, the police have confirmed that no note written by Dr Kelly was ever recovered from anywhere in connection with his death.

Conceivably, Dr Kelly's professionally high-ranking status guaranteed that the police responded more briskly and in greater numbers than they might otherwise have done. After all, it was found after his death that his MoD security clearance was distinctive in that it gave him access to material of UK and US origin marked 'Top Secret' for a period of seven years, until 2007. In the eyes of the State, Dr Kelly was a very important man.

And yet, until anything to the contrary was known, it must have seemed at least possible that night that Dr Kelly might simply have taken himself off to spend some time alone, as reflective people are prone to do. As well as the absence of a note of intent, there had been no special words when he bade farewell to his wife on leaving at about 3 p.m. He hadn't even said goodbye. Furthermore, when he left he had a Yale house key and a Renault car key with him. This suggested that he wanted to be able to let himself into the house on his return, owing to Mrs Kelly having been sick that afternoon. Had he not bothered to take a house key with him, he would have put his unwell, arthritic wife to the trouble of having to get up to open the front door to him. What husband would want to do that? Likewise, carrying his car key showed he may have planned to drive somewhere at some future point.

Records show that at 3.44 a.m. Dr Kelly's disappearance was upgraded to a 'critical incident'. His wife had not seen or heard from him for just over twelve hours at that point.

Two portable communications masts were erected around the Kellys' property during the early hours of Friday, 18 July, apparently because the area was in a communications black spot, potentially hampering officers' ability to speak to each other via radio. The first was thirty-five feet high and was initially parked next to the Kellys' house but was found to be of insufficient strength. It was later replaced by an eighty-five-foot mast set up in the Kellys' back garden.

The helicopter which had been buzzing around for the previous forty-five minutes or so was forced to leave the area at 4.05 a.m. to refuel. Having done so, it was back on the scene at 4.35 a.m., where it remained for a further ten minutes. At that point the pilot was running out of legal flying hours so was forced to turn back and land. Nobody on board had spotted anything.

In the meantime, police activity on the ground was being stepped up. At 4 a.m. a Detective Sergeant (DS) Geoffrey Webb was telephoned and asked to report to Abingdon Police Station to receive a briefing about Dr Kelly. He arrived there at 4.45 a.m. – exactly the same time Mrs Kelly and her daughters Rachel and Sian had just been asked by the police to go and sit in their garden while a search dog was put through the house. This was the second time that an undisclosed number of police officers had checked the Kellys' property within five hours. Despite the fact that the police had already gone over it once in search of Dr Kelly, ACC Page decided that this second exercise, involving the dog, was necessary in case one of the five bedrooms had been overlooked.

At 5 a.m. Paul Chapman, a searcher with the South East Berkshire Emergency Volunteers who lived in the Reading area, received a message on his pager, followed by a text message, asking if he was free to assist with an undisclosed search operation. He replied that he was and got his equipment ready before heading off to Abingdon Police Station. His co-searcher, Louise Holmes, and her search dog, Brock, would join Chapman there.

Meanwhile ACC Page had called a meeting, also at Abingdon Police Station, which began at 5.15 a.m. It was attended by the area Detective Inspector (DI), Ashleigh Smith; Katherine Govier, the area Commander; Sgt Paul Wood, a qualified police search adviser; and a sergeant from Milton Keynes who specialized in the assessment of missing persons but whose identity has never been revealed. The head of Special Branch at Thames Valley Police – effectively the police arm of the intelligence and security services – was also present. This was the first time Special Branch is known to have been involved in the operation, which had by now been given the code-name 'Mason'.

Page was told at what time Dr Kelly had left home; what he was wearing; and given an insight into his mood plus general background information about what had happened to him over the previous two weeks and what impact those events might have had on him. At that stage he decided that he was overseeing a missing person investigation, albeit one with possibly sinister undertones. His chief concerns were that Dr Kelly might have become ill while out walking, or had had an accident. He also believed it was possible that Dr Kelly had been abducted, though hypothetically by whom has never been established. However, notably absent from his list of potential occurrences, carefully compiled by Thames Valley Police in conjunction with Dr Kelly's family and senior police colleagues, was anything to do with suicide or death by whatever means.

Page asked the police search adviser and the specialist sergeant from Milton Keynes to make an assessment of where to begin looking for Dr Kelly, based on what his family had said were his favourite haunts and walks. A list of six places was identified. Harrowdown Hill was second on the list.

He also organized for Special Branch officers from the Metropolitan Police to visit the three offices in London from which Dr Kelly was known to work in his capacity as a senior civil servant, in case he was to be found in one of them. Page knew that, as Dr Kelly was a government employee, it would be easier to access his offices with the assistance of Special Branch officers.

By 6 a.m. DS Webb, who had been rung two hours earlier and asked to assist with the search for Dr Kelly, had just left Abingdon Police Station. He had been briefed by Sgt Morris about Dr Kelly's disappearance, and was making his way to the Kellys' house to try to gain a better understanding of why Dr Kelly might have disappeared.

At the same time, 6 a.m., Detective Constable (DC) Graham Coe of Thames Valley Police CID was called in from Wantage Police Station and soon after began making door-to-door inquiries near Dr Kelly's house.

When DS Webb arrived at the Kellys' house at 7.15 a.m., he found that the Kelly family believed collectively that

Dr Kelly was alive. They were even in an 'upbeat' mood, in his opinion, and were apparently under the impression, like ACC Page, that he might just have become ill somewhere.

Also at 7.15 a.m., volunteer searchers Paul Chapman and Louise Holmes arrived at Abingdon Police Station to be briefed on their task by their manager, Neil Knight, plus two officers. They were given a photograph and description of Dr Kelly and were asked to search the area around Harrowdown Hill, including the track that runs alongside it from the village of Longworth to the River Thames. The search helicopter had already covered this territory from the air a few hours previously, but they drove there and set off on foot with Brock. They were the only volunteer searchers who were looking for Dr Kelly but were to play a key role in the investigation.

Also at 7.15 a.m., PC Andrew Franklin, normally based at the Royal Lodge in Windsor Great Park, arrived at Abingdon Police Station for a briefing from Sgt Paul Wood and about eight other officers. Franklin lived in Windsor, some fifty miles away, indicating just how important Operation Mason had become. He was shortly joined by his colleague PC Martyn Sawyer, who was specially trained to search major crime and murder scenes and was also based at the Royal Lodge at Windsor Great Park.

Franklin informed Sawyer that they were looking for a 'high-risk' missing person, signifying that by this time fears for Dr Kelly had reached their peak and the possibility that he had come to some harm was now considered greater than it had been seven hours previously. It is not clear what circumstance, apart from the passage of time, had determined the police to raise Dr Kelly's risk status. Like the volunteer searchers, Franklin and Sawyer were handed a photograph and description of Dr Kelly before discussing where they would begin looking for him, based on the places he was known to frequent.

By 7.30 a.m. a search pattern was established. About forty officers were asked to start combing a wider area around the Kellys' house than had previously been covered. A mounted unit from Milton Keynes was also on its way to help, as was an underwater search team.

At about 8 a.m., Thames Valley Police were preparing to publicize Dr Kelly's disappearance. Acting Superintendent David Purnell, of Abingdon Police, said in the statement which the force released shortly before 8.30 a.m.: 'We are concerned for Dr Kelly's welfare and need to hear from anyone who recalls seeing a man of this description in the area since yesterday afternoon. Due to the bad weather and the fact it is unlikely he was wearing a coat he would have been distinctive and people who may have seen him in the area are urged to contact police as soon as possible.'

This was odd. Firstly, the weather was not bad, though neither was it brilliant for high summer, a little light rain having fallen overnight. Secondly, when Dr Kelly was eventually found he was wearing a Barbour coat. Not only that, but his house had been searched twice by police during the early hours and his family had been spoken to by several police officers at some length. The straightforward matter of whether he had been wearing his coat had been overlooked by them.

Records show that the police initially said in their statement that Dr Kelly was last seen wearing an off-white cotton shirt which was possibly striped; blue jeans; a brown leather belt; and brown shoes. They described him as an avid walker with good local knowledge of the many footpaths surrounding his house, and said that it was not unusual for him to walk for two or three hours at a time, but it was unusual for him to do so alone.

At 8.30 a.m. DS Webb returned from the Kellys' house to Abingdon Police Station to give ACC Michael Page a progress report, leaving family liaison officer WPC Karen Roberts with the Kellys.

According to Webb, after a conversation with Page lasting fifteen or twenty minutes, a call came in to the police station confirming that a body had been found at Harrowdown Hill by the volunteer searchers, Paul Chapman and Louise Holmes. It appeared to match Dr Kelly's description.

On hearing this, Page sent Webb back to the Kellys' house to tell them the grim news in person. Of course, although the body appeared to the volunteer searchers to be that of Dr Kelly, based on the photograph of him which they had been given, nobody had been able to confirm as much by that stage, even unofficially. This is known because the police have verified that there was no wallet and no identifying documentation on Dr Kelly at Harrowdown Hill.

Chapman and Holmes had only managed to locate Dr Kelly's body with the help of Brock. Having searched the track towards Harrowdown Hill, and then the southern edge of the wood, they walked as far as the River Thames before deciding to check in the wood itself.

On arrival at the river they found four people moored on a boat, who asked what the searchers were doing and then said that they had heard the helicopter the previous night but had not seen anybody or anything else. Their identities have never been published, even if they ever were known to police.

The volunteer searchers then walked the north boundary of the wood until Brock picked up a scent within it. They approached the wood from the east, whereupon Brock signalled that he had a scent to follow and ran ahead. He quickly returned to Holmes, who was a few hundred yards into the wood by this point, barking to indicate that he had found something. The dog then lay down, leaving Holmes to go further into the wood alone.

From a distance, she saw what she described as the body of a man slumped against a tree. She did not touch the body. Paul Chapman was some way behind so she shouted to him to ring the police.

Chapman tried to contact the control team but the mobile numbers he had been given went straight to answerphone. He then rang 999 and asked to be put through to Abingdon Police Station. The operator wouldn't transfer him so he asked to be rung back immediately. Within a couple of minutes he heard from an officer and was able to report the location of the body. The discovery was logged as having been made at 9.20 a.m.

Three policemen – DC Graham Coe, DC Shields, plus a third man whom Thames Valley Police have refused to name – were soon at the scene. Coe volunteered to stand guard alone over the body until more help came. It's not known where Shields and the 'third man' went.

On hearing of the discovery, the police rang for an ambulance. At about 9.45 a.m. paramedic Vanessa Hunt and ambulance technician David Bartlett parked three-quarters of a mile from the wood – the closest they could get to it – and encountered several armed police. Having been told they were on their way to a 'Kilo 1' call – a call involving a dead body – they immediately assumed there had been a shooting.

They were directed up the bridle path to the wood on foot carrying heavy equipment including an oxygen tank and defibrillator machine, and led to the scene. Two PCs, Franklin and Sawyer, had arrived before them and were fixing aluminium posts into the ground to indicate the route they had taken up to the body.

The paramedic team lifted Dr Kelly's eyelids to check for pupil reaction and felt his neck for a pulse. They then placed heart monitor paddles used for defibrillation onto his chest over his shirt to check for signs of life. They declared Dr Kelly dead at 10.07 a.m.

Back at the Kellys' house, DS Webb, who had broken the news to the Kelly family that a body had been found, began a further search of the property. He examined Dr Kelly's briefcase and found a sealed letter dated 9 July 2003 addressed to Dr Kelly from Richard Hatfield, Personnel Director of the MoD, headed 'Discussions with the media'. He took this back to the police station along with a notebook; some business cards; various papers relating to Dr Kelly's appearances before the select committees; his 2003 diary; plus a number of booklets. One was entitled *Iraq's Weapons of Mass Destruction* and another *The Decision to Go to War in Iraq, Volumes 1 and 2*.

Later that morning, Thames Valley Police's Special Branch unit was ordered by ACC Page to conduct a yet more detailed search of Dr Kelly's house and to remove anything which was considered to be of interest, including 'documents of a secret nature', because Special Branch officers are cleared to handle such material. Eventually, five computers plus a hand-held digital device were removed from Dr Kelly's study by the police Hi Tech Crime Unit along with a zip drive and some zip discs, a stack of floppy discs, some CDs, three mobile phones, a microcassette recorder and two memory cards.

'SUSPECTED SUICIDE'

On the plane, Tony Blair had been glued to the phone speaking to colleagues in London to find out what was going on.

Among them was Sir Kevin Tebbit, Dr Kelly's ultimate boss at the MoD. He also spoke to Geoff Hoon, the Defence Secretary and the man who had played such an instrumental role in making life uncomfortable for Dr Kelly over the previous two weeks following his admission that he had spoken to Andrew Gilligan.

Perhaps surprisingly, Blair appears to have gone back to sleep after the initial flurry of phone calls he made and received. It was apparently left to his adviser, Sir David Manning, who was also on the flight, to wake him up and tell him the worst when an update on the situation came through from the UK.

The morning's dramatic events in Oxfordshire were being followed closely by members of the government, in particular Blair's friend and former flatmate Lord Falconer of Thoroton, who had been appointed Lord Chancellor and Secretary of State for Constitutional Affairs the previous month.

In his autobiography, published seven years after Dr Kelly's death, Blair described the scene as follows: 'In the middle of the night Sir David Manning woke me. "Very bad news... David Kelly has been found dead," he said, "suspected suicide."' Because Blair was flying between Washington and Tokyo he was crossing the international dateline, meaning that his sense of time might perhaps have been confused.

If the official version of events is true, however, it now seems highly unlikely that Sir David Manning could have been told much before 10 a.m. London time – roughly nine hours into Blair's flight – that Dr Kelly was dead, let alone that his death was a 'suspected suicide'.

This can be posited because, as described above, the two volunteer searchers who, officially, were the first to find Dr Kelly's body at about 9.20 a.m. did not touch it or spend enough time near it to know the manner of his death. They merely observed that Dr Kelly looked dead and were the first – officially – to inform the police of this. They did so by phone a couple of minutes after making the discovery.

DCs Coe and Shields were the next people at the scene, arriving on foot at about 9.30 a.m. Coe was with the body by himself for about twenty-five minutes. He would have had ample opportunity to inspect it more closely than the volunteer searchers had done and presumably to notice that Dr Kelly appeared to have a bloodied wrist, but no other obvious signs of injury. Having seen a knife lying by Dr Kelly's side, it is quite probable that Coe assumed that Dr Kelly had died from a self-inflicted wound and equally likely that he or perhaps his colleague DC Shields rang a senior officer or Thames Valley Police HQ to let them know of this.

Assuming what Blair wrote in his memoir is accurate, and working on the basis that the official story is true, it does not seem fanciful to suggest that the following chain of events (or something very like them) therefore occurred: DC Coe or DC Shields, or perhaps another colleague, would have contacted Thames Valley Police shortly after 9.30 a.m., at the earliest, to report their belief that Dr Kelly had committed suicide. Next, Falconer or one of his colleagues would have been rung in London by someone from Thames Valley Police and informed of this. Somebody from Falconer's office would then have had to contact the plane on which Blair was flying in order to alert Sir David Manning to the situation.

It remains very difficult to understand why Falconer – or whichever official in Whitehall was first told that the police were searching for Dr Kelly – was even associated with this matter at this very early stage. True, Dr Kelly had been in the eye of a media storm thanks to Alastair Campbell's obsessive behaviour towards Andrew Gilligan and the BBC, but that does not explain why a senior political figure was personally involved in the police operation to find Dr Kelly to the extent that he was being briefed by police so soon after the discovery of his body. Who instructed Thames Valley Police to inform Falconer, or one of his colleagues, the minute Dr Kelly was found?

After these three phone calls had been made, Sir David would have been in a position to wake up Blair to break the news to him, just as Blair described in his memoir, of Dr Kelly's 'suspected suicide'. Conveying all of the relevant information during each of these phone calls would have taken a little time. A window of forty minutes from the point at which the searchers located the body in an Oxfordshire wood to Blair hearing of the death while cruising at 35,000 feet over the Pacific Ocean therefore seems reasonable.

It is important, however, to remember that the details initially given to Blair would have been sketchy at best, being based solely on the opinion of Coe or whichever of his colleagues first saw Dr Kelly's dead body at about 9.30 a.m. For, other than the volunteer searchers, nobody except the police had seen the body by that point – if the official version of events is to be taken at face value.

Thanks to Blair's memoir it is also known that he and

Falconer then spoke about the situation in a separate phone call in which they decided that they were going to hold a public inquiry into Dr Kelly's death. Of this, Blair wrote mysteriously: 'I often go over the decision to hold the inquiry into Dr Kelly's death, taken in those early hours, exhausted, on the flight across the Pacific, by means of the unsecured plane phone. I spoke to Charlie Falconer... He agreed to find a judge.'

Falconer, for his part, was able to expand slightly on what he and Blair talked about when he spoke about it publicly a year later, in June 2004. He told the House of Commons Public Administration select committee: 'I had a conversation with the Prime Minister... in which we discussed the possibility of setting up an inquiry into the events leading up to the tragic death of Dr Kelly.' Then, striking a more tentative note, he added: 'I think at the time I had the conversation the position was that Dr Kelly's body had been found in Oxfordshire although I do not think it had been made public that that was the position.'

The time at which these key conversations were held, and who knew what and when, has never been revealed by Falconer. The Press Association news wire was the first to report on 18 July that a body had been found at Harrowdown Hill. It did so at 11.05 a.m., meaning that, as long as Falconer's memory was correct, he and Blair spoke some time before then. Falconer went on: 'I agreed as a result of the conversation I had with the Prime Minister that we would seek to find a senior judge to head the inquiry, without drafting any terms of reference.'

This all but proves categorically that a tired, probably jet-lagged Blair instructed Falconer by phone from his plane sometime between 10 a.m. and 11.05 a.m. that there should be a public inquiry into Dr Kelly's death – a public inquiry, we are expected to believe, almost certainly established thanks to nothing more than a police officer looking at a dead body that was assumed to be Dr Kelly's, noticing he had an injured wrist, seeing a knife nearby, and merely joining the dots as he saw them to conclude that he had killed himself.

Whether or not the original source of the suicide theory – possibly Coe or one of his colleagues – was accurate is irrelevant at this point. What is worth emphasizing is that, according to the official version of events, before midday no medical professional had examined Dr Kelly's body, so nobody knew exactly how he had died.

Two paramedics had seen the body, but their job was to do nothing more than confirm the fact of death. Having done so at 10.07 a.m., they left the scene shortly afterwards. Yet, as shall become clear, at no stage did these experienced professionals ever think that Dr Kelly did commit suicide, based on what they saw that morning. If the paramedics weren't sure how Dr Kelly had died, what made Sir David Manning and, in turn, Tony Blair so certain that this was a 'suspected suicide'?

Furthermore, as it is known that no note of intent was found on Dr Kelly's body, and that he had no identification with him, not only was it being presumed by the Prime Minister from a plane thousands of miles away that Dr Kelly had committed suicide, but also that the body found actually was that of Dr Kelly. It seems remarkable that so many assumptions were being made at this very early stage, and equally extraordinary that Blair's immediate instinct was to go to the trouble of setting up a public inquiry into a matter about which nobody had anything approaching a full understanding.

In 2004 Falconer also told the Public Administration select committee that after his call to Blair ended, he spoke to the Permanent Secretary in his department, Sir Hayden Phillips, a hugely powerful though not universally popular career civil servant. Separately, he also spoke to the senior Law Lord, Lord Bingham. As a result of these chats, it was decided that Lord Hutton, a seventy-two-year-old Law Lord and former Lord Chief Justice of Northern Ireland, was the man to head the public inquiry which Blair decided he wanted. Falconer told the committee: 'After some thought and discussion, Lord Hutton was a name that emerged quite quickly as a suitable person to do it.'

There is no evidence that Falconer had any idea where Hutton was on that particular Friday morning. Indeed, as 18 July 2003 was the final day of the parliamentary session for the House of Lords, it would have been quite possible that Hutton might already be abroad on holiday, or in his native Ulster, or perhaps just at home in London.

Moreover, I have been told by staff who worked in the House of Lords at the time that, as a Law Lord, Hutton was seldom seen there except on what was known as Judgement Day – always a Wednesday – when he and whoever of his eleven colleagues was required to do so would deliver their legal judgements. Yet, most conveniently, Hutton apparently happened to be working in the Law Lords Corridor, a group of offices on the second floor of the House of Lords.

It is claimed that Falconer rang Hutton and, having found him to be in the Lords, asked him to come downstairs to his office on the first floor. Hutton later described the events of that morning to the House of Commons Public Administration select committee as follows:

> Lord Falconer telephoned me. I was in my chambers at the House of Lords. He asked me to go to see him in the House of Lords, and I did that, and he then told me of the discovery of the body of a person who it was believed was Dr Kelly; and he said that the government had decided to hold an inquiry into the circumstances of the death if it was confirmed that the body found was that of Dr Kelly. He asked me to be the chairman, and I thought it was my duty

to agree to that request. So it all happened in a very short space of time.

Hutton also revealed in a letter in January 2007 to then MP Norman Baker that he was rung by Falconer at about midday. This means that over the course of the two hours following his conversation with Blair, Falconer held a meeting with Sir Hayden Phillips, spoke to Lord Bingham, then decided that Hutton should head the inquiry, rang Hutton, found him to be working in the Lords, and invited him to chair the inquiry into Dr Kelly's death – an undertaking to which Hutton was apparently able to agree on the spot without hesitation.

The wheels of power were certainly turning remarkably effectively in the Whitehall machine. But is this sequence of events really plausible? Nobody by this stage had, formally, the faintest knowledge as to how Dr Kelly had died.

How did Blair, Falconer, Phillips and Bingham know that Dr Kelly hadn't had a heart attack while walking, tripped and accidentally cut his wrist? Come to that, how did they know that Dr Kelly hadn't been the victim of a random assault by a psychopath? How did they know Dr Kelly hadn't been murdered in a premeditated attack by somebody who knew him – or who didn't know him?

The answer is they didn't know because they could not possibly have known. Yet the speed of their reaction, and the decision taken to hold a public inquiry, suggests that *somebody* had some advance warning before 9.20 a.m., when the volunteer searchers found his body, that Dr Kelly was dead.

This hugely sensitive incident was addressed by the government with such alacrity as to suggest that, in realizing the potential scandal of Dr Kelly's sudden and mysterious death, the government prejudged its nature before any official police or medical investigation had taken place, let alone the Hutton Inquiry getting under way. Well before midday on 18 July, it seems that the government had determined that Dr Kelly had killed himself, as opposed to having been unlawfully killed or dying of natural causes.

Falconer also spoke to Alastair Campbell on the day Dr Kelly's body was found. Campbell had been with Blair in Washington the day before, Thursday, 17 July, but had decided not to accompany him to Japan, returning to London instead. According to Campbell's diary, he landed at Heathrow Airport at about 9 a.m. on Friday, 18 July, and while waiting to get off the plane received a message from Whitehall's media monitoring unit that Dr Kelly had disappeared. This was followed by a further message asking him to ring the Downing Street duty clerk urgently. He then learned that a body had been found. According to Campbell he was rung by Blair sometime after 11 a.m. Blair told him: 'We should announce a judicial inquiry

now.' Campbell also noted in his diary: 'Charlie Falconer…
called me re the inquiry.'

As Campbell tells it, Falconer and Blair spent part of
their respective phone calls to him urging him not to step
down as Downing Street Communications Director, as
he had apparently been planning to do, because of how
the timing would be perceived by the public. Campbell
wrote: 'TB [Blair] said it would be a disaster for me if I did
that. Falconer… said I would be mad to do it.' Persuading
Campbell not to quit certainly shows that in the heat of
a crisis, Blair and Falconer were able to keep their heads
cool enough to carry on thinking one move ahead of
their critics.

Within twenty-one hours of Dr Kelly slipping out of
his front door in Southmoor without saying goodbye to his
wife as he left for his 3 p.m. stroll, a public inquiry into
his death had been ordered personally by Tony Blair while
in transit and Lord Hutton had agreed to chair it – even
though, technically, it had not yet even been established
as fact that he had died, never mind when, where or how
his life had ended.

Hutton was an Establishment man, educated at Shrews-
bury School and Balliol College, Oxford. He had been a
barrister since 1954, a QC since 1970 and had been given
a knighthood on his elevation to the post of Lord Chief
Justice of Northern Ireland in 1988. Such was his commitment to the Establishment, it appears that he didn't

even need to consult his second wife, Lindy, whom he had married exactly two years before, to notify her that he had been asked and was intending to take on this very public, time-consuming commitment. Although it must have been clear to him that he was going to have to spend the entire summer and several months beyond dealing with the Dr Kelly affair, he was apparently quite happy simply to jump to attention.

While Dr Kelly's body lay cooling in the woods the government spin operation was running at top speed, having recruited the man that *it* wanted to explore this problematic death. Falconer's swift move, made on Blair's order, put in place the mechanism by which the government could – and would – take control of the examination of this tragic event. For while any sudden, violent or unnatural death in England or Wales is always subject to the rigours of a coroner's inquest, and has been for centuries, Falconer was busy doing the groundwork which would eventually allow the government to bypass such an examination and instead hold a much looser, non-statutory public inquiry chaired by its own hand-picked official. Perhaps even more surprisingly, Hutton had only chaired one public inquiry in his life – and that was into the diversion of a river in Northern Ireland.

As an experienced legal figure, Falconer would have been only too aware that a coroner's inquest is an independent inquiry with a potentially unpredictable outcome such as an open verdict, whereby a coroner states that it is not possible to conclude how an individual died. A public inquiry, on the other hand, chaired by a man appointed by the government of the day, can be the very opposite of transparent if set up accordingly.

Records released under the Freedom of Information Act by the Cabinet Office show that, having retained the services of Hutton, Falconer made two further telephone calls to the aeroplane on which Blair was flying towards Japan. The first took place between 12.10 p.m. and 12.13 p.m.; the second between 12.20 p.m. and 12.25 p.m. Perhaps these were the calls confirming to Blair that Hutton had agreed to do his duty.

What made Blair so certain of the circumstances of Dr Kelly's death and the urgent need for a public inquiry? Was it merely the words of Sir David Manning, who, we are told, woke him to tell him of the 'suspected suicide'? Or was it something else?

Some have argued that by setting up the Hutton Inquiry Blair was simply following his well-honed media instincts and knew that when he landed in Tokyo a few hours later it would look best if he had something tangible to say to reporters about this grave inconvenience involving a man who had been appallingly treated by his government – something which could also be used as a shield to hide behind. What better than a public inquiry?

But wouldn't he have looked very foolish if it transpired

Dr Kelly had been murdered in a random attack or had suffered an accident of some kind? Setting up the Hutton Inquiry so quickly was certainly a risk. Of course, it only comes across that way if the official story surrounding Dr Kelly's death is followed. The possibility that Blair, Falconer and Hutton, to name but three, had a head start on events cannot be excluded – particularly when the police seemed to think that Dr Kelly had been found lying 'face down', even though the volunteer searchers who discovered his body had never reported any such thing.

An early warning that Dr Kelly had died might have signalled to the government that establishing a public inquiry was its best route out of a potentially career-threatening crisis. Reputations were at stake, and nobody was immune from having their career cut short.

BUMPY LANDING IN TOKYO

When Blair's plane left Washington, and nobody on it had even been aware that Dr Kelly had gone missing, the original plan had been for the Prime Minister's spokes-man, Godric Smith, to give the reporters a briefing during the last three hours of the flight as a result of talks Blair and President Bush had held shortly before their supper. The journalists were to be told that military proceedings against two British prisoners in Guantánamo Bay were to be suspended, a story which would easily have made front-page news in London.

At about 10 a.m. UK time, however, one of the reporters on the plane rang their office and was told that Dr Kelly had disappeared. Inevitably, the news circulated around the plane straight away. With about four and a half hours of the flight remaining, the media wanted to know what on earth was going on. In a clear sign of panic by officials on board, they were kept waiting. Smith did not address the journalists as a group until the plane was preparing to land and it was far too late for a lengthy briefing. And even when he did begin speaking, he was summoned back to Blair's cabin before returning a few minutes later. Blair himself was nowhere to be seen.

According to reports at the time, by this stage the plane was flying at just 4,000 feet, with Tokyo Airport within landing distance. Smith spoke to the press pack over the standard speaker system used on such occasions, saying: 'The Prime Minister is obviously very distressed for the family. If it is Dr Kelly's body the Ministry of Defence will hold an independent judicial inquiry into the circumstances leading up to his death.'

At about 2.35 p.m. UK time – and 10.35 p.m. Tokyo time – a photographer working for Agence France Presse reported that Blair's plane touched down at Haneda Airport in the Japanese capital. Blair and his wife, Cherie, disembarked and were photographed looking tired and ill at ease.

A few minutes later the then Sky News political editor Adam Boulton reported: 'While he [Blair] understands there will be no formal identification until tomorrow, if it is Dr Kelly, the Prime Minister is obviously very distressed for the family and the Ministry of Defence intends to hold an independent judicial inquiry and there will be an announcement this afternoon as to the name of the judge.'

Little did Boulton realize that by then Blair appeared to have known for several hours that the body was indeed Dr Kelly's – or that the judge who would chair the public inquiry had already been secured in what now appears to be record time.

DR KANAS AND DR KELLY

If there had been a painstaking search taking place at Harrowdown Hill during the morning of Friday, 18 July, unbeknown to police and any other authority at that point another careful search – into missing documentation – was being conducted a few miles away at the Ock Street dental practice in Abingdon, where Dr Kelly had been a patient.

On hearing the news that morning that a body believed to be that of Dr Kelly had been found, his dentist of nine years' standing, Dr Bozena Kanas, wanted to read his notes urgently. There were two reasons for this. Firstly, Dr Kanas remembered that Dr Kelly was due for his six-month check-up shortly. Protocol dictated that a receptionist would ring a patient's house forty-eight hours before an appointment by way of reminder and Dr Kanas was keen to avoid causing any distress to the Kelly family by such a call being made.

The second reason why Dr Kanas wanted to see her patient's dental records was more personal: Dr Kelly had also become something of a friend to her. Their purely platonic friendship extended to him occasionally sending her postcards when abroad. Having heard during a radio report that morning that Dr Kelly had apparently been 'depressed' before being found dead, Dr Kanas wanted to check his notes to see whether he had ever mentioned suffering from such a condition, for if he had, she had no recollection of it.

There was an extensive refurbishment project taking place in the surgery at the time. Despite the ongoing building work, however, the filing cabinet containing her patients' notes remained outside her practice room in its usual place. Patients' notes were kept in alphabetically ordered cardboard files. Before midday on that Friday, the dentist looked under 'K' for Kelly but could not locate his records. She looked again several times but still found nothing. She widened the search, checking at least fifteen sets of records either side of Dr Kelly's but, again, there was no sign of them. Baffled, Dr Kanas eventually alerted two other members of staff and asked them to help her search, including her boyfriend – who was also the practice manager – Nick Barnes. Nobody could find Dr Kelly's notes anywhere.

Every available patient record was combed in every conceivable corner of the surgery to see whether Dr Kelly's notes had mistakenly been moved from the place where they should have been. A member of staff working there at the time who did not wish to be named has revealed that the practice was searched for hours. And yet still there was no sign of them.

Dr Kanas was very uneasy about the situation, which was obviously compounded by the sense of shock she felt at the sudden loss of her friend Dr Kelly. But what was she to do?

Her surgery had opened for business at 8 a.m., yet no trespassers had walked into the practice between that time and her realization sometime before midday that the records were missing. It then dawned on her that the records must have been taken before she had heard on the radio about Dr Kelly's disappearance earlier that morning. This also meant that the records must have disappeared before Dr Kelly's body was found by the volunteer searchers at Harrowdown Hill at about 9.20 a.m.

Where were they?

'MOST HONOURABLE
OF MEN'

While Westminster and Whitehall leaped into action, former BBC journalist Tom Mangold – who had used Dr Kelly as a source and spoken to him by telephone periodically – with lightning-quick speed publicly advanced the theory that the scientist might have taken his own life. Having heard at 9 a.m. that Dr Kelly was missing, Mangold telephoned Mrs Kelly just a few minutes before the volunteer searchers found the body. Mrs Kelly took his call, perhaps thinking that he knew something of her husband's whereabouts. He did not.

After this, Mangold acted as an unofficial spokesman for the Kelly family, giving an interview to ITV News which was broadcast at lunchtime, when the body found at Harrowdown Hill still hadn't been identified and no cause of death established. In this interview, Mangold said: 'If Dave Kelly is dead, he is dead because of something that happened in journalism which means that we all have to look to our consciences.' Clearly, Mangold was not suggesting that Dr Kelly had been murdered by a journalist – or indeed by anybody. He was linking Dr Kelly's death to the previous ten days' worth of media coverage.

Mangold also found time that morning to write an 870-word first-person piece for the *Evening Standard*, which warrants scrutiny. A news reporter familiar with the *Standard*'s four daily edition deadline times in 2003 said that Mangold would have had to file his copy by about 1 p.m. in order to guarantee publication in the later editions on 18 July, which were on the streets of central London from about 4 p.m.

Headlined 'Most honourable of men with the very best of motives', the piece initially appeared on page four and opened rather chillingly: 'I write this knowing that a body has been found five miles from David Kelly's home. I do not wish to assume the worst at this very moment, but the signs are not good.' It went on, referring to Dr Kelly in the present tense: 'He is at his very best one on one, a cup of tea or a pint in hand, explaining slowly, patiently, the complexities of biological warfare.' The funny thing is, Dr Kelly was teetotal and had been for several years since taking a close interest in the Bahá'í faith, which forbids its adherents from drinking alcohol.

Another strange comment followed this one when Mangold stated: 'David is often a guest at my home.' Mangold had known Dr Kelly for five years and later estimated that they saw each other no more than twice a year because they usually spoke by telephone. This means they had met about ten times in total. Mangold also subsequently said of their contact: 'It was not that frequent. I spoke to him whenever I had a query about biological warfare or occasionally chemical warfare subjects. But it was not a frequent relationship.' And yet in the *Standard* article, Mangold presented himself as a close friend, and has done ever since.

Mangold also referred to Dr Kelly's appearance at the FAC hearing which had taken place three days earlier, on Tuesday, 15 July, writing: 'His wife Janice told me this morning that this experience had traumatized him, that he had come home from the committee hearing very stressed and physically sick, and very, very angry at what had happened. The committee hearing had not been a catharsis, nor had it made him feel any better.' Yet Mrs Kelly has never said anything publicly about her husband being 'physically sick' after the FAC hearing. Nor has anybody else. And the FAC had exonerated him as Gilligan's primary source.

Poignantly, by the time the final edition of the *Standard* was being sold during the early-evening rush hour, Mangold's copy had been rewritten – presumably by a member of the *Standard*'s editorial staff – to refer to Dr Kelly in the past tense. The piece had been cut by 200 words and pushed back to page six, it having been confirmed unofficially that the body was indeed Dr Kelly's.

But Mangold didn't finish there. He also gave an interview to Radio 4's *PM* programme that day, which is broadcast for an hour from 5 p.m. until 6 p.m., repeating the line that Dr Kelly had taken his own life. He told the BBC programme: 'I guess he couldn't cope with the firestorm that developed after he gave what he regarded as a routine briefing to Gilligan.'

Might Mangold have been guilty of over-egging his role in Dr Kelly's life? It certainly appears so. He has written about Dr Kelly in several newspapers in the years since his death, insisting that he committed suicide, and spoken about the affair on television, notably claiming during a *GMTV* interview in 2006 that Dr Kelly's death was 'investigated by the local police, the county police, Scotland Yard, Special Branch, MI5; MI6 had a man present [at the scene where the body was found] and the CIA had a man present because the Americans were interested in this'.

It is unclear how Mangold was able to make this assertion about these various intelligence agencies and impossible to know how accurate he was being, but as a journalist whose work had often focused on security matters he would have expected anybody watching to have taken him seriously as he reeled off this list of official inquisitors. However, given that Dr Kelly's death was regarded so quickly as a simple case of suicide – not least by Mangold himself – it seems extraordinary that so many British and American representatives of the spy world would have shown such an interest in it.

As it was, even before the full facts about the manner of Dr Kelly's death were known, and before his friend's blood was cold, Mangold maintained publicly that he had taken his own life. The parallel with Tony Blair's assumption is obvious. But who, or what, made both men so sure?

CONSTRUCTING THE INQUIRY

To recap: the government reacted eerily quickly to the discovery of a dead body at Harrowdown Hill on the morning of Friday, 18 July, if the official chronology is accepted. In the space of about two and a half hours, Lord Hutton had been secured to chair a public inquiry into Dr Kelly's death, even though the body which had been discovered had not by that point been formally identified; nobody knew how it had come to be in a wood; and no medical or forensics team had examined it. This meant that a public inquiry had been established by the government into the death of a man whose demise had not even been officially confirmed, let alone the manner of his death. All of this happened on the orders of Tony Blair while he flew between Washington and Tokyo. There has not been a situation like it before or since.

As all sudden, violent or unnatural deaths are always investigated fully by a coroner, the government's decision to set up a public inquiry was extremely unusual in itself, never mind the speed with which Hutton had been named as Chairman. Having secured Hutton, however, the government was able to use an obscure law to all but guarantee that only he, and nobody else, would be able to scrutinize Dr Kelly's death.

It is vital to examine briefly how Hutton was appointed in order to appreciate the legal basis of his inquiry and its ramifications, given that they are still felt to this day. As it was Lord Falconer who appointed Hutton, we must look at how Falconer came to be in a position to do this.

On 12 June 2003, exactly five weeks before Dr Kelly was found dead, Tony Blair abruptly released his Lord Chancellor, Derry Irvine. The precise reason for this defenestration has never been clear but, as Irvine was only sixty-two at the time, it seems odd that it was presented to the world as a retirement. Having served Blair faithfully for six years, Irvine is known to have been deeply unhappy about the way he was treated. Apart from anything else, he had introduced Blair to his future wife, Cherie, in the early 1980s when they were young barristers, so he might have expected a less brutal exit from public life.

Falconer, a well-off Scot, was a successful commercial barrister and, like Irvine, another long-standing friend of Blair. As plain Charles Falconer, he had attempted, with Blair's blessing, to become the Labour candidate for the safe seat of Dudley North in 1997, but it is said that at the meeting to formalize his candidacy he dismayed local party bigwigs by refusing to take his children out of private education. As a result, they hadn't selected him.

Falconer's consolation prize after Blair's landslide victory in the May 1997 election was a life peerage – the first Blair created – and, with it, the government post of Solicitor General. Over the ensuing six years he was given a variety of other senior government jobs, despite never having been elected.

As part of his desire to be seen as a radical reformer, Blair's grand plan was to scrap the ancient post of Lord Chancellor altogether and transfer some of its powers to a new ministry, the Department for Constitutional Affairs. And so, on the day of Irvine's 'retirement', Falconer was unveiled as the first ever Secretary of State for Constitutional Affairs. In what is surely the greatest of ironies, however, there was a constitutional glitch. It quickly became apparent that, for various historic reasons, getting rid of the post of Lord Chancellor, which dated back to Norman times, and replacing it was far trickier than had been anticipated. This is why Falconer ended up serving simultaneously both as Secretary of State for Constitutional Affairs, a political role, and as Lord Chancellor, a judicial role. He wore two wigs, as it were.

In Falconer's new post it was certainly within his gift to appoint Hutton to head a public inquiry into Dr Kelly's death. However, on the same day as Hutton was appointed, the Oxfordshire coroner, Nicholas Gardiner, was also told by Thames Valley Police, as they were obliged to do, about the discovery of the body at Harrowdown

Hill. Gardiner's involvement was a matter of routine and entirely in keeping with legal requirements, but it meant that there were now effectively two competing parties looking into the matter of Dr Kelly's death – Hutton, the government appointee, and Gardiner, who normally dealt with deaths in his county.

Falconer would have known that a coroner's inquest is held to establish the identity of the deceased, the place of their death, the time of their death, and how they died – also that a coroner is entirely independent of local and central government. Furthermore, he would have been sufficiently versed in the law to be aware that witnesses can be compelled to attend an inquest; that they always swear an oath before giving evidence and face a charge of perjury if they are found to have lied; and that a jury may be called to an inquest.

None of these standards applied to the Hutton Inquiry, however, because it had already quietly been decided at the highest level that it was not even going to be a formal public inquiry convened under the Tribunal of Inquiries (Evidence) Act 1921. Had it been a formal inquiry, the resolution of both houses of Parliament would have been required. With the summer recess having just begun, it would have been difficult to reconvene MPs and peers. This meant the Hutton Inquiry had no parliamentary authority.

The Hutton Inquiry was an ad hoc public inquiry with no formal powers – witnesses could not be compelled to attend, no evidence was given on oath, and Hutton had total control over who would appear and what documents could be disclosed. In fact, the very term 'public inquiry' is a misnomer: being set up so quickly, it had no legal weight at all. It was, in essence, a private inquiry which Blair and Falconer established. When all is said and done, the findings of the Hutton Inquiry were nothing more than the opinions of one man, albeit a senior judicial figure. Aside from the Hutton Inquiry's proceedings still being publicly available to read online, the only thing that was public about it was the source of the funds that would pay for it.

Coroners' inquests often have an unpredictable outcome such as an open verdict being reached, where it has not been possible to determine an exact cause of death. Falconer would also have known that coroners are often reluctant to record a verdict of suicide unless they are satisfied 'beyond reasonable doubt' that an individual intended to take their own life and then did so. This level of proof is often not met, even when someone has been found with a ligature around their neck, as inquests in England and Wales demonstrate most weeks of the year. By contrast, Hutton's public inquiry would have been required by its government appointees to reach a firm conclusion, not an ambiguous one.

Had the normal course of events been allowed to continue under the auspices of a coroner, the government would have faced the possibility of an open verdict. It is unthinkable that this did not cross the minds of those in Whitehall piecing together the jigsaw on the day that Dr Kelly's body was found. Somebody close to the government must have calculated on Friday, 18 July 2003 what type of inquiry would be preferable.

Why was Hutton chosen for the delicate task of inquiring into Dr Kelly's death? There were clearly other judges who might have been suitable, yet Falconer later admitted that Hutton was the first and only person he asked to do it. Falconer said:

I was very conscious of the fact that the person taking on this job would be stepping into the eye of a great storm that was then raging, that the person appointed to do the job would have to be somebody of real experience, of real steadiness, and somebody whom everybody, the public in particular, would have confidence in being able to do the job in a fair and objective way. So somebody not experienced, a recently appointed, quite junior judge would not have been appropriate for the job. Somebody who had been a judge for a long time who had had experience of the potential dangers of being a judge – I do not mean physical dangers but the dangers inherent in being a judge in somewhere like Northern Ireland – and somebody who had ended up in the House of Lords Judicial Committee was plainly somebody with that experience and that weight to do the job. Was I aware of the sensitivity of the job that Lord Hutton was being asked to do? Yes I was. Was I aware of the fact that it would require incredibly sensitive handling? Yes I was.

Falconer agreed that there were only a certain number of suitable judges in the country who were available at the time, and estimated this to be 'in the tens'. He said Hutton 'was, as it were, my first choice and he, as he said and I say, accepted it without demur on the basis of it was his public duty to do it'.

At the same committee hearing, Falconer justified Hutton's appointment by saying: 'After some thought and discussion, Lord Hutton was a name that emerged quite quickly as a suitable person to do it. Lord Hutton's particular qualities that made him suitable were that he was a senior judge of unimpeachable standing, he had been a successful Lord Chief Justice of Northern Ireland, he looked completely beyond reproach and he had the right skills to investigate – the skills coming from being a senior judge – a series of facts leading up to somebody's death.'

The clear inference is that Hutton had specific skills suited to the task, but Falconer made no mention of factors in his professional background which might not have made him everybody's automatic first choice.

Hutton was a judge in Northern Ireland during 'the

Troubles'. As such, he needed round-the-clock protection by the security services and police, and unarguably owed a huge personal debt to these men who guarded his life. Might he therefore have been reluctant to look at any possible involvement or negligence in regard to Dr Kelly's death on the part of MI5, MI6 or Special Branch? Certainly, as a judge who was known to be conservative as opposed to radical, he was unlikely to rock the boat.

When I asked to speak to Falconer about the case in 2010, before entering into a discussion he took the precaution of asking me what sort of articles I had written in the past on the subject of Dr Kelly's death. I sent him a selection by email – each emphasizing the lack of a coroner's inquest – and rang him back the following day, as agreed. He must have read the articles because when we spoke on that second occasion he told me he did not want to talk to me and our contact, such as it was, ended.

On the same day that Hutton was appointed, he rang a young QC, James Dingemans, and asked him to act as senior counsel to the inquiry. Dingemans was working late when this call came through to his chambers at 3 Hare Court, in the heart of London's legal district but, like Hutton, he also agreed on the spot to do his duty. Who knows what work he abandoned to accept the challenging case of investigating Dr Kelly's sudden death?

Aged only thirty-eight, Dingemans was the son of Rear-Admiral Peter Dingemans, who had commanded the landing ship *Intrepid* during the Falklands conflict in 1982. He had often appeared before Hutton as counsel in appeals to the Judicial Committee of the Privy Council, and the Ulsterman rated him highly.

Dingemans had a track record of which a barrister ten years his senior would be proud. His practice included commercial and business law in which he represented insurance firms, construction companies, banks and local authorities. He also undertook constitutional and appellate work in the Privy Council and administrative and human rights work, including claims for and against governments; cases raising issues of freedom of expression; and ones relating to the European Convention on Human Rights, the International Covenant on Civil and Political Rights and the Inter-American Convention on Human Rights. He had also undertaken personal injury work, defamation cases, professional negligence and product liability.

Yet despite such impressive legal experience, Dingemans, like Hutton himself, had no known track record in the field of public inquiries or in the coroners' courts. Nevertheless, Hutton considered this rugby-playing product of Radley College and Oxford University to be among the finest young barristers he had come across and therefore the best man for this hugely important job. The loyalty Hutton showed to him in picking him for this career-defining exercise would be acknowledged months after the Hutton Inquiry finished, when Dingemans was asked some questions by a newspaper reporter about the inquiry and his role in it. Dingemans told the journalist that he could only imagine one occasion on which he would ever discuss any aspect of the Hutton Inquiry. He said: 'Perhaps on my deathbed.'

FORENSIC FINDINGS

At midday, exactly the same time as Falconer and Hutton held their impromptu meeting in the House of Lords, forensic pathologist Dr Nicholas Hunt was logged into the outer cordon of the police scene at Harrowdown Hill. That morning Hunt had been on a course at the National Crime Faculty in Bramshill, Hampshire when, in his capacity as a Home Office-accredited pathologist, he took a phone call from the office of Nicholas Gardiner, the Oxfordshire coroner, summoning him urgently to Harrowdown Hill. He was told that a body believed to be that of Dr Kelly had been found and, if he hadn't already worked it out for himself, he would have been made aware that he was about to embark on the highest-profile case of his career up to that point.

Hunt had been on the Home Office list of forty-three names since only 2001 and was by no means the most experienced in his field, having spent less than ten years working in pathology. However, Nicholas Gardiner had appointed him because he was the first person available; it was the summer and many people were away. Gardiner and ACC Page had spoken earlier that morning about the need to achieve the most thorough examination of the scene possible, based on the police's decision to treat Dr Kelly's death as 'suspicious', which clearly meant that murder had not been ruled out.

Having arrived, Hunt then made his way to the inner cordon, where he was logged in at 12.04 p.m. There he was met by scene-of-crime officers John Sharpley and Mark Schollar, along with DI Ashleigh Smith of Thames Valley Police. He was given a background briefing into what the police knew at the time including, according to the notes which appeared in his subsequent post-mortem report, that Dr Kelly had last been seen walking 'northwards' at 3.30 p.m. the previous afternoon.

Strangely, Ruth Absalom, Dr Kelly's neighbour and the last person known to have seen Dr Kelly alive, saw him walk down the Appleton Road – that is to say in an easterly direction away from Harrowdown Hill. Had he been walking in a northerly direction from where Mrs Absalom last saw him, he would indeed have been walking towards Harrowdown Hill. Hunt could have made a mistake, but it is far likelier that he was given incorrect information by the police when he arrived.

At the inner cordon Hunt was shown a video of Dr Kelly's body – which he described to the Hutton Inquiry as 'lying on his back fully clothed with his boots on' – by scene-of-crime officer Andrew Hodgson. Hunt noticed 'bloodstaining around his left wrist'. Hunt then spoke to Chief Inspector Alan Young of Thames Valley Police, who ran the investigation into Dr Kelly's death, before walking up into the wood wearing fully protective clothing, latex gloves and a mask. At 12.35 p.m., after just a visual observation, he reconfirmed that Dr Kelly was dead, the paramedics having already done so.

He withdrew from the area while a fingertip search of the common approach path was conducted by PC Sawyer and others, wearing forensic kit, on the orders of Chief Inspector Young. It began just after 1 p.m., with Young apparently telling the searchers to 'look for medicine or pill bottles, pills, pill foils or any receptacle or bag that may contain medicines'. Nothing was found, though the searchers combed the ten yards running along either side of the seventy-yard-long path, meaning they covered a fair amount of ground. Incidentally, this was the first inkling that Dr Kelly's death might be linked to some sort of overdose, suggesting that somebody might have already gone through his pockets and found the three blister packs of co-proxamol tablets which Hunt was about to discover. Who first found these pills has never been established, however.

Hunt returned to the body at 2.10 p.m., again in fully protective clothing. This time he was with Roy Green and Green's colleague, Dr Eileen Hickey, both employees of the private company Forensic Alliance Ltd, then the country's largest independent supplier of forensic science. Their role was to interpret whatever blood evidence they found, with a view to assisting with what the police thought at the time could be a crime scene. Hickey accompanied Green in his examination by taking notes, photographs, and helping with various tests to establish what might have happened. Also there was David McGee, a police photographer. A blue tent had by this time been put up over Dr Kelly's body to protect it from the elements. A larger, white tent had been erected in the field at the edge of the wood to provide shelter for those involved in the search who had to fill in paperwork.

Hunt had a closer look at the body and, according to his notes, was able to see that Dr Kelly's left arm was extended out at approximately shoulder level and his right arm was over his chest. He wore jeans, a striped shirt, a green waxed Barbour coat, beige socks and Timberland walking boots, and also a brown leather belt which had a Virgin Atlantic mobile phone pouch clipped to it. On the ground next to him was an open Sandvik knife with a slightly curved blade, and a Casio digital watch.

After the knife was discovered at the scene, it was not seen by anybody other than the police, Hunt and forensics officers. A photocopy of the knife was shown to Mrs Kelly in the hope that she could identify it. The ownership of the watch was never established by the police. Rather, it was assumed that it belonged to Dr Kelly.

Hunt first checked the Barbour which Dr Kelly wore and found, in the front right-hand pocket, his glasses, a key fob and a mobile phone. It is assumed, because there is no evidence to the contrary, that he was the person who also officially found the three blister packs of co-proxamol prescription painkillers. Each pack could hold ten tablets. Two packets were empty and the third contained one pill, giving the impression that Dr Kelly had swallowed up to twenty-nine pills. No outer packaging was found, however, so there was no way of knowing from where these pills originated.

A search for 'trace evidence' on Dr Kelly's body, such as fibres or third-party DNA, then began. The body was undressed at the scene and thirty swabs taken from it. Dr Kelly's clothes, shoes and personal items were also checked for DNA and fibre contamination. Speaking into a tape recorder, Hunt logged any item at the scene on which there was a bloodstain or traces of blood, as well as the places on Dr Kelly's body where he could detect any blood.

Hunt's post-mortem report notes record that at the scene he found blood on Dr Kelly's left wrist, which at that time showed 'five incised wounds'. There was also bloodstaining on the front of Dr Kelly's shirt; on the right knee of his jeans; in the left-hand sleeve of his Barbour coat and over the coat itself; and on the fingers and palm of his right hand. There was a small spot of blood on his right ear, right cheek and the right side of his neck.

Blood was also present on the items found to the left of his body: the watch, which had been taken off and was face down; the knife handle and its open blade; and his Barbour cap. An upright Evian bottle, positioned against some broken branches about a foot to the left of Dr Kelly's left elbow, and its top were also bloodstained, suggesting that Dr Kelly might have drunk from the bottle while injured, thirst being a natural consequence of profuse bleeding. Hunt also recorded that there was further bloodstaining to his left side, running across the undergrowth and the soil, over an area of 'two to three feet'. Blood was also seen 'around the knife and underneath it' on the ground.

Two trails were observed of what Hunt speculated was vomit, from either side of Dr Kelly's mouth towards his ears and around the lips. There was some vomit staining over the left shoulder of the Barbour and also on the ground near Dr Kelly's left shoulder.

Throughout this time Roy Green and his assistant Dr Hickey were taking notes and measurements, walking back to the white tent periodically to update Chief Inspector Young on what might have happened to Dr Kelly. Green told the Hutton Inquiry that he observed 'blood distribution' which he thought had originated from Dr Kelly's left wrist and that he saw 'arterial rain' – spurts of blood which had exited Dr Kelly's body at high pressure when he severed an artery – on the stinging nettles beside his body. Green said there was 'a fair bit of blood' and it had been absorbed by detritus on the wood floor such as leaves, rather as blotting paper absorbs ink. Green added that in his opinion the bloodstain on the right knee of Dr Kelly's jeans would have been caused by his kneeling on the ground at some point, and coming into contact with his own blood on the ground. Green also examined a gate which led from the field below up to the wood, but he found no trace of blood on it.

Hunt's post-mortem report recorded rigor mortis present in all muscle groups at 5.30 p.m., after he had finished taking the thirty swabs from Dr Kelly's body. Rigor mortis, triggered by chemical changes in muscles following death, is affected by a range of factors including age, weight, sex and build. It begins in the head and neck area and can take between two and six hours to be established. It lasts, typically, between twenty-four and thirty-six hours depending on temperature.

Green and Hickey were at the scene for roughly five hours and left at about 7 p.m. According to Green, approximately fifty items were sent to his laboratory for DNA profiling and further investigation, which he was to supervise.

The last thing Hunt did before leaving the scene shortly afterwards was to take Dr Kelly's body temperature. He did so at 7.15 p.m. Many medical experts have pointed out that this was potentially reckless in terms of working out a time of death as accurately as possible. Having been at Harrowdown Hill for seven hours, and having had permission to conduct a full assessment of the area for at least five hours, Hunt might have taken the body temperature as early as possible in order to narrow the window of time in which Dr Kelly died.

As it was, Hunt's decision to leave it until after 7 p.m. meant that he could only speculate that Dr Kelly had died at some point over the previous twenty-seven hours – that is to say between 4.15 p.m. on 17 July, an hour after he had left his house, and 1.15 a.m. on 18 July, eight hours before his body was found. He recorded a body temperature of 24 Celsius (75 Fahrenheit) using the Henssge nomogram.

As soon as Hunt had finished at the scene, a fingertip search of the area inside the tape where the body had been found was conducted by PC Franklin. It took twenty minutes and was completed by 7.45 p.m. but, like the other searches carried out earlier that day, it turned up no results. Officers said they found no sign of any struggle in the wood either.

Hunt was logged out of the outer cordon at 7.35 p.m. and headed back to the John Radcliffe Hospital in Oxford, where he had a long night's work ahead of him performing the post-mortem on Dr Kelly's body once it had been transferred there. The Press Association reported that a private ambulance believed to contain Dr Kelly's body left the scene at Harrowdown Hill shortly before 8 p.m. and drove off through the village of Longworth, also heading to the John Radcliffe Hospital. It is believed to have been driven by undertaker Quentin Silas, an employee of the local firm A. Baker & Sons. For reasons which are not clear, Mr Silas was later required to give a statement to Thames Valley Police. It has never been published.

POST-MORTEM

Nicholas Hunt began the post-mortem examination of Dr Kelly at 9.20 p.m.

Those listed on Hunt's notes as being present were the senior investigating Thames Valley Police officer, Chief Inspector Alan Young; the exhibits officer, DC Charles Boshell; and scene-of-crime officers Mark Schollar, Michelle Sapwell, Andrew Hodgson and Katie Langford. Two CID officers, DC Paul Kingsley and DC Mark Bray, were also there along with coroner's officer Sally Hunt (who is not believed to be a relation of Nicholas Hunt) and a mortuary technician, Kate Tompkins. The presence of ten people at a post-mortem is itself something of a mystery. Some police will claim it is standard procedure for such a large gathering where a death which is being treated as 'suspicious' is concerned. However, that day the police had already been more than happy to leave the press and the public with the impression that Dr Kelly's death was attributable to suicide, surely eliminating any sense of suspicion.

Hunt examined Dr Kelly's skin for any marks, concentrating on his left wrist initially. He recorded a series of incised wounds of varying depths running across its front. He found that the ulnar artery had been completely severed and the ulnar nerve partially severed. The radial artery was intact, as was the radial nerve. There were also many 'hesitation marks' on the wrist – less severe wounds caused by apparent slashing attempts – though it has never been clear on what side of the wrist these marks were made. Hunt's conclusion about the wrist injury was that the reddening around it indicated that the wounds were inflicted while Dr Kelly was alive.

Hunt's examination of the cuts on Dr Kelly's left wrist elicited that they were five to eight centimetres long and one of them had punctured his ulnar artery, which is about the width of a matchstick and located on the outer side of the wrist – that is to say, in line with the little finger.

Hunt then examined the head. It showed several

'abrasions' just behind the left ear, all less than three centimetres. He concluded that these were 'consistent with scraping against rough undergrowth such as the small twigs, branches and stones which were present at the scene'.

The legs showed four minor red lesions at calf and thigh level, three of which were described by Hunt during the post-mortem as being 'of uncertain origin'. These lesions were apparently typical of areas of hair follicle irritation or skin irritation, and were not injuries or puncture wounds, in his opinion.

Hunt's internal examination showed a small abrasion in the midline of the lower lip, consistent, he thought, with contact against the teeth or biting of the lips. The teeth were uninjured.

Subcutaneous dissection of the left leg showed a small area of bruising over the outer part of the upper end of the left shin below the knee one centimetre in diameter. Subcutaneous dissection of the right lower limb showed two areas of bruising just below the right knee.

Hunt concluded that the main factor which caused Dr Kelly's death was bleeding from the wounds to his wrist; later views of medical experts regarded this as unlikely. He also sent samples to be tested for 'stupefactants' – drugs that could have been used to tranquillize Dr Kelly, such as the sedative Rohypnol. None were found.

Hunt's other discovery from the post-mortem – that

Dr Kelly had without realizing it been suffering from a severe form of coronary heart disease called atherosclerosis – was odd as well. Seemingly, this condition had not been identified when he had undergone an MoD medical check earlier that month on 8 July – nine days before he disappeared. Yet two of his main coronary arteries were found to be much narrower than normal, creating a significant risk of cardiac arrest. This apparently left his heart vulnerable to sudden blood loss, and may have rendered him more susceptible to stress. According to Hunt, it also made his heart less able to withstand a synthetic opiate in the painkiller which it was assumed he had taken, co-proxamol. This prescription painkiller was withdrawn in 2007 after it emerged that overdoses, either accidental or deliberate, were causing up to 400 deaths a year. The synthetic opiate it contains – dextropropoxyphene – can cause the heart to develop an abnormal rhythm, leading to cardiac arrest.

Hunt finished the post-mortem at midnight, but it is clear that he must have been tired when he began it almost three hours earlier. His notes state that, early on in the autopsy, he weighed and measured Dr Kelly and found him to be an 'adequately nourished' man of fifty-nine kilos, or nine stone four pounds, who was about five feet six inches tall. Yet earlier that day police had issued a description in which they said he was five feet eight. And his weight at death as recorded by Hunt was also surprising, for at the

MoD medical he was found to be seventy-four kilos, or eleven stone six pounds.

These apparent miscalculations – later blamed on faulty hospital scales – are considered by some scientists to have had a significant impact on Hunt's estimation of time of death, because accurately recorded body weights and measurements are vital in this regard. Earlier that evening, at Harrowdown Hill, Hunt had taken Dr Kelly's body temperature and speculated he must have died sometime between 4.15 p.m. on Thursday, 17 July and 1.15 a.m. on Friday, 18 July, meaning that Hunt's analysis is certainly open to question.

During the post-mortem he also stated that Dr Kelly's liver weighed 134 grams – less than the weight of either of his kidneys, which were logged as weighing 159 grams and 166 grams. This makes no sense: the liver is the largest internal organ in a human body and usually weighs about 1.5 kilos.

These discrepancies aside, Hunt deduced that there was no forensic evidence to support the idea that a third party was involved in Dr Kelly's death.

THE NEW YORK TIMES

By the time the sun rose in Oxfordshire on 19 July, the day after David Kelly's body was discovered, *The New York*

Times had published the first and, to date, only newspaper interview given by Janice Kelly. In it she spoke about her husband's sudden death.

The story was written by Dr Kelly's American journalist friend Judith Miller, to whom Mrs Kelly had spoken by telephone the previous evening, 18 July, just hours after Dr Kelly's body was discovered. Mrs Kelly told Miller that Thames Valley Police had informed her that her husband had committed suicide.

The *New York Times* story read: 'Janice Kelly said the police had confirmed that the body was her husband's and that the cause of death was suicide. She declined to say what led police to that conclusion, saying that they had asked her not to discuss details of her husband's death.' It continued: 'Janice Kelly said her husband had worked on Thursday morning on a report he said he owed the Foreign Office and had sent some email messages to friends.' Mrs Kelly was then quoted as saying: 'After lunch, he went out to stretch his legs as he usually does.' The story said that Mrs Kelly 'had no indication that her husband was contemplating suicide'. She then reportedly said: 'But he had been under enormous stress, as we all had been.'

The news story went on:

> In an email message to a reporter sent hours before he left for his walk, David Kelly gave no indication

that he was depressed. He said he was waiting 'until the end of the week' before judging how his appearance in front of the [Foreign Affairs] Committee had gone, and referred to 'many dark actors playing games'. Based on earlier conversations with Kelly, the words seemed to refer to people within the MoD and Britain's intelligence agencies with whom he had often sparred over interpretations of intelligence reports.

What readers of the *New York Times* article that day would not have known was that the 'reporter' to whom the paper referred and to whom Dr Kelly had sent that dramatically worded email was, of course, also the author of the *New York Times* story, Judith Miller.

Under the circumstances it seems surprising that on the same day that Dr Kelly had been found dead, Mrs Kelly had given any interview to any newspaper reporter. What was odder still, however, was that she told Miller not only of her own certainty, and the police's, that her husband had taken his own life, but also of her fears of upsetting Thames Valley Police by explaining publicly how they, and indeed she, were so convinced of this.

Taking into account the five-hour time difference between Britain and New York, at the same time that Mrs Kelly gave Judith Miller that interview, the post-mortem being conducted on Dr Kelly's body would almost certainly have been under way and its results therefore unknown.

FORMAL IDENTIFICATION

During the late morning of Saturday, 19 July Mrs Kelly and her daughter, Sian, were driven in an unmarked police car with blacked-out windows to the John Radcliffe Hospital in Oxford to formally identify Dr Kelly's body. At the same time, a team of police officers in white forensic overalls continued to search at the bottom of Dr Kelly's garden and also checked his car, which was parked in the driveway of the house.

Records show that at 11.25 a.m., just over twenty-four hours after the volunteer searchers had found the body on Harrowdown Hill, Janice Kelly identified her late husband in the hospital's Chapel of Rest.

While the Kellys were at the hospital, a second Thames Valley Police search team, dressed in black polo shirts and combat trousers, arrived at their house. The seven men and one woman carried several silver-coloured cases to the back of the property. DC Graham Coe, who had stood guard alone over Dr Kelly's body for twenty-five minutes after it was first found, was drafted in to act as 'exhibits officer' in this search of Dr Kelly's home the day after his body was found.

In an interview with *The Mail on Sunday* years later, Coe recalled: 'We were looking for documents relating to Iraq. No one knew whether he kept any papers of a sensitive nature at home. We had to search. If someone writes a suicide note, you'll find it. We were looking for politically sensitive documents.' Coe would go on to spend three days the following week examining the documents retrieved from Dr Kelly's house with a Special Branch officer from Thames Valley Police. He later said the documents related to 'all sorts of things' but would not elaborate. Still, he told the newspaper far more than he would be required to tell the Hutton Inquiry.

The Kellys returned to the house in the same unmarked police car at 12.45 p.m. They were escorted into the house by police officers, ignoring the news crews, photographers and reporters waiting outside. Sian Kelly was then asked to give a sworn statement to WPC Karen Roberts confirming that her father was right-handed in order to prove, presumably, that he had been capable of cutting his own left wrist.

STATEMENTS

At 2.05 p.m. the Press Association reported that Dr Kelly had bled to death from a cut to his wrist, according to Thames Valley Police. Twenty minutes later, speaking on the steps of Wantage Police Station, Acting Superintendent David Purnell said:

> I can confirm that the body on Harrowdown Hill found yesterday at 9.20 a.m. has been formally identified as Dr David Kelly, fifty-nine, of Faringdon, Southmoor, Abingdon. A post-mortem has revealed that the cause of death was haemorrhaging from a wound to his left wrist. The injury is consistent with having been caused by a bladed object. We have recovered a knife and an open packet of co-proxamol tablets at the scene. Whilst our inquiries are continuing there is no indication at this stage of any other party being involved. We would ask the press to respect the privacy of Dr Kelly's family at this difficult time.

Unusually, no attention was paid by the police to the notion that the manner of Dr Kelly's death would have to be considered by a coroner's inquest or – in this case – a public inquiry.

Just after 5 p.m., the Kelly family released a statement through Thames Valley Police. It was again read out at Wantage Police Station in Oxfordshire by Acting Superintendent David Purnell. The full statement ran:

> We are utterly devastated and heartbroken by the

death of our husband, father and brother. We loved him very much and will miss his warmth, humour and humanity. Those who knew him will remember him for his devotion to his home, family and the community and countryside in which he lived. A loving, private and dignified man has been taken from us all. David's professional life was characterised by his integrity, honour and dedication to finding the truth, often in the most difficult of circumstances. His expertise was unique and universally respected and his life and achievements will always be a source of great pride to us. Events over recent weeks made David's life intolerable and all of those involved should reflect long and hard on this fact. We have been deeply moved by the many expressions of support from friends, family and the local community. We would also like to pay tribute to the professionalism and compassion of the officers of the Thames Valley Police Force. It is hard to comprehend the enormity of this tragedy. We appeal now to everyone to afford us the privacy to grieve in peace and to come to terms with our loss.

A few minutes later the Conservative leader of the Opposition, Iain Duncan Smith, released a copy of a letter he had written to Tony Blair in which he said that the public inquiry which had just been announced 'must be able to compel witnesses on oath'. His plea fell on deaf ears.

'HAVE YOU GOT BLOOD ON YOUR HANDS, PRIME MINISTER?'

Having touched down in Tokyo on 18 July, Blair was determined to carry on with his long-planned eight-day tour of the Far East. It soon became obvious that his judgement in doing so was questionable.

On Saturday, 19 July he made a statement during a press conference in which he described Dr Kelly's death as 'an absolutely terrible tragedy' and said he was 'profoundly saddened for David Kelly and for his family'. He then paid tribute to Dr Kelly, saying:

> He was a fine public servant who did an immense amount of good for his country in the past and I'm sure would have done so again in the future. There is now, however, going to be a due process and a proper and independent inquiry and I believe that should be allowed to establish the facts. And I hope we can set aside the speculation, and the claims and the counter-claims, and allow that due process to take its proper course. And in the meantime all

of us, the politicians and the media alike, should show some respect and restraint. That's all I intend to say.

This was a clear attempt to block any awkward questions from the reporters travelling with him and, inevitably, some of them had other ideas. One was Jonathan Oliver, then the deputy political editor of *The Mail on Sunday*. He put Blair on the spot at a joint press conference later that day in such a memorable way that it is likely Blair's own obituaries will record the moment.

With Blair at the front of the packed room alongside the Japanese Prime Minister, Junichiro Koizumi, Oliver stood up as the press conference was nearing its end and asked: 'Have you got blood on your hands, Prime Minister? Are you going to resign over this?'

Photographers' cameras clicked at high speed as Blair, appearing stunned, stood at a lectern trying to buy himself time. He gave the impression that he hadn't heard the question but was obviously unsure what to say, so said nothing. Looking around the room from side to side for a few seconds, it was an obviously embarrassed Mr Koizumi who rescued Blair by shaking his hand to indicate that proceedings had finished.

This was no act of spontaneity on Oliver's part but a carefully thought-through plan hatched in London. His editor, Peter Wright, had told him to forget about protocol and to hold Blair to account by whatever means necessary.

The effect of the question was instantly damaging, reinforcing many people's view that little appeared to be straightforward when it came to the circumstances surrounding this very unusual death – and that Blair's government was mired in it.

DR KELLY'S
DENTAL RECORDS

Dr Kelly's dentist, Dr Kanas, had spent the weekend worrying about what appeared to her to be the theft of his dental records from her surgery.

As we have noted, she had spent a considerable amount of time looking for the records on the day she had heard that his body had been found, but drawn a blank. There is even a well-sourced story told to me by an individual who worked at the surgery at that time that Dr Kanas and the practice manager Nick Barnes had laid out on the floor of the practice every set of her patients' records – amounting to the high hundreds – in an effort to find Dr Kelly's, without success.

Weighing heavily on Dr Kanas's mind was the fact that, the previous week, she had noticed that one of the surgery's windows had been left open all night because it was warped. It did not appear that anyone had broken in through the window, but Dr Kanas could not rule out a connection between this and the apparent disappearance of Dr Kelly's records.

On the afternoon of Sunday, 20 July, Dr Kanas returned to the surgery to have another look. Once again she opened the filing cabinet. This time she noticed that the notes of the patient next to Dr Kelly's were raised by three-quarters of an inch. Immediately behind them, in their correct place, were Dr Kelly's records. Nothing appeared to be missing from the cardboard envelope. Even a post-card which he had once sent to Dr Kanas from Iraq was still there.

Dr Kanas waited for several hours. Then, at 10.21 p.m., she rang Thames Valley Police and told a rather unusual and, perhaps, slightly confusing story over the phone. She informed the police officer on the other end of the line that she had looked for Dr Kelly's notes two days earlier, on the morning that his body had been discovered at Harrowdown Hill, and found nothing, but had returned to her surgery that Sunday afternoon and located them in their rightful place.

Sixty hours after Dr Kelly's body was found, a new and potentially criminal line of inquiry had been opened into Dr Kelly's death thanks to the conscientiousness of his dentist. The police had to react – but the truth of what happened next would stay secret for years.

'DID YOU ASSASSINATE HIM?'

On Monday, 21 July an inquest was opened by the Oxford-shire coroner, Nicholas Gardiner. None of Dr Kelly's family attended the hearing. Uniformed police flanked the entrance to the coroner's court in Oxford. During proceedings lasting a mere four minutes Ruth Rees, the coroner's officer for south Oxfordshire, said that a preliminary post-mortem examination revealed that the likely cause of death had been an incision wound on Dr Kelly's left wrist, pending the results of toxicology reports. Rees's words were based on the initial conclusions of the pathologist, Dr Nicholas Hunt. It is worth noting that Hunt's preliminary report has never been published. As is routine, the inquest was adjourned.

That same morning in Downing Street, a Lobby briefing was held at which journalists were beginning to air their own theories about the manner of Dr Kelly's mysterious death. One Middle Eastern journalist who was present asked if Dr Kelly might have been murdered. Then the BBC's political editor, Andrew Marr, asked point-blank: 'Did you assassinate him?' The reply from Tony Blair's Official Spokesman, Tom Kelly – not a relation of Dr Kelly – was emphatic: 'I would simply say, categorically no.' No matter how inevitable these sorts of questions were, it was obviously most unhelpful to the government that reporters were asking them.

Also on 21 July, Hutton put out a press release confirming the terms of reference of his public inquiry and stating what steps he had taken to get this examination of events up and running. His statement read:

The Government has invited me to conduct an investigation into the tragic death of Dr David Kelly which has brought such great sorrow to his wife and children. My terms of reference are these: 'urgently to conduct an investigation into the death of Dr Kelly'. The Government has further stated that it will provide me with the fullest co-operation and that it expects all other authorities and parties to do the same. I make it clear that it will be for me to decide as I think right within my terms of reference the matters which will be the subject of my investigation. I intend to sit in public in the near future to state how I intend to conduct the Inquiry and to consider the extent to which interested parties and bodies should be represented by counsel or solicitors. In deciding on the date when I shall sit I will obviously wish to take into account the date of Dr Kelly's funeral and the timing of the inquest into his death. After that preliminary sitting I intend to conduct the Inquiry with expedition and to report as soon as possible. It is also my intention to conduct the Inquiry mostly in public. I have appointed Mr James Dingemans QC

to act as Counsel to the Inquiry and Mr Lee Hughes
of the Department for Constitutional Affairs will be
the Secretary to the Inquiry.

With the benefit of hindsight, it is surely of the utmost importance that Hutton's terms of reference were only to 'conduct an investigation into the death of Dr Kelly' and that he was not required to investigate the *cause* of Dr Kelly's death. Again, the contrast with a coroner's duty is stark.

Although Hutton acknowledged that the timing of the coroner's inquest might have a bearing on when his inquiry would open, the reality was that he – or Falconer – knew that it would have no impact. Having been adjourned, the inquest could, as shall become clear, very conveniently be paused until further notice.

SPECULATION

The next day, 22 July, Blair agreed to speak to the journalists accompanying him on his Far East tour while they flew to Hong Kong. Having avoided them since he had been asked if he had 'blood on his hands', this was the least he could do. When asked by *The Times* – which had named Dr Kelly as having been Gilligan's source in its 10 July edition – whether he was involved in unmasking

Dr Kelly, Blair reacted angrily, saying: 'That's completely untrue… That is emphatically not the case.' He added: 'I did not authorize the leaking of the name of Dr Kelly. I believe we have acted properly throughout.' He also said: 'When you set up an inquiry you can speculate for ever about what the inquiry might find but let's let the inquiry do its work.'

Again the forthcoming public inquiry acted as a doughty shield in the face of awkward questions being fired in his direction. It may also have occurred to him that there was an upside to having some of Westminster's brightest reporters alongside him on his trip, for it meant that they were unable to probe what was taking place in London. This included, on Thursday, 24 July, Falconer sending a short and what appears to be hastily written letter to Lord Hutton at an office which had been set up for the purposes of the inquiry. It was formally addressed to 'The Right Honourable The Lord Hutton, Hutton Inquiry, 81 Chancery Lane, London WC2' and headed 'Investigation into the circumstances surrounding the death of Dr David Kelly'. It read:

DEAR BRIAN,

I am writing to confirm my request of 18th July, on behalf of the Government, to you to conduct an inquiry with the following terms of reference: 'urgently to conduct an investigation into the circumstances surrounding the death of Dr Kelly'. The Department for Constitutional Affairs will be the sponsor Department for the inquiry and I would be grateful if, when your report is complete, it could be delivered to me, on behalf of the Government.

YOURS, CHARLIE.

Having taken six days to put into writing the verbal contract agreed between them in the House of Lords the previous week, and Hutton having quoted the terms of reference in his press statement three days earlier, sending this letter appeared to be something of an afterthought on Falconer's part. For one thing, as Falconer evidently knew, the Hutton Inquiry office was already operational. For another, its simultaneously formal and casual wording makes it seem Falconer could not decide whether he was addressing Hutton professionally or as a friend.

That day it was also announced that Hutton had asked Peter Knox to act as junior counsel to the inquiry. Knox, like Dingemans, was a member of 3 Hare Court Chambers. He was forty-five years old, had attended Westminster School and had a First in Classics from Wadham College, Oxford. His main practice areas at the time were commercial and business law and appellant work in the Privy Council. Yet, as with Dingemans, it is now clear that nowhere in his impressive CV was there any case pointing to solid experience of coronial law or a track record of acting in public inquiries.

A couple of days later, on Saturday, 26 July, Hutton and Dingemans left London and headed for Southmoor to see Dr Kelly's widow and three daughters at home. Having made it past the police guard which had been outside the Kellys' house for a week, the two men spent an hour inside. It was explained to an inquisitive press that Hutton had wanted to inform the Kellys exactly how his inquiry would function, but, there being no written record of the meeting, it is impossible to know exactly what was said during this unorthodox visit.

THE HUTTON INQUIRY

Less than a week later, on the morning of Friday, 1 August, Hutton opened his inquiry with a preliminary session lasting about two hours.

The inquiry was held in Court 73 at the Royal Courts of Justice, situated in a modern, functional annexe beside the forbidding Victorian Gothic building in the Strand. Microphones hung from the ceiling and lawyers' computer screens crowded almost every available flat surface in this austere, strip-lit setting. A large coat of arms was apparently removed from the wall to give the room an entirely neutral appearance.

Although wigs and gowns were not worn because this was not a legal trial, in other respects the court was set up as though it were just that. For example, Hutton sat in an elevated position looking down from a dais. Wearing half-moon spectacles, he spoke methodically in a rich baritone voice which blended his first-class English education and his Northern Irish roots. The overall effect of formality was rounded off by him being addressed by witnesses and counsel as 'My Lord' or referred to as 'his Lordship'. And yet, as previously observed, the Hutton Inquiry had no legal powers. Indeed, on 1 August Hutton even found the time to pose, alone, for a Getty Images photographer in the car park of the Royal Courts of Justice, wearing a grey suit and clutching a file in his left hand. This is not something a sitting judge – or coroner – would ever dream of doing.

Court 73 was able to accommodate all of the various parties' legal representatives, plus seventy members of the press, twenty-five officials and ten members of the public at any one time. A second decommissioned court-room next door, for use as an overflow for the public and the media, had space for a further sixty journalists and thirty members of the public. Such was the interest in the death of Dr Kelly, however, that it quickly became clear when hearings began in earnest that more space would be required. A marquee with TV screens lining its walls was therefore erected in the car park next to the courts to provide 200 extra spaces for the media – leaving the overflow room available solely for the public.

The Hutton Inquiry was seemingly, for many, a spectacle of the summer to be experienced like a Prom or a sporting occasion. Photographs from the morning of 28 August 2003, the day on which Tony Blair gave evidence, even show rows of people in sleeping bags having camped out overnight in the hope of getting a ticket, while armed police in combat suits stationed on nearby rooftops scanned the area with binoculars.

In his opening statement, Hutton first said that a minute's silence should be observed as a mark of respect to Dr Kelly. He then explained the ground rules. He alone would decide which witnesses would be called to give evidence, and in what order. Significantly, as previously described, he confirmed that witnesses would not swear an oath as he had no power to compel them to do so. He said that witnesses would include Blair, Alastair Campbell, Geoff Hoon, Andrew Gilligan and Janice Kelly, among others. An application for proceedings to be televised was also lodged that day by ITN and other commercial television companies, which was rejected on Tuesday, 5 August. And tucked away in his opening address was an acknowledgement by Hutton that he had been 'given information' by Mrs Kelly during the visit he and Dingemans had made to her house the weekend before. Hutton did not elaborate on this at the time, but it is safe to say that no coroner would have thought it acceptable to start taking testimony of any kind – no matter how trivial – from a widow in such an informal way.

Nine of London's top lawyers appeared at the Hutton Inquiry for the various parties. Dingemans and Knox were counsel for the inquiry, effectively putting questions to witnesses on Hutton's behalf. Representing the BBC was Andrew Caldecott QC, a leading media barrister. Gilligan was represented by Heather Rogers QC while the BBC *Newsnight* reporter Susan Watts elected to be represented by her own solicitor, Fiona Campbell. The Kelly family, at public expense, was represented by Jeremy Gompertz QC and Jason Beer. Government ministers and officials were represented by a Treasury lawyer, Philip Sales. And MPs from the FAC and ISC select committees who were called to appear were represented by Nigel Pleming QC. The solicitor to the inquiry was Martin Smith of the City law firm Clifford Chance. Normally a Treasury solicitor would have been provided for this role, but Hutton said that 'public confidence would best be served by the appointment of an independent firm of solicitors'.

Career civil servant Lee Hughes, of the Department for Constitutional Affairs – Falconer's – had been chosen to tackle the crucial duties of Secretary to the Inquiry. Aged fifty-two, Hughes's background was different to those of Hutton, Knox and Dingemans. Unlike them, he had not attended Oxford University but had instead read

Business Studies at Middlesex Polytechnic before heading to Whitehall, where he made steady progress advancing through the Home Office.

Hughes was effectively a Man Friday figure, assisting Hutton in whatever way necessary, from writing press releases to managing the inquiry's budget and overseeing practical matters such as negotiating with government departments over the availability of witnesses and the collection of their evidence.

The Hutton Inquiry aimed to set new standards in how it used technology and, as a result, how transparent it was compared to its predecessors. All evidence submitted to the inquiry was fed into a database which could be retrieved immediately and displayed on monitors for the public and media in the hearing room. Transcripts and evidence were published twice daily on the inquiry's website so that the public could follow proceedings. A live transcription service called Livenote was also used for the benefit of legal teams, the public and the media, who could follow what was being said on monitors in the hearing room itself and in the annexes.

The inquiry was divided into two parts. The first phase, which consisted of neutral examination of witnesses by counsel to the inquiry, was to begin on Monday, 11 August. It was to last for fifteen working days, until 4 September. Its purpose was to establish the sequence of events from September 2002, when the government published the 'forty-five-minute' dossier, up to Dr Kelly's death in July 2003. Witnesses were invited to give evidence, with their invitation specifying the areas on which they would be questioned. They were also asked to submit a written statement and, if necessary, documents, beforehand. None of the witness statements has ever been published, so in fact a qualified kind of transparency operated.

At the end of stage one, Hutton decided which witnesses might be liable to criticism in his report. They were told about this and invited to appear in phase two of the inquiry so that they could answer those criticisms. The second phase ran across eight working days between 15 September and 25 September, the day on which Hutton made his closing statements. In the event a further day of hearings took place on 13 October so that Sir Kevin Tebbit, the Permanent Secretary at the MoD, could give evidence. He had been unable to attend when scheduled following an eye operation.

During that second phase, witnesses were examined by their own counsel, and limited cross-examination by counsel to other parties to the inquiry was also allowed. Other witnesses were recalled in stage two to provide further evidence, even though they were not under any threat of potential criticism. A few witnesses were also called for the first time. Cross-examination was limited to agreed areas, and time limits were imposed. No formal written submissions or experts' reports were published.

In total, 110 hours of evidence was heard from seventy-four witnesses across twenty-three separate days, after which Hutton began writing his report. In practical terms the inquiry was generally considered to have gone well.

On 27 January 2004, however, four months after its conclusion, its smooth running was derailed spectacularly by a leak. In what has gone down as one of the most memorable scoops in recent British journalism, *The Sun* was given a read-out of the essential conclusions of Hutton's report the day before the judge was able to announce his findings personally to the public. The *Sun*'s story, billed as a world exclusive, appeared in its first edition on Wednesday, 28 January. Its top lines were that Tony Blair had been 'cleared of using [a] sneaky ploy to name Dr Kelly'; the BBC was 'at fault'; and Andrew Gilligan's report was 'unfounded'.

Hutton's thunder had been stolen, but – far more significantly – the thrust of what turned out to be *The Sun*'s completely accurate coverage was that he had let the government off the hook. To the amazement of most, it was Gilligan and the BBC who came in for the heaviest criticism from Hutton.

And so at lunchtime on 28 January 2004 – when Hutton had been expecting to deliver his report exclusively at the Royal Courts of Justice – every newspaper, radio and television programme already had a fair idea of his conclusions. An inquiry into the leak took place, but the source has never been identified. With the benefit of hind-sight, this episode itself is something of a mystery. Who leaked the Hutton Report and why?

Though it was hotly denied by *The Sun* at the time, it does not seem unreasonable to suggest that someone close to the government was responsible and perhaps acted as they did to put newshounds off the scent of a troublesome line of inquiry that was splashed on the front page of the *Evening Standard* the previous afternoon. Headlined 'Was Dr Kelly Murdered?', the *Standard*'s article focused on a letter written by three medical professionals and published in that day's *Guardian* which raised doubts about the manner of Dr Kelly's death. The doctors – surgeon David Halpin, radiologist Stephen Frost and anaesthetist Searle Sennet – said it was 'improbable' that Dr Kelly could have died by slashing his wrist and called for a full coroner's inquest. If the leak to the *The Sun* was part of a plan to switch attention back to Hutton's findings, it certainly worked.

As *The Sun* had warned, over 750 pages comprising thirteen chapters and eighteen appendices, Hutton's report determined that Dr Kelly had taken his own life and that nobody could have anticipated this. His report said that 'the principal cause of [Dr Kelly's] death was bleeding from incised wounds to his left wrist which Dr Kelly had inflicted on himself with the knife found beside his body'. It added: 'It is probable that the ingestion of an excess amount of co-proxamol tablets coupled with apparently clinically silent coronary heart disease would have played a part in bringing about death more certainly and more rapidly than it [sic] would have otherwise been the case. I am further satisfied that no other person was involved in the death of Dr Kelly and that Dr Kelly was not suffering from any significant mental illness at the time he took his own life.'

The report lambasted Gilligan, declaring that the allegations he had made against the government were baseless. Gilligan quit the BBC shortly afterwards. Hutton also drove a stake into the BBC's management and editorial processes, labelling them 'defective'. This resulted in the immediate resignations of its Chairman, Gavyn Davies, and Director-General, Greg Dyke.

At the same time, the government was cleared of any 'underhand strategy' to name Dr Kelly as Gilligan's source. In Hutton's view the September dossier had not been 'sexed up', as Gilligan had claimed, but reflected the available intelligence. The MoD was lightly admonished for not telling Dr Kelly it would give his name to any journalist who guessed it. Having cleared the government, Hutton said that any failure of intelligence assessment was outside the remit of his inquiry, essentially allowing the intelligence services to escape censure.

Following this lengthy build-up, Hutton's findings were greeted with derision by the press, which pretty much collectively concluded that his inquiry had been an Establishment 'whitewash'. Memorably, a *Daily Mail* editorial fumed: 'We're faced with the wretched spectacle of the BBC Chairman resigning while Alastair Campbell crows from the summit of his dunghill. Does this verdict, my lord, serve the real interest of truth?' Even its political opposite, the *Daily Mirror*, opined that the Hutton Inquiry 'stinks to high heaven'.

Hutton's inquiry, however, which cost at least £2.5 million and was conducted and written over five months, had reached a very definite conclusion. For better or for worse, the controversy surrounding the death of Dr Kelly was at an end as far as the government was concerned.

Or was it?

What nobody knew at this point was that when he had finished writing his report, Hutton made a secret recommendation to the State. He asked that all records provided to his inquiry which were not produced in evidence be closed to the public for thirty years. Added to this, he sought permission for all photographs of Dr Kelly's body and all medical reports relating to his death – including Dr Kelly's post-mortem report – to be sealed for seventy years.

When, by chance, all of this came to light six years later, the overwhelming question to which thousands wanted the answer was: what was it about Dr Kelly's death that prompted Hutton to hide this material away without the public knowing?

PART 2

CONCERNS

HOW TO SIDE-STEP AN INQUEST

As many people are not familiar with the relatively arcane workings of the coroners' courts, at the time it was set up the Hutton Inquiry probably appeared to the wider public to be a rigorous investigation into Dr Kelly's untimely death. The idea that some of the highest-profile Establishment figures in the country – from Tony Blair and Alastair Campbell down – had agreed to be questioned demonstrated its apparent robustness. They were even joined in giving evidence by Sir Richard Dearlove, the head of MI6, whose voice had never even been heard in public before. Truly, this was an exceptional situation.

Yet this public inquiry was nothing like a coroner's inquest for one simple reason: its premise from the outset was that Dr Kelly had killed himself. Not only were Hutton's conclusions favourably tilted in the government's favour, but less than half a day of the twenty-four days on which the inquiry sat was spent going through the medical evidence relating to Dr Kelly's death.

The inquiry very successfully gave the impression of investigating Dr Kelly's death and holding the powers that be to account while also examining the circumstances leading to the invasion of Iraq, including the role of the intelligence services. But a large number of the high-profile witnesses who gave evidence – many of whom could shed no light on the circumstances of Dr Kelly's death simply because they had no knowledge of it – were effectively red herrings.

After Hutton's findings were known, the sense of trust there had been in the process of his inquiry ebbed away rapidly.

As already described, a full coroner's inquest would have been entirely different to the Hutton Inquiry. Had the inquest into Dr Kelly's death run its course, it would have been a thorough examination of how, where and when he had died. It would have made no pre-judgements or assumptions in the way that the Hutton Inquiry seemed to do, knowingly or otherwise. Furthermore, it would have had the full force of the law behind it. The Hutton Inquiry had no legal significance per se. Hutton's conclusion, that Dr Kelly had taken his own life, was merely his opinion based upon the oral evidence he had heard and the written evidence which had not been aired publicly.

It is now apparent that those who were aware of the differences between a coroner's inquest and Hutton's ad hoc public inquiry felt some unease at these distinctions. Indeed, while the Hutton Inquiry was getting under way at the Royal Courts of Justice, a behind-the-scenes dispute between the government and the Oxfordshire coroner, Nicholas Gardiner, was playing out.

On Monday, 4 August, three days after the Hutton Inquiry opened, Falconer metaphorically removed the political wig he wore as Secretary of State for Constitutional Affairs – which had enabled him to set up the inquiry – and put on the legal wig he wore as Lord Chancellor. He did this in order to exercise a unique power available to him in that post. Falconer asked his private secretary, Sarah Albon, to write to Gardiner making it clear that he would be invoking Section 17A of the 1988 Coroners Act. The consequence of applying this law was simple: it negated the role of the coroner and, to all intents and purposes, meant that the Hutton Inquiry would replace the coroner's inquest.

The relevant part of the 1988 Act states:

> If on an inquest into a death the coroner is informed
> by the Lord Chancellor before the conclusion of
> the inquest that (a) a public inquiry conducted or

chaired by a judge is being, or is to be, held into the events surrounding the death; and (b) the Lord Chancellor considers that the cause of death is likely to be adequately investigated by the inquiry, the coroner shall, in the absence of any exceptional reason to the contrary, adjourn the inquest and, if a jury has been summoned, may, if he thinks fit, discharge them.

Section 17A of the 1988 Coroners Act was created in order to simplify the task and cut the expense of dealing with multiple deaths as a result of a tragedy such as a ferry disaster or a motorway pile-up. At the time of Dr Kelly's death it had only ever been used twice: first, in 2000, when investigating the thirty-one deaths caused by the Ladbroke Grove rail crash; then in 2001 to inquire into the 311 murders committed by Dr Harold Shipman. Both of the resulting public inquiries were held on a statutory basis.

Dr Kelly's death marked the third time Section 17A was used, but the context was entirely different from the previous occasions for two reasons. Firstly, it was employed to examine a single death, not multiple deaths. Secondly, as has been observed, the Hutton Inquiry was established on a non-statutory basis, meaning that it had no legal powers. It was confirmed by Parliament in November 2015 that Dr Kelly's death is the only ever occasion on record when a coroner's inquest into a single death has been adjourned using this obscure law so that a non-statutory public inquiry could be held instead.

The letter of 4 August which Gardiner received from Falconer's office stated that he 'should, in the absence of any exceptional reason, adjourn the inquest. One of the purposes is to prevent duplication of proceedings... He [the Lord Chancellor] has asked if you would kindly signify within seven days your agreement that there is no exceptional reason why the inquest should not continue to be adjourned.'

This was in keeping with the strict application of the provisions of Section 17A, but it is hard to conclude from this distance that it wasn't a cynical manoeuvre by the government to seize full control of the situation. It also seems a bit rich for Falconer to have cited 'duplication of proceedings' as a reason for asking Gardiner to stand down. If anything, Falconer was surely duplicating the proceedings which Gardiner, as a coroner independent of local and central government, should by rights have been able to launch without interruption from Falconer's department.

Did Falconer, as Lord Chancellor, really believe that the cause of Dr Kelly's death was 'likely to be adequately investigated by the [Hutton] inquiry'? Hutton's terms of reference – 'urgently to conduct an investigation into the circumstances surrounding the death of Dr Kelly' – were in fact so vague as to be obscure compared to what a coroner always sets out to achieve. It is also worth reiterating that there was no requirement in the terms of reference for Hutton to determine the *cause* of Dr Kelly's death in the way that a coroner would have had to do.

If Falconer *was* in any doubt about the differences between a coroner's inquest and a public inquiry, Gardiner was quick to point them out to him. He replied to Falconer's office by letter on Wednesday, 6 August – the day of Dr Kelly's funeral in Oxfordshire, which both Hutton and Dingemans attended – sounding perplexed.

Gardiner wrote: 'I had envisaged that it might be possible to conclude the Inquest during September.' He also raised concerns about the less meticulous nature of the Hutton Inquiry as opposed to a coroner's inquest, stating: 'As you will know, a Coroner has power to compel the attendance of witnesses. There are no such powers attached to a Public Inquiry. If I do adjourn under Section 17A(1), I would be unable to resume, if at all, until after the Public Inquiry has been concluded and thus would not be in a position to assist Lord Hutton.'

Gardiner further used the letter to point out to Falconer that as a coroner he had to be 'scrupulous' in following the Coroners Rules 1984 – the rules by which, legally, he had to abide. Point 16 of the Rules states: 'Every inquest shall be opened, adjourned and closed in a formal manner.' In other words, some further formal sitting would have to be conducted by the coroner.

Finally, in the same letter of 6 August, Gardiner also divulged the hugely important matter of the pathologist, Dr Nicholas Hunt, wanting to change his opinion as to what had caused Dr Kelly's death. Gardiner wrote: 'The preliminary cause of death given at the opening of the Inquest no longer represents the final view of the Pathologist and evidence from him would need to be given to correct and update the evidence already received.'

It is now known that after finishing the autopsy on Dr Kelly, Hunt went on to produce two reports: a preliminary report dated Saturday, 19 July 2003 and a final report dated Friday, 25 July 2003. Yet, bizarrely, it seems that Hutton was unaware of the latter report when he opened his inquiry on 1 August. The preliminary report, which has never been published, must have placed little or no importance on a potential co-proxamol overdose. This can be posited because when Hutton opened his inquiry on 1 August he referred only to the preliminary report of 19 July, stating: 'It is the opinion of Dr Hunt that the main factor involved in bringing about the death of Dr Kelly was the bleeding from incised wounds to his left wrist.' In other words, Hunt made no mention of the co-proxamol tablets.

Yet five days later, on 6 August, Nicholas Gardiner stated in his letter to Lord Falconer that Hunt's 'preliminary cause of death… no longer represents [his] final view'.

Despite the seriousness of the matters raised, Falconer's department was apparently not minded to allow Gardiner to resume his inquest – or indeed to formally close his inquest. Gardiner was sufficiently concerned to request, on Monday, 11, August a special meeting at the Department for Constitutional Affairs to discuss the situation.

The Hutton Inquiry had begun in earnest that very morning, yet a parallel meeting was taking place just down the road in Whitehall to try to straighten out what appears to have been the very unusual set of circumstances relating to the way in which Dr Kelly's death was being examined. Also present at that meeting were Victor Round, the Coroner for Worcestershire; a parliamentary clerk called Michael Collon; and Judith Bernstein, a solicitor and civil servant who specialized in inquests.

There are no known minutes of this meeting between Gardiner and the government officials, but in an unpublished interview three years later with the *Sunday Telegraph* reporter Nina Goswami, Gardiner referred to it briefly. He told Goswami that in his view the officials were 'reluctant' to allow him to resume the inquest until he managed to persuade them of its importance. Gardiner revealed: 'I took the opportunity to see the Lord Chancellor's department about the Kelly matter. It just seemed convenient to pop down and meet them. I wanted to make sure the cause of the death was accurately stated to the registrar. To do that, I had to resume the inquest very briefly to admit pathologist's reports which hadn't been available at the opening of the inquest.'

If nothing else, this is evidence of the legal tangle the government had got itself into by trying to take over the investigation into Dr Kelly's death by means other than a coroner's inquest. But it seems extraordinary that Gardiner had to go to such lengths to ensure that the law was adhered to in a matter involving the death of any person, let alone Dr Kelly. It is unlikely that any other coroner has been in such a situation where officials including a government Minister were, apparently, 'reluctant' for him to obey the letter of the law.

The meeting cut little ice. Falconer's office wrote back to Gardiner the next day, 12 August, saying: 'The Lord Chancellor considers that the cause of death of Dr David Kelly is likely to be adequately investigated by the judicial inquiry conducted by Lord Hutton... Accordingly, I am instructed by the Lord Chancellor to request (i) that you adjourn the inquest in compliance with Section 17A(1); and (ii) that you resume the inquest only if, pursuant to Section 17A(4) there is in your opinion an exceptional reason to do so.'

Section 17A(4) could be triggered only after the outcome of a public inquiry was known. Gardiner had effectively been swatted out of the way by the might of the office of Tony Blair's closest political ally.

In the same letter, a copy of which was sent to Hutton, Falconer's office did agree that Gardiner could take evidence from Dr Hunt and from the forensic toxicologist,

Alexander Allan, but it was stipulated: 'He [Falconer] has asked that you keep the proceedings as short as possible and, so far as the Coroners Rules allow, take the evidence in writing.'

Gardiner followed the instruction, taking evidence from Hunt and Allan on Thursday, 14 August – the same day as he adjourned his inquest pending the outcome of the Hutton Inquiry. Gardiner later confirmed to me that Hunt's evidence was given in writing. It is believed that Allan's was as well. Whether they swore an oath or signed an affidavit is not clear.

Why was Falconer so keen that the hearing be so short? Why was it specifically requested that neither Hunt nor Allan should appear in person? What was being hidden? It is remarkable for a government Minister in Falconer's position to have told an independent coroner how to run his affairs.

In the event, somebody appeared determined that as few people as possible were even aware that Gardiner's inquest was to be resumed at all. Falconer's Department for Constitutional Affairs put out a press release on Wednesday, 13 August stating that Falconer had 'directed that the coroner's inquest into the death of Dr David Kelly should be adjourned'. No mention was made of where and when this adjournment would take place the following day. It later came to light that on 14 August some members of the press were rung so soon before it started that they were unable to attend and no press reports of it exist.

At the resumed inquest on 14 August – some two weeks after Hutton's inquiry had begun – Gardiner considered the evidence of Hunt and Allan, but he took evidence from nobody else. No minutes from Gardiner's resumed, and then quickly adjourned, inquest of 14 August have ever been made public so it is impossible to know what importance was attached to the proceedings or the evidence by Gardiner himself at the time.

Gardiner having formally adjourned his inquest on 14 August, on 18 August a death certificate was registered with the Oxfordshire registrar's office. But there were – and are – problems with it, which lists the three separate causes of death as: 1a Haemorrhage; 1b Incised wounds to the left wrist; 2 Co-proxamol ingestion and coronary artery atherosclerosis. Other than listing the causes of death, however, it appears to be an irregular document.

Firstly, it does not identify the place where Dr Kelly died. In the box where the place of death should be stated are the words: 'Body found at Harrowdown Hill.' This clearly demonstrates that the coroner was not able to determine where Dr Kelly died because he had been forced to shut down his inquest. Had he been allowed to carry on, he might have been able to establish the place of death more categorically.

Secondly, the certificate states that an inquest into Dr

Kelly's death took place on 14 August 2003. This is, to put it generously, misleading. The inquest was adjourned on that day having taken evidence from only two witnesses. It can hardly be described as a full inquest, for it was nothing of the sort.

Thirdly, the date when Dr Kelly died was listed on the death certificate as being 18 July. Not only is it the case that nobody has ever established on what day Dr Kelly died, but the forensic pathologist who conducted the autopsy believed he had died sometime between 4.15 p.m. on 17 July and 1.15 a.m. on 18 July, making it far more likely that the date of death was 17 July. Indeed, the headstone on his grave stated the date of his death as 17 July 2003 though, confusingly, a simple plaque that was used as a preliminary grave marker and which predated his gravestone gave the date as 18 July 2003.

Fourthly, neither the coroner nor the registrar ever signed the only publicly available copy of Dr Kelly's death certificate, but, strictly speaking, they should have done so.

Apart from these inexactitudes and oversights, the most extraordinary thing of all about this death certificate is that it was completed and registered more than five weeks before the Hutton Inquiry stopped hearing evidence from witnesses. In other words, the Hutton Inquiry may as well not have been conducted at all, because as far as the authorities were concerned they already 'knew' how

Dr Kelly had died and could point to a death certificate for proof.

The Hutton Inquiry – which the public was led to believe was a replacement inquest into Dr Kelly's death to establish how he died – was therefore a waste of time if its aim, as Hutton has claimed, was to take the place of a coroner's inquest. Gardiner's truncated and adjourned inquest of 14 August effectively closed the case. Once again, the manner of Dr Kelly's death had been pre-judged, though most people seemed oblivious to this at the time. The public's lack of awareness was hardly surprising when Hutton had promised them that Blair, Campbell and senior intelligence chiefs were about to take the stand at the Royal Courts of Justice.

Having met Nicholas Gardiner once and spoken to him by telephone on several occasions, I regard him as a committed public servant whose reservations about what was going on would have been genuine. He does not seem to be the sort of man who would have considered it wise to put up a serious fight with Falconer's department, how-ever, even if the law had allowed him to do so. A solicitor by training, he took over as Oxfordshire Coroner from his father, Thomas, in 1981, and retired aged sixty-nine in 2012. He continued to work as an assistant coroner in Oxfordshire into his seventies.

In an interview with *The Oxford Mail* on 28 February 2012, Gardiner said of the Kelly case: 'I was never under any political pressure... Whatever conspiracy theories people bring forward – and I think they will be brought forward for ever – I don't think I would have done anything differently. My duty is to determine whether there are exceptional reasons that warrant an inquest and if I thought there had been, I would have. The Government was always very proper.'

Gardiner claims publicly that the government followed the letter of the law in dealing with the Kelly affair, yet he had had to remind officials how to act regarding admission of the revised cause of Dr Kelly's death. Having come out of that discussion second best, he was hardly likely to tell his local paper, or indeed anybody else, that he had been put under pressure by the government in relation to the very politically sensitive death of Dr Kelly.

That aside, it is still remarkable that the government expected people to regard its public inquiry – which had fewer powers than a coroner's inquest – as the best way of examining this most controversial of deaths. It is hard to believe that on 18 July, when Blair and Falconer set up the Hutton Inquiry, Falconer, as Lord Chancellor, was not fully aware of his legal ability to be able to force the coroner to stand down and therefore of the possibility of a less stringent form of investigation via the Hutton Inquiry.

As for Hutton, he believes his inquiry 'took the place of an inquest and carried out the functions of an inquest'. We know this because he said so to the then Attorney

General Dominic Grieve in a letter dated 3 September 2010. In reality, it did no such thing.

During 2004's Public Administration select committee investigation into public inquiries, both Hutton and Falconer gave evidence, but neither man uttered a word about the fact that Section 17A was invoked in the Dr Kelly affair. They were interviewed by the committee separately and asked a total of 270 questions. Could it be that none of the committee members had an awareness or understanding of the consequences of Section 17A, or that it had even been used to set up the Hutton Inquiry?

FOUND WANTING: THE KELLY FAMILY'S EVIDENCE TO THE HUTTON INQUIRY

Aside from the sheer haste with which the Hutton Inquiry was set up, there are some equally pressing questions about how Dr Kelly spent his last days alive, his disappearance, his death, and the discovery of his body – alongside a series of holes in the Hutton Inquiry itself.

Janice Kelly's evidence concerning the events of Wednesday, 9 July – the evening on which she and her husband allegedly fled to Weston-Super-Mare following Dr Kelly's unexpected encounter with the *Sunday Times* reporter, Nick Rufford – provides a natural starting point for exploring many of these unresolved matters.

Mrs Kelly gave her evidence over a period of sixty-five minutes on 1 September 2003 during phase one of the Hutton Inquiry – the phase which sought only to establish facts.

Firstly, it is important to note that although she was recorded by press photographers and TV news crews arriving at the Royal Courts of Justice, she never appeared in Court 73, where the hearings took place. Instead, she answered questions from a private room in a different part of the building via an audiolink. A still photograph of her was displayed on a computer screen in Court 73 while she was questioned by James Dingemans, but in effect Mrs Kelly was nothing more than a voice over a loudspeaker.

It is not known whose idea it was that she should give evidence in this fashion, but an application for what amounted to this semi-anonymity was lodged with Hutton by or on behalf of Mrs Kelly after his inquiry began and was approved without any fuss. This meant that the precious opportunity for those present to see Mrs Kelly's face, and to view her body language as she spoke, was denied.

Even allowing for the understandable idea that Mrs Kelly was afforded this special treatment to protect her from prying eyes and distress, it is difficult to avoid asking: what was the point of her travelling all the way to central London from Oxfordshire and being photographed walking into the High Court if she wasn't even going to give evidence in the conventional way? Why not simply remain in Oxfordshire and do so from there via a digital telephone line or videolink, as another witness to the inquiry did the following day? Was her arrival in London a staged event, perhaps to demonstrate that the inquiry had her support? Whatever the truth, analysis of what she said at the Hutton Inquiry raises important questions about her recollections of 9 July and beyond.

Mrs Kelly's evidence session on 1 September was not the first time that she had ever spoken to Hutton or Dingemans. As already noted, both men visited her and her daughters for a private meeting at the Kellys' house in Oxfordshire on the morning of 26 July, eight days after Dr Kelly's body was found. Hutton later defended this meeting by claiming: 'The sole purpose of my visit was to express my sympathy to her and her daughters and to assure them that I intended to investigate Dr Kelly's death fully and carefully. I took no evidence from her.'

Not only was it irregular of Hutton to spend time with Mrs Kelly before his inquiry began, but his memory of the visit also appears to be completely wrong. In his opening statement on 1 August 2003 Hutton had said: 'At my request I have been sent a considerable quantity of documents by the BBC, the Ministry of Defence and the Cabinet Office and I have also been given information by Dr Kelly's widow when I met her at her home on the morning of Saturday, 26th July.' So according to Hutton himself, he and Dingemans were in fact given information – which has never been divulged publicly – by Mrs Kelly before the Hutton Inquiry got under way.

Hutton and Dingemans had, as previously noted, also attended Dr Kelly's funeral at St Mary's Church in Longworth, Oxfordshire on 6 August, even though neither man had ever met him. One is inclined to ask whether they did so with the encouragement of the government first and foremost, rather than out of some instinctive sense of moral duty. Certainly, as the inquiry's two most senior figures, it was no bad thing that the media might get to hear that they had taken the trouble to pay their respects.

During her evidence session, Mrs Kelly admitted that her husband had not in fact been in London working at any point on 9 July, contrary to what she told Nick Rufford when he rang the Kellys' house that morning. Dr Kelly, known as something of a workaholic, had instead uncharacteristically decided to take the day off and spent much of it gardening at home. Mrs Kelly said she was 'quite surprised' by this, though she added that Dr Kelly did find the time to do some work, making and receiving phone calls.

Later, the Kellys ate an early supper and then drank coffee in their garden before Mrs Kelly returned to watering plants and Dr Kelly went to put away some gardening tools which he had been using. This involved him going into the yard which lay between the house and the main road outside. It was at this point, at about 7.30 p.m., that she noticed Rufford had arrived. Mrs Kelly said: 'I suddenly looked up and there was David talking to somebody. I had not got my glasses on so I moved a little bit closer with the hosepipe to see who it was and I recognized it as Nick Rufford. Nick had been to our house before but only by arrangement, he never just turned up before this. No journalist just turned up before this, so I was extremely alarmed about that.'

According to Mrs Kelly, Rufford and Dr Kelly chatted for 'four or five minutes maximum' – not the fifteen minutes Rufford estimated – after which she claimed she heard her husband instruct the reporter: 'Please leave now.'

She then said Dr Kelly approached her and told her: 'He, David, was to be named that night and that the press were on their way in droves. That was the language David used, I am not sure Nick used that. He also added – he was very upset and his voice had a break in it at this stage. He got the impression from Nick that the gloves were off now, that Nick would use David's name in any article that he wrote and he was extremely upset.' She also said that her husband told her his friendship with Rufford was 'at an end'.

Of course, two people can have entirely different recollections of the same event. But it is noteworthy that in describing Rufford's chat with her husband, Mrs Kelly gave the impression that Rufford had revealed to Dr Kelly that he was to be named that night. When he gave evidence, however, Rufford said that things happened the other way around: Dr Kelly had seemed shocked because the MoD had just told him they had leaked his name to the press minutes earlier – something now known to be true.

Furthermore, in his evidence Rufford certainly gave no clue that their conversation was heated. Neither did he say Dr Kelly had seemed upset. When questioned at Hutton, he also denied categorically that Dr Kelly had asked him to leave. Yet if Mrs Kelly, who didn't hear the whole conversation, is to be believed, Rufford was effectively ordered off the property by a very angry Dr Kelly.

The Kellys must have felt dazed by what was happening. Everything seemed to be going in the wrong direction for them and within hours their humiliation at the hands of the MoD would be known publicly.

Mrs Kelly told the Hutton Inquiry that she and her husband 'hovered' for a while after Rufford left. She, it seems, eventually took the initiative. 'I said I knew a house that was available to us, if we needed it, down in the south-west of England, and he [David] did not pick up on that initially.' According to her, 'The phone rang inside the house and he [David] went in to answer it, came out and he said: "I think we will be needing that house after all. The MoD press office have just rung to say we ought to leave the house and quickly" so that we would not be followed by the press.'

Again, there are some problems with Mrs Kelly's account. According to the MoD's Chief Press Officer, Kate Wilson, things happened in the very opposite way to that which Mrs Kelly described: Dr Kelly rang Wilson from his house at 8 p.m. and 'said that Nick Rufford had been in contact with him and asked him why he was not now in a hotel. He was now minded to go to family and friends and he would be heading to the West Country, but he would let me know where he was when he got there.' Wilson added that Dr Kelly sounded 'calm' during their 'very short call'.

Telephone records produced by Dr Kelly's line manager, Bryan Wells, also show that he rang Dr Kelly's mobile at 7.54 that evening. Presumably it was this call, which lasted only ninety-two seconds, that Mrs Kelly heard, and this call which prompted Dr Kelly to ring Wilson in the MoD press office straight afterwards, at about 8 p.m. This call came after Rufford had left the scene.

Mrs Kelly next told the inquiry that after Dr Kelly had finished on the telephone: 'We immediately went into the house and packed and within about ten minutes we had left the house.' It is known, thanks to the Hutton Inquiry testimony of Leigh Potter, the part-time barmaid at the Waggon and Horses, that, as well as packing his bag, Dr Kelly also crossed the road outside his house and went into the pub at about 8 p.m. Dr Kelly asked Miss Potter to tell the publican, Graham Atkins, that he was going away for a few days because the 'press were going to pounce'.

Miss Potter told Dingemans, who examined her at the inquiry, that Dr Kelly was in the pub for no more than thirty seconds. It is worth adding that as well as giving verbal testimony to the inquiry, Miss Potter gave two separate witness statements to Thames Valley Police. Neither statement has ever been published.

Putting all these details together, Mrs Kelly's account would mean that the Kellys must have fled Southmoor at about 8.15 p.m. at the latest. Not having prepared for this unexpected event, ten minutes is a short space of time for two people who had just been doing some gardening to go into their house; to pack a bag each with enough clothes to last an unknown number of days; to secure the property; to tie up any other loose ends, such as Dr Kelly leaving a message at the Waggon and Horses; and to drive away. Further complicating matters, Mrs Kelly described herself to the Hutton Inquiry as 'disabled'. Friends of hers have said that she has for many years suffered from painful arthritis, restricting her mobility.

Despite these obstacles, this was the sequence of events which Mrs Kelly told the Hutton Inquiry had unfolded, and since they had taken place less than seven weeks before, the details of what had happened would be expected to be fairly fresh in her mind, notwithstanding the shattering loss of her husband.

She went on: 'We headed along the road towards the M4 and got to – about 9.30, 9.45 we got as far as Weston-

Super-Mare and decided to pull in at a hotel there for the night.'

She was asked by Dingemans whether any telephone calls were made on the way to Weston-Super-Mare and she replied: 'Yes. He [Dr Kelly] was driving, very, very tense and I was trying to persuade him not to take or make any calls while we were actually driving. So before we got onto the M4, we pulled over and tried to get hold of Bryan Wells. I cannot remember at that time exactly when he did make contact with Bryan, it may have been rather later. It did take some time to get hold of him but he did make contact with someone called Kate at the MoD press office.'

The telephone records produced by Wells at the Hutton Inquiry confirm that Dr Kelly used his mobile to ring Wells's mobile at 8.40 p.m. which, if Mrs Kelly's account is accurate, would be about twenty-five minutes into their journey. The call lasted for only thirty-four seconds. Wells, again using his mobile, rang Dr Kelly's mobile back at 8.44 p.m. That call lasted for just thirty-two seconds. It looks very likely that Dr Kelly and Bryan Wells therefore left messages for each other but did not speak directly.

However, the call which Mrs Kelly alleges her husband made to 'Kate' – the MoD Chief Press Officer, Kate Wilson – cannot have taken place. The only time Wilson spoke to Dr Kelly that evening, as far as she mentioned, was at 8, while Dr Kelly was at home. She recalled clearly that

Dr Kelly rang her at that time because, she said, she had been about to ring him when his call came through.

The sheer speed with which events were moving, and the number of personalities involved, may have caused some confusion in Mrs Kelly's mind. Of course, nobody would be surprised if Mrs Kelly made some small mistakes on such matters of fact in her evidence. The evening of 9 July would have been a stressful time for her and seemingly straightforward incidents might have blurred more quickly than usual in her memory due to the pressure she would have felt. Giving evidence at a public inquiry into her husband's death might have added to the confusion.

Dingemans then asked Mrs Kelly: 'Do you know what he spoke about to Kate?' Mrs Kelly answered: 'No, he was – I think he used a phrase like "cut and run". David would never use that phrase in normal terms. He was obviously exceedingly upset, we both were, very anxious, very stressed.' The phrase 'cut and run' is memorable, but it now appears that Mrs Kelly may have been mistaken as to when Dr Kelly used it. Dr Kelly's friend Dr Olivia Bosch, his fellow weapons inspector, also gave evidence to the Hutton Inquiry. Her testimony provides some important clues about this.

According to Bosch, who appeared at the Hutton Inquiry on 4 September, three days after Mrs Kelly, she rang Dr Kelly by arrangement on the evening of 9 July, and she said they spoke sometime between 7 and 8. Bosch told Peter Knox, junior counsel to the inquiry, that the conversation began as follows: 'I said: "Hello" and he said "I have cut and run." I said "What?" I was not sure what he said. He said "I have cut and run." It was not a phrase that I expected him to use.'

Bosch was asked if Dr Kelly had explained why he had 'cut and run', to which she replied: 'he was advised that he should go because the press were coming to his house and that he would have to be leaving his home'.

Bosch was then asked: 'Did he say he was with anyone?' She said: 'Yes, he was with his wife.' She was then asked by Knox: 'Was it apparent he was in a car or not, or was he stationary?' 'I am not sure if he was in a car or a train but he was moving, yes. He was on the road or whatever, yes,' she answered.

It therefore seems most likely that the phrase 'cut and run' lodged in Mrs Kelly's mind during a phone call she heard between her husband and Bosch – not between her husband and Kate Wilson. And yet, confusingly, if the Kellys didn't leave home until 8.15 p.m., Bosch's conversation with Dr Kelly, which took place between 7 p.m. and 8 p.m., probably didn't happen when they were on the move but earlier, when they were at home.

'How did he seem at this stage, his appearance?' Dingemans asked. Mrs Kelly replied: 'Very taut. His whole demeanour was very tight. I was extremely worried because he was insisting on driving. I asked if I could drive, he would not let me. He was very, very tired and so was I by this time.'

Dingemans asked: 'Do you know if he spoke to Dr Wells at all that night?' Mrs Kelly replied: 'I think he did as we were driving along the M4.' Dingemans then asked: 'What was said?' Mrs Kelly answered: 'Only that we had left home and that we were heading towards the south-west of England and was this okay because it was going further away from London, and he got the assurance that for the time being that was fine.'

Dingemans asked: 'Which town did you drive to?' Mrs Kelly replied: 'Weston-Super-Mare. We stayed overnight. We had a rather sleepless night but we stayed overnight there en route to Cornwall.'

The Kellys' daughter, Rachel, appeared at Hutton on the same day as Mrs Kelly. Like her mother, Rachel spoke only via radio link from a separate room. She corroborated some of what her mother said had taken place on the evening of 9 July. Of course, neither of them was on trial, and their accounts were being given to help establish the circumstances surrounding Dr Kelly's death, but since there appear to be a number of inconsistencies in Mrs Kelly's evidence, it is important to be able to find a witness to support it.

Speaking about 9 July, Rachel Kelly told the Hutton Inquiry:

On the Wednesday Mum phoned to say when they were leaving for Cornwall... She said they were leaving. They were travelling in the car, they had just left home. She sounded quite distressed. Dad was driving and she told me that Dad was to be named as the source... for Andrew Gilligan's story and the report. She sounded very upset, very distressed. More because I think it was more adrenalin, they had had to pack and put their things together in minutes and then they had had to leave because I think Nick Rufford had been and the MoD press office had called to say they really should leave because there were a lot of press on their way.

Rachel added that she did not speak to her father because he was driving, but 'promised that I would look after their cats and their house for them whilst they were away. They did not think they would be away for that long, they very much hoped the media interest would subside quickly. They thought they might be away for a couple of days.'

Rounding off this part of her evidence, Rachel added, almost as an afterthought: 'I did actually speak to them several times on their way down to Weston-Super-Mare.'

If, as Rachel claimed, she and her mother did speak more than once during the eighty-five-mile journey from Southmoor to Weston-Super-Mare on 9 July, it seems strange that Mrs Kelly did not mention these conversations among the other phone calls which she thought she could remember. It is also pertinent to bear in mind that there were no witnesses who could verify that Mrs Kelly was driven by her husband to Weston-Super-Mare that night.

Bosch said she spoke to Dr Kelly between 7 p.m. and 8 p.m. – when Dr Kelly is in fact known to have been at home – and thought he was on the road at the time, but Bosch's perception of where Dr Kelly was proves nothing of Dr Kelly's whereabouts. The same could be said for Rachel Kelly's testimony.

At this juncture, conflicting evidence regarding Mrs Kelly's account of her dramatic journey to Weston-Super-Mare with her husband, and some of the many deficiencies of the Hutton Inquiry, come to the surface. For although, as described, Mrs Kelly's memories of 9 July chime in some ways with the recollections of Bryan Wells, Kate Wilson and Olivia Bosch – and although the trip to Weston-Super-Mare was referred to by Rachel Kelly – the Hutton Inquiry did not ask Mrs Kelly to comment upon an altogether different activity which Dr Kelly is said to have been involved in that night: playing cribbage at the Hinds Head pub, about a mile from his home in the neighbouring village of Kingston Bagpuize.

Dr Kelly had played cribbage for the Hinds Head team for several years and, as a teetotaller, even used to drive the team minibus to away fixtures, such was his devotion to his hobby.

Immediately after his death, investigating police officers took the trouble to speak to the landlord of the Hinds Head, Steve Ward. Upon request, Ward produced for Keith Jones of Thames Valley Police a list of sixteen regular cribbage team members. The email in which Ward supplied these names was sent to the police on 22 July – four days after Dr Kelly's body was found – and was among thousands of pieces of evidence considered by the Hutton Inquiry team. In his email, Ward wrote: 'On checking fixture list last night [*sic*] my memory was put right by some of the team – David did NOT play the league game on Monday, 7th [July] but was here for the friendly session on Wednesday 9th.' Ward then listed for the police those team members who had been present at the Hinds Head on the evening of 9 July.

His assertion that Dr Kelly was not present on 7 July made sense, because it is now known that he was on a training course at RAF Honington in Suffolk that day in preparation for a forthcoming trip to Iraq.

Acting on Ward's information, Thames Valley Police contacted every member of the Hinds Head cribbage team and interviewed them. This is a certainty because between late 2010 and June 2011 the then Attorney General, Dominic Grieve, confirmed as much in an official review of the Dr Kelly case which he oversaw and then presented to the House of Commons. The months-long review – which he said was independent of the government – took place after a group of doctors launched a legal challenge in a bid to trigger a full coroner's inquest into his death. In the dossier Grieve produced in June 2011, he stated: 'Dr Kelly was a member of the Hinds Head crib team. He last played for them on 9th July 2003. Every other member of that team was interviewed by officers from the investigation team.'

Independently, surviving team members present at that friendly session on 9 July have also confirmed to me subsequently that Dr Kelly was there. Among them are married couple Brian and Pat Forster, who told me that such games, which they referred to as a 'practice match' as opposed to a league match, would normally begin at about 8.30 p.m.

When I spoke to Mrs Forster, she was adamant that David Kelly played cribbage on the night of 9 July and provided a robust reason for having such a strong recollection. During our five-minute telephone call in January 2015, Mrs Forster told me: 'The only reason I remember he was there is because he was my partner and we won the game. It was a really close match and we won.' She added that she could remember that the game had lasted a long time, and she found it unlikely that Dr Kelly would have left the pub much before 10.30 p.m. at the earliest.

As this was the last time Mrs Forster saw Dr Kelly alive, and because they were partners in the game, it seems fair to believe that she would have had a strong recollection of the occasion and furthermore would have made her best effort to provide the police with accurate information. She described her police interview as follows: 'My husband and I were interviewed because we were among the last people to see him alive. We were interviewed in separate rooms at our house.' When I asked after Dr Kelly's mood on the night of 9 July, Mrs Forster said: 'He seemed fine.'

Mrs Forster, who spoke without hesitation during our conversation and said that she was as sure as she could be that she last saw Dr Kelly alive on the evening of 9 July, was sixty-six years old at the time we spoke. There is no reason to doubt her memory. Presumably the other team members who gave police witness statements in July 2003 were also able to recall that they had seen their friend at the pub on 9 July.

This fundamental contradiction suggesting that Dr Kelly was in two places at once, courtesy of multiple witnesses in the pub, should surely have posed a serious question for Hutton and for Dingemans. Since the police interviewed all of the cribbage team members, and then passed their findings to the Hutton Inquiry, it appears that Hutton was content to allow the inquiry to proceed without securing a definitive conclusion from available witnesses as to what the Kellys actually did on the night of 9 July. Indeed,

Hutton appears to have left unchallenged the idea that Dr Kelly was in two places simultaneously, even though the police were aware of an alternative narrative.

As for Dingemans, he made no attempt to discover whose story was accurate: Mrs Kelly's, or that of those present at the Hinds Head that night. Why did they allow this contradiction to remain in place? This particular knot also raises questions about the evidence of Janice Kelly. For how can Dr Kelly have been driving her to Weston-Super-Mare at the same time as he was playing cribbage with friends in the pub? Did the timing allow both events to be possible? Might any of the witnesses have been mistaken about any of the information they gave to police? The integrity of the Hutton Inquiry is undermined by such unresolved details.

It is hard to know why this wasn't clarified at the Hutton Inquiry. It could be that, having given the police a witness statement within a few days of her husband's death on which her evidence to Hutton was based, Mrs Kelly was not given the chance to review it. Perhaps she or the Hinds Head witnesses were mistaken. Or for some reason she may have wished to give the MoD the impression that both she and her husband had obeyed their instructions and left Southmoor immediately. Even though her husband had died, perhaps she still feared what this department might do if it found out that Dr Kelly had ignored official advice.

But it is troubling that the police had already been told by several witnesses that Dr Kelly did not, so far as they could tell, escape to the West Country on the evening of 9 July. Instead, demonstrating a certain coolness of character, he apparently visited his local pub to play – and win – a game of cribbage. So why was Mrs Kelly's story about driving to Weston-Super-Mare not scrutinized by Hutton? What is particularly striking is that none of the cribbage players whom the police interviewed so carefully within a few days of Dr Kelly's death was called as a witness to the Hutton Inquiry. Neither was Steve Ward, the pub landlord. Indeed, in contrast to others who gave police witness statements, the cribbage players were omitted from the Hutton Inquiry altogether. Were they sidelined as the result of an accidental oversight or for some other reason?

It could be argued that the Hutton Inquiry was so large, complex and unwieldy that nobody noticed the glaring divide between Mrs Kelly's evidence and that of those at the Hinds Head that night. However, that wouldn't say much for the intelligence of Hutton, the counsel to his inquiry, or Thames Valley Police.

Mrs Kelly's account certainly escalated the drama and tension of the evening of 9 July and, whether it occurred to her or not, underscored the story the authorities were pushing, namely that Dr Kelly was a vulnerable figure who fled the press on the advice of the MoD, leaving his house in the space of ten minutes, and who then felt under such dreadful pressure that he took his own life the following week.

Looking back, it seems remarkable that the Hutton Inquiry called Leigh Potter, the Waggon and Horses bar-maid who had never met Dr Kelly before, to give evidence based on nothing more than the thirty-second conversation she had with him in which he delivered a rather cryptic message, but not Pat Forster or Steve Ward, who was something of a trusted friend to Dr Kelly.

While there is no question that Miss Potter was telling the truth about the brief conversation which she had with Dr Kelly that night, which was witnessed by a customer in the Waggon and Horses, it seems quite possible that Dr Kelly changed his mind and remained in Oxfordshire. What is certain is that both stories cannot be right. For reasons best known to themselves, however, Hutton and Dingemans chose not to pursue the evidence.

Special mention must be made here of the former Attorney General. Dominic Grieve appears to have done such a poor job of 'reviewing' the Dr Kelly case that, while confirming that Dr Kelly played cribbage, he did not address the contradiction his confirmation produced. Did Grieve even realize that Dr Kelly is supposed to have been in two places simultaneously? Whatever the answer, his oversight meant that no awkward questions about this peculiar period of time have ever been satisfactorily settled. There is no doubt, however, that if Dr Kelly really was playing cribbage that night, rather than speeding down the motorway to Weston-Super-Mare, it calls into question his supposed fear of the press, his allegedly weak state of mind, and the testimony of Janice Kelly at the Hutton Inquiry.

A further benefit to the government of the official story that has been allowed to take root is that the MoD was portrayed as a caring organization which showed sensitivity to Dr Kelly at a time of need by, supposedly, advising him that it would be in his best interests to disappear for a few days.

Another member of the cribbage team I spoke to about this series of events is Nigel Cox. In 2003 he was the team captain and had known Dr Kelly and his family well for several years. He was on holiday in Cornwall on 9 July and therefore couldn't attest to Dr Kelly's whereabouts that night. Nonetheless, the police still interviewed him, and, according to Mr Cox, did so in the beer garden of the Hinds Head shortly after his return to Oxfordshire and Dr Kelly's death. During their conversation, Mr Cox informed the police that he had received an answerphone message from Dr Kelly on or about 14 July stating that he was looking forward to seeing Mr Cox for a cribbage game on 23 July. Mr Cox thought it important to tell the police this, presumably because it proved that Dr Kelly was making future plans at the very time he is supposed to have been feeling under so much pressure that he eventually killed himself. Officers said they would be interested to listen to this message and promised to call round to Mr Cox's house to do so but, according to him, they never did. Dominic Grieve, however, stated otherwise. In the official review of the case which he conducted he wrote: 'Thames Valley Police did listen to the answer machine message and included the details of the message in the subsequent statement provided by Mr Cox.' Again, one is compelled to ask: what is the truth about this seemingly straightforward event?

Among the differing versions of what happened on 9 July, one thing is certain: Mrs Kelly was not entirely clear about another matter that day. She told Nick Rufford when he rang Dr Kelly's house on the morning of 9 July that Dr Kelly was not at home because he was working in London. In fact, as she admitted at the Hutton Inquiry, Dr Kelly was at home, tending to his vegetable patch and doing some gardening. Of course, those who do not wish to speak to the press often find an expedient way to dodge reporters, and may feel they do so legitimately. Giving evidence to an inquiry also carries more weight than being doorstepped. But the fact remains that on 9 July at least one incorrect piece of information passed Mrs Kelly's lips. The question is, why was she not asked by the Hutton Inquiry to clear up other, more significant details?

WESTON-SUPER-MARE

According to Janice Kelly, she and her husband woke up early on the morning of Thursday, 10 July in a hotel in Weston-Super-Mare. Its name has never been made public and Mrs Kelly was never asked for it during the inquiry. After the unwanted excitements of the previous evening, in which she claimed they had fled their house in Southmoor at ten minutes' notice, it is perhaps unsurprising that she said they slept badly.

They ate breakfast in the main dining room of the hotel, reading some articles in *The Times* as they did so. 'The first one if I remember correctly – I am sure I do – was written by Nick Rufford giving a brief outline of his contact with David, naming him in his article,' Mrs Kelly told the Hutton Inquiry.

While it may seem pedantic to point this out, Mrs Kelly cannot have been correct. Nick Rufford – the man who, according to Mrs Kelly, had been ordered off her property by Dr Kelly twelve hours previously – works only for *The Times*'s sister title, *The Sunday Times*. The two are entirely separate newspapers for editorial purposes which happen to be owned by the same proprietor. Dingemans would almost certainly have known this.

Mrs Kelly said her husband ate little breakfast and then made a few calls to the MoD on his mobile phone from the garden of the hotel. She was asked by Dingemans:

'Do you know what was said? Did he report back?' She replied: 'No, he did not. He just said I was okay to continue down towards Cornwall.' Mrs Kelly's response, using the singular 'I', was perhaps odd, suggesting that she and her husband had for some reason agreed that she would travel on to Cornwall alone.

Another possible explanation is that she was alone in Weston-Super-Mare already. This theory is not as far-fetched as it might seem when what happened next is considered. Mrs Kelly said: 'I did my packing. He had already more or less done his own. He had a briefcase and we each had a small suitcase each.' She then said they set off directly to Cornwall, leaving the hotel at about 8.45 a.m. and arriving in Mevagissey at about midday.

Her account so far ties in with the rough length of time this 143-mile journey would take: the AA Route Planner estimates it at about three hours. It does not explain the testimony to the Hutton Inquiry of Rod Godfrey, however.

Like Dr Kelly, Godfrey was a weapons expert. He knew Dr Kelly well and appeared at the inquiry on 3 September – two days after Mrs Kelly. For security reasons he did so under the pseudonym 'Mr A', but his identity later became public. What Godfrey had to say triggers more questions about the failure of the Hutton Inquiry to establish and pursue certain key facts.

As Mrs Kelly did, Godfrey gave evidence to the inquiry via audiolink, meaning that his voice could be heard in

Court 73 at the High Court but he could not be seen. Again like Mrs Kelly, he was examined by Dingemans. Godfrey said that the last time he had seen his friend Dr Kelly was at his house near Swindon on the morning of Thursday, 10 July. Earlier that week the pair had undergone some training together at RAF Uxbridge near London and at RAF Honington in Suffolk in preparation for their imminent deployment to Iraq, then scheduled for Friday, 11 July. Dr Kelly was in possession of a batch of the anti-malarial drug Paludrine, which had been prescribed for both of them, and needed to give Godfrey his share of these pills, since they would not be travelling to Iraq together.

In Godfrey's account of the arrangements for the hand-over, it was apparent that he was rather baffled by Dr Kelly's behaviour that morning. The two men lived about thirty minutes' drive from each other, Southmoor to Swindon being a distance of about twenty miles. Godfrey told Dingemans: 'It was slightly odd. He rang me on the morning of the 10th to tell me he had the medication for me... He rang to say he had the medication and was quite happy to drop it off. This was quite odd. I was quite happy to travel the short distance to his home to pick it up. But he almost insisted he dropped it off. Within about half an hour to an hour he arrived at my house.'

Dr Kelly certainly didn't deny to Godfrey that he was at home during their chat, and said nothing about Weston-Super-Mare either. Considering so many witnesses told the police that they had spent the night before playing cribbage with Dr Kelly in the Hinds Head – a fact confirmed by Dominic Grieve in 2011 – the idea that Dr Kelly never went to Weston-Super-Mare but remained in Oxfordshire must again be considered seriously.

Strangely, Mrs Kelly made no mention in her evidence of the cumbersome sixty-mile detour from Weston-Super-Mare to Godfrey's house in Swindon, which would have taken her and her husband towards Wiltshire and therefore in the opposite direction of Cornwall – and all at a time of considerable stress to the couple. The journey by road takes about two hours.

Godfrey was in no doubt about Dr Kelly's visit on 10 July, even providing a good description of it. He said: 'David had parked some distance from my house and walked a hundred yards up the road to my house... He was distracted. Our conversation would normally include a significant part relating to work, but he seemed to want nothing more than to have a cup of coffee and walk through my garden talking about the garden, so that is what we did... I would characterize his behaviour as being somewhat distracted at this point and he clearly did not want to talk much about work.'

Significantly, Godfrey did not see Mrs Kelly at all that morning, but he did explain that the location of his house, and the fact that he had no driveway, meant visitors' cars could only be parked well away from his front door.

When asked where Mrs Kelly was at this point, he said: 'It is possible that she could have been in the car. I myself did not understand how the whole Weston-Super-Mare/ Cornwall trip works in the chronology.'

Since Mrs Kelly made no mention in her evidence of having visited Swindon that morning, and was not seen there either, it would not be unreasonable to conclude that she was never there. Did she even know at the time she gave evidence to the Hutton Inquiry that Dr Kelly's visit to Swindon had taken place? If she and Dr Kelly were travelling separately, it is entirely possible she did not. Conceivably, her husband died without ever mentioning to her that he had made this stop-off on his way from Oxfordshire to Cornwall, which is why it didn't crop up in her evidence on 1 September, but why Rod Godfrey *did* refer to it in his evidence two days later.

If Mrs Kelly was in Swindon with her husband, it was a curious decision on the Kellys' part that she should remain outside while Dr Kelly went into Godfrey's house to drink coffee and wander around his friend's garden. And bearing in mind that the Kellys had, according to Mrs Kelly, been forced to leave Southmoor at such short notice the previous evening, Dr Kelly did extremely well to remember to pack the Paludrine for Godfrey in the first place.

In any case, Mrs Kelly's story of her and her husband leaving Weston-Super-Mare at 8.45 a.m. and arriving in Mevagissey at noon on 10 July would have been physically impossible, in the light of Godfrey's evidence. Mevagissey is 200 miles from Swindon. Add this distance to the sixty or so miles which Dr Kelly had supposedly had to drive from Weston-Super-Mare to Swindon that morning, and he apparently undertook a 260-mile round trip that day.

Covering these 260 miles would have taken at least five hours. Mrs Kelly claimed she and her husband were on the road for only three hours. And to these five hours must also be added the thirty or so minutes that Dr Kelly spent drinking coffee in Godfrey's garden. In terms of timings, this makes no sense, but neither Dingemans nor anybody else associated with the Hutton Inquiry seemed bothered by this discrepancy, for they asked no questions about it – even when Godfrey made it clear that he himself was puzzled by the chronology.

It is also worth introducing the account of another witness who appeared at the Hutton Inquiry, Dr Richard Scott. He was Dr Kelly's line manager at Porton Down. Scott revealed in his evidence on 15 September – two weeks after Mrs Kelly gave evidence – that he, too, had received a call from Dr Kelly on the morning of Thursday, 10 July. It was at 9 a.m., and Dr Kelly rang him to cancel a meeting which had been due to take place at Porton Down at exactly that time.

Scott told Peter Knox, who examined him at the inquiry: 'He said that he had been told by the press office, and I inferred the MoD press office, that his name was likely to become known and that he should leave home to avoid press intrusion'. One impression given by the wording of Scott's evidence is that Dr Kelly had not in fact left Southmoor at the time they spoke but was about to do so, albeit reluctantly.

Knox then asked Scott: 'Do you know from where he was speaking?' Scott answered, addressing Hutton: 'I think he was speaking from home, my Lord, but I could not be certain... I also asked David again to keep me informed of any significant developments. He was calm but, as I say, I sensed that he was under some pressure... The reason I say that was because the conversation was very brief. He wanted to get the telephone conversation over and done with, which was not really like David.'

Was their chat brief because Dr Kelly was in fact gearing up to drive from his house to Swindon and then on to Cornwall, rather than being in Weston-Super-Mare? If Hutton found any of the evidence he heard about the events of the morning of 10 July as confusing and conflicting as it undeniably is, he kept his thoughts private.

CORNWALL

Exactly one week after the Kellys' arrival in Cornwall, Dr Kelly would go missing and never be seen alive again, his body eventually being found in the grimmest of circumstances in a lonely Oxfordshire wood a few miles from his front door.

Given the almost instantaneous conclusion among the authorities upon Dr Kelly's body being found that he had taken his own life, it would have been second nature to a coroner investigating a death like this to hear evidence from those with whom Dr Kelly spent his final days in order to form a full picture of his activities and his mood. No coroner would be prepared to reach a suicide finding unless he or she could convince himself or herself beyond reasonable doubt that Dr Kelly had intended to kill himself, and then did so.

This being the Hutton Inquiry, however, the key period of his final weekend alive was left almost entirely unclarified. Indeed, there is a strong sense that it was kept deliberately vague.

Mrs Kelly's evidence about what she and her husband did in Cornwall amounted to very little. She told Dingemans that, understandably, she wanted this unexpected trip to be almost like a holiday for her husband in order that he might feel more relaxed and less upset. She said that they visited two local tourist attractions; ate well; relaxed; and tramped around the beaches and bays of south Cornwall. At no stage was she asked where they stayed or whether they saw anybody else while they were there; she was therefore not required to mention any socializing which they did.

1. Andrew Gilligan, nemesis of Tony Blair's spin doctor Alastair Campbell. Dr Kelly always insisted he wasn't Gilligan's prime source. If he wasn't, who was? (© Jim Watson/Getty Images)

2. Dr Kelly's notorious appearance at the FAC hearing, 15 July 2003. Many believe the pressure he was put under led to his death but anyone who watches a recording of the entire event will see he cracked jokes and performed fluently. (© PA/PA Archive)

3. Port Mellon, Cornwall, to where the Kellys escaped after Dr Kelly's name was given to reporters. Despite this being where he spent his last weekend alive, details of his activities when there were kept oddly vague at the Hutton Inquiry. (© Niall Woods/Alamy Archive)

4. Lord Hutton poses in the High Court car park on the first day of his inquiry. He agreed to investigate Dr Kelly's death less than three hours after his body was found. He secretly requested that key documents and photos connected to the inquiry be sealed for between 30 and 70 years. (© Ian Waldie/Getty Images)

(Clockwise from top)
5. Lord Falconer of Thoroton. He masterminded the setting up of the Hutton Inquiry on the orders of his ex-flatmate, Tony Blair, within minutes of Dr Kelly's body being found. How did they know the circumstances of his death so soon? (© Bloomberg/Getty)

6. Tony and Cherie Blair land in Tokyo hours after Dr Kelly was found dead. Blair was visibly stunned to be asked at a packed press conference the next day whether he had 'blood on his hands'. (© Koichi Kamoshida/Stringer)

7. Nicholas Gardiner, the Oxfordshire coroner, who battled with Lord Falconer to ensure he was able to do his professional duty. No full coroner's inquest into Dr Kelly's death has ever been heard. (© *Oxford Mail*)

8. Janice Kelly arrives at the High Court in London to give evidence to the Hutton Inquiry. Despite travelling 70 miles to be there she only answered questions via audiolink from a room adjoining Court 73, triggering suspicions her presence was for effect only. (© Dan Chung/Stringer)

9. Ock Street Clinic, Abingdon, from where Dr Kelly's dentist believes his dental records were stolen before his body was found. The records were recovered with six unidentified fingerprints on them, a fact not mentioned at the Hutton Inquiry. (© Alamy Stock Photo)

10. *(right)* Dr Kelly in London the month he died. Note he holds his briefcase in his left hand. His right arm was weak following a 1991 horseriding accident. This arm injury was not mentioned at the Hutton Inquiry. (© Eddie Mulholland/Rex)

11. *(below)* Alastair Campbell after giving evidence to the Hutton Inquiry. Years later he claimed to 'think about Dr Kelly often'. This alleged sense of remorse did not stop him and Cherie Blair autographing a copy of the Hutton Report which was auctioned at a Labour Party fundraiser for £400. (© PeerPoint/Alamy Stock Photo)

CERTIFIED COPY OF AN ENTRY

Pursuant to the Births and Deaths Registration Act 1953

DEATH

Entry No. 190

Registration district	Oxfordshire	Administrative area County of Oxfordshire
Sub-district	Oxfordshire	

1. Date and place of death

Eighteenth July 2003
Found dead at Harrowdown Hill, Longworth, Oxon

2. Name and surname

David Christopher KELLY

3. Sex   Male

4. Maiden surname of woman who has married

5. Date and place of birth

14th May 1944   Pontypridd, South Wales

6. Occupation and usual address

Civil Servant
Westfield, Faringdon Road, Southmoor, Oxon

7(a) Name and surname of informant

Certificate on inquest adjourned received from N G Gardiner Coroner for Oxfordshire. Inquest held
Fourteenth August 2003

(b) Qualification

(c) Usual address

8. Cause of death

I (a) Haemorrhage
(b) Incised Wounds to the Left Wrist

II   Co-proxamol ingestion and coronary artery atherosclerosis

9. I certify that the particulars given by me above are true to the best of my knowledge and belief

Signature of informant

10. Date of registration	11. Signature of registrar
Eighteenth August 2003	Val Farrant Registrar

Certified to be a true copy of an entry in a register in my custody.

C Bowden   {   Deputy *Superintendent Registrar   Date 28ᵗʰ April 2004
Registrar

*Strike out whichever does not apply

CAUTION: THERE ARE OFFENCES RELATING TO FALSIFYING OR ALTERING A CERTIFICATE AND USING
OR POSSESSING A FALSE CERTIFICATE. ©CROWN COPYRIGHT
WARNING: A CERTIFICATE IS NOT EVIDENCE OF IDENTITY.

12. Dr Kelly's death certificate. It fails to name his place of death; wrongly claims an inquest was held on 14 August 2003; and states he died on 18 July 2003 even though the date of his death has never been established.

THAMES VALLEY POLICE

Witness Statement
(CJ Act 1967, s.9 MC Act 1980, ss.5A(3a) and 5B, MC Rules 1981, r.70)

Statement of   **Karen Lesley ROBERTS**

Age   **over 18**

This statement (consisting of 1   pages each signed by me) is true to the best of my knowledge and belief and I make it knowing that, if it is tendered in evidence, I shall be liable to prosecution if I have wilfully stated in it anything which I know to be false or do not believe to be true.

Dated the   **3rd**   day of   **January**   **2004**

Signature   **KL Roberts**

On Saturday 19th July 2003, I was on duty performing the role of Family Liaison Officer for Thames

Valley Police.

On this date I spoke to Sian KELLY, the daughter of Dr. David KELLY who confirmed that her father

was right handed.

KL Roberts

Signature KL Roberts   Signature Witnessed by

NMG11-LAN(02/00)

13. The witness statement of WPC Karen Roberts confirming she was told in July 2003 by Dr Kelly's daughter, Sian, that her father was right-handed. It was only made three months after the Hutton Inquiry ended. There was no mention in the inquiry of the injury which caused permanent weakness in Dr Kelly's right arm.

14. Dr Kelly's local pub, The Hinds Head, in Kingston Bagpuize. The official story is that he fled Oxfordshire on 9 July 2003 to escape the press. But his friends told police he was playing cribbage with them here that night. (© *Oxford Mail*)

15. *(above left)* Mai Pederson, Dr Kelly's close friend. Thames Valley Police interviewed her just after his death but she didn't appear at the Hutton Inquiry and her observations were never referred to during it. She later said he couldn't have killed himself. (© *Mail on Sunday*)

16. *(above right)* Dr Kelly's grave in St Mary's Church, Longworth, Oxfordshire. In July 2017 his remains were exhumed, apparently at the request of his family, and all trace of the grave removed. No authority will say what happened to his remains. (© David Hartley/Rex Features)

I have established that the three nights which the Kellys had together in the Mevagissey area were in fact spent a mile to the south of the village in the tiny cove of Portmellon in a holiday property which some friends told them they could use. They had the place to themselves.

Shortly after arriving on the afternoon of Thursday, 10 July, Mrs Kelly rang John and Pamela Dabbs, a couple who live locally and who Mrs Kelly knew slightly through Mrs Dabbs's sister. The Dabbses had been rung at 10.30 the previous night and, as the keyholders to the property where the Kellys were to stay, alerted to the Kellys' imminent arrival. Mr Dabbs had never met Dr Kelly before, but it was agreed that they would all see each other at some point over the weekend.

When we spoke, Mr Dabbs told me: 'We understood they arrived [in Portmellon] together. Obviously we've got no direct proof but we have no reason to doubt that.' When asked, Mr Dabbs conceded that at no point had either of the Kellys told him they had been together at Weston-Super-Mare.

The Kellys ate lunch together that Thursday afternoon, a meal which Mrs Kelly recalled easily because she told the Hutton Inquiry that her husband was 'more upset at that stage and very tense'. She added: 'He seemed to withdraw into himself completely. And I decided that the best I could do, and I made a policy thing here then that I would keep him properly fed, good food, attractive food and then keep him occupied as pleasantly as possible. So although he was less stressed in one sense, he was more upset by now... We both had a meal and then lay down for a little while before going out into the local village for a walk.'

She went on to say that the former weapons inspector Olivia Bosch rang Dr Kelly as they were looking over the harbour that afternoon. Bosch wanted to bring her friend up to speed with the press coverage about him of which she was aware. This apparently seemed to unsettle him further. Mrs Kelly said: 'He was upset. He did not like his name being in the public domain. He did not like being – becoming the story.' The couple also spoke to their daughter, Rachel, that evening, who by then had gone to Southmoor to feed her parents' cats and keep an eye on her parents' house.

The next day, Friday, 11 July, was another charged one for Dr Kelly. He and his wife visited the Lost Gardens of Heligan, a popular botanical garden near Mevagissey. Dr Kelly's MoD line manager, Bryan Wells, rang him at 10 a.m. and they spoke for about five minutes, during which they discussed the fact that he would have to appear before the ISC the following week, and also the FAC, to discuss the red-hot topic of his contact with the media. It was also conveyed to Dr Kelly that the FAC hearing would be televised. This meant it would likely be broadcast live on the specialist BBC *Parliament* channel and excerpts could also be shown on the main TV news bulletins.

According to his wife he was 'ballistic' at the prospect of this event being held in public in front of TV cameras. She said: 'He just did not like that idea at all. He felt it – he did not say this in so many words but he felt it would be a kind of continuation of a kind of reprimand into the public domain. That was not going to be very comfortable for him.'

The trip to the gardens was ruined. Dr Kelly was so upset that he apparently retreated into 'a world of his own' and conversation became difficult. After returning for lunch to the cottage in Portmellon where they were staying, they went for a walk. Dr Kelly and Bryan Wells then spoke by phone a further nine times that afternoon, during which it was agreed that they would meet in London on Monday, 14 July to prepare for the forthcoming select committee hearings.

Dr Kelly was 'very unhappy', according to his wife, but he did manage to ring his half-sister, Sarah Pape, at her house in north-east England that evening at about 9. According to the evidence of Ms Pape at the Hutton Inquiry Dr Kelly said to her: 'I presume you have heard the news [about the accusation that he had been Andrew Gilligan's source].'

Ms Pape had, of course, heard the news – as had anyone who had read the papers over the previous thirty-six hours. She went on: 'He explained that the MoD press office had given him a sort of five-minute warning to leave the house because the press were on their way. He said it had actually taken ten minutes to pack, but they had then left and gone to stay with friends.'

Significantly, there was no mention by Ms Pape of Weston-Super-Mare – nor was she asked at the Hutton Inquiry whether she had any knowledge of her half-brother having stayed in a hotel there. Yet, unwittingly, she had just added a further, third, layer of confusion as to the Kellys' whereabouts on the evening of 9 July by stating that her half-brother had told her he and his wife had gone to stay with friends, having fled from home. Hutton showed not the slightest interest in this.

Dr Kelly did not tell Ms Pape from where he was ringing on that Friday evening, but out of curiosity she looked at the caller display device on her telephone after the conversation had ended and saw that he had rung from a landline number which she did not recognize. She checked a telephone code book which she owned and realized he was in the Mevagissey area. She then apparently remembered that Mrs Kelly had friends who had a holiday cottage there. Ms Pape told the Hutton Inquiry: 'That would have been a very sensible place to go to hide from the press for a few days. So I was actually quite reassured. He said Janice was with him. I felt he was in the best place at that time.'

Dr Kelly told his half-sister during their call that he would have to appear before the FAC the following

Tuesday; he also said he would be appearing before the ISC. He explained that the FAC would be a public hearing and that it would be televised, but apparently expressed no concerns about this.

Ms Pape offered him the kind of reassurance any man in Dr Kelly's position would no doubt have welcomed, telling him that the family loved him and wanted the best for him. When asked how he seemed during their conversation, Ms Pape replied: 'He sounded a little tired but other than that he sounded his normal self.'

This represented quite a contrast to the message about Dr Kelly's mood conveyed by Mrs Kelly's evidence. She said he was 'very upset' but, in her defence, she was actually with her husband so would have been able to see his physical reaction to the situation in which he found himself. In any case, Dr Kelly may have wanted to sound relaxed when speaking to his half-sister so as not to alarm her.

Dr Kelly also spoke to his daughter, Rachel, on the evening of Friday, 11 July. She told him and Mrs Kelly that Graham Atkins, the landlord of the Waggon and Horses, a man whom she described as a family friend, had told her that several journalists had been hanging around all day, asking his staff a lot of questions about Dr Kelly. Again showing initiative and strength of character, according to Rachel Kelly her mother was sufficiently concerned by this news to take it upon herself to ring Atkins at the pub to establish exactly what was going on in Southmoor.

TEA AND SYMPATHY

One of the first phone calls Dr Kelly made on the morning of Saturday, 12 July was also to a publican, but in his case, according to the evidence of Rachel Kelly, the man in question was Steve Ward, the landlord of the Hinds Head, who would later tell the police of his belief that Dr Kelly had been playing cribbage in his pub on the evening of 9 July and would also supply them with the names of sixteen of Dr Kelly's cribbage team mates. It was about 8 a.m. and Dr Kelly was trying to establish from Ward the lie of the land back in his corner of Oxfordshire. Thanks to the recent tip-off from Graham Atkins, Dr Kelly was aware that journalists had been waiting to speak to him the previous day. By contrast, Dr Kelly was told by Ward that his end of the village was completely clear of the press.

By this stage, Dr Kelly was plotting his return home in preparation for the select committee hearings he was to attend the following week. According to Rachel Kelly, he even gave serious consideration to parking his car in the car park of the Hinds Head, walking the mile or so home, and sneaking back into his house to retrieve undetected whatever he needed.

It is impossible to understand why Hutton thought that his inquiry was improved by not questioning Steve Ward. Not only had Ward told the police, who had in turn informed the Hutton Inquiry, that Dr Kelly was apparently playing cribbage in the Hinds Head at the exact time Mrs Kelly claimed she and her husband were supposedly driving to Weston-Super-Mare – but his chat with Dr Kelly that Saturday morning may have elicited some further insight into Dr Kelly's frame of mind.

In any case, Dr Kelly's plan to use the Hinds Head car park was abandoned after he spoke to his daughter Rachel at about 8.30 a.m. She suggested instead that her father should simply drive directly to her house, close to Oxford Station, whenever he returned from Cornwall and she would collect whatever he needed from his house and make sure that it was waiting for him when he arrived.

Dr Kelly agreed to this. When Rachel went to her parents' house later that Saturday to feed their cats, she picked up some clothes for her father, plus a copy of the 'infamous' forty-five-minute dossier, as he put it, which was in his study. That he was able to refer to it with something approaching a sense of humour despite it being the document which had plunged him into his unsavoury predicament was testament to his ability to retain an unemotional perspective on the situation.

In discussing with Mrs Kelly at the Hutton Inquiry what she and her husband did in Cornwall on 12 July – Dr Kelly's last Saturday alive – one of the few probing questions which Dingemans asked related to the Eden Project. Having been told that the Kellys had visited this major tourist attraction that day, Dingemans asked Mrs Kelly to describe it, which in retrospect seems to be without obvious relevance. Mrs Kelly replied to Dingemans as though reading from a tourist brochure: 'It is a huge quarry which has some biospheres in it with tropical and warm temperate plantings within.'

Asked if Dr Kelly enjoyed himself, Mrs Kelly said bluntly: 'No. He seemed very grim, very unhappy, extremely tense, but accepting the process he was going through. He knew he would have to go forward the following week. I was trying to relax him. He was eating, he was drinking soft drinks but it was a very grim time for both of us. I have never, in all the Russian visits and all the difficulties he had in Iraq, where he had lots of discomforts, lots of horrors, guns pointing at him, munitions left lying around, I had never known him to be as unhappy as he was then.'

Having heard this poignant but vivid description of Dr Kelly's steely disposition, which clearly showed that in his wife's opinion he had experienced far more hardship and danger than most people in their day-to-day lives, Dingemans evidently wasn't satisfied. Instead of asking Mrs Kelly to tell the Hutton Inquiry about the sort of work her husband did which had put him in life-threatening situations in Russia and Iraq, thereby drawing out from her a fuller portrait of a man who was evidently used to being in complex and stressful situations, and who therefore might not necessarily be the type of person to take his own life, Dingemans probed the grieving widow for more emotional details.

'His unhappiness you could feel?' Dingemans asked, in what now sounds like pidgin English. Mrs Kelly answered: 'It was tangible.' As if those listening had still not got the message, Dingemans went on: 'You could see it as well?' She replied: 'Absolutely, palpable.'

Dingemans had squandered a valuable opportunity to show that Dr Kelly was not, in fact, the weak, middle-ranking civil servant whom many had assumed but had instead been prepared to chance his own safety in the name of his country by involving himself in incredibly risky situations overseas. If anything, the QC appeared intent on emphasizing Dr Kelly's allegedly fragile state of mind, as depicted by his widow. This fed into the narrative of his suicidal disposition which the Hutton Inquiry seemed concerned to maintain.

Switching to the historical present tense, Dingemans then asked Mrs Kelly: 'What else do you do on the Saturday?' She answered: 'Somehow we got through the day. I am not terribly sure what we did now. We certainly went back home [to the cottage in Portmellon]. We wandered along the beach at some stage. That was not easy for him. It was just a nightmare. That is all I can describe it as.'

Having encouraged Mrs Kelly to speak in this fashion, Dingemans asked her no further questions about how the couple had spent the Saturday, therefore establishing few hard facts and leaving the impression that nothing else had happened that day which was worth mentioning. Without the commendable candour of John Dabbs, things would have remained that way.

Mr Dabbs was not called to give evidence to the Hutton Inquiry but he and his wife Pamela were both required to give a witness statement to Thames Valley Police on 28 July, four days before the inquiry was opened. Their statements were then passed to inquiry officials. Like those of others who gave such statements, the Dabbses' were never released publicly, but when I tracked down Mr Dabbs he turned out to be in possession of some important information which triggers more uncomfortable questions about the police investigation of Dr Kelly's death, Mrs Kelly's evidence to Hutton, and Hutton's management of his inquiry.

Mr Dabbs told me that the Kellys visited him and his wife by arrangement for a couple of hours on that Saturday afternoon at their house in the village of Gorran Haven, about a mile from where the Kellys were staying. The invitation to tea was issued as a token of friendship at what was clearly a very unsettling time for the Kellys.

The Kellys arrived at their house at about 4 p.m. According to Mr Dabbs, nothing about their behaviour appeared strange to him – for example, neither of them seemed to be upset. Indeed, they told Mr and Mrs Dabbs they had earlier been in the nearby village of Charlestown watching a local gig boat race.

Mr Dabbs acknowledged to me that, not knowing Dr Kelly, it was hard for him to judge his mood, but he did say of the weapons inspector: 'He seemed to me to be relaxed.' Mr Dabbs also asked me to make it clear that, in contrast to him, his wife, Mrs Dabbs, apparently thought Dr Kelly seemed rather tense.

Tea was made and then Mrs Kelly went into the kitchen with Mrs Dabbs, leaving their husbands in the sitting room together. The two men were alone for about an hour, bar the occasional interruption from their wives. Mr Dabbs said that during this time he and Dr Kelly were able to have an open conversation.

He confirmed that Dr Kelly spoke to him about the situation he was in but, having voluntarily pledged to Dr Kelly that he would keep what was said between them private, he would not elaborate, only confirming that their conversation related to work as opposed to anything in Dr Kelly's personal life. He said: 'I did promise Dr Kelly it would be confidential – that I'd keep whatever he said confidential. And his wife, Jan, heard me say this as well.'

While honouring these self-imposed commitments, however, Mr Dabbs has rightly identified himself as some-one who could have been a useful witness to the Hutton Inquiry had he been asked to give evidence, and it remains an inexplicable oversight on the part of Hutton that he, like Steve Ward, was not called upon to appear.

Both Mr Dabbs and his wife were contacted by Thames Valley Police following Dr Kelly's death after it had been established – presumably via Mrs Kelly – that they had spent some of that Saturday in Dr Kelly's company. Mr Dabbs said that two male officers, one of whom was senior, drove the 250 or so miles to their house to interview them, but he remains perplexed by the encounter.

He said that when the police had initially rung him, they were very interested to know about any telephone conversations he or his wife might have had with the Kellys and the times these calls took place. When they arrived to take their statements, such questions were again asked. The police, however, seemed less concerned about anything else Mr and Mrs Dabbs might have had to say.

Mr Dabbs added that he made a point of offering to show the officers around the property where the Kellys had stayed in case they found something important there. They accepted this offer but, according to Mr Dabbs, took hardly any interest in the place when they got there, merely putting their heads around the door in a cursory fashion. Luckily, Mr Dabbs had checked over the house himself as soon as he heard about Dr Kelly's death, which was swiftly labelled a 'suicide' in the media. He found no note of intent or anything else suggesting Dr Kelly might have been planning to take his own life. Mr Dabbs said:

The police contacted us. Two of them came down all the way from Oxford especially to see us. At the time we weren't quite sure what the circumstances [of Dr Kelly's death] were but the assumption was it was suicide, and you'd expect then to be asked questions about his mental state and so on, but they weren't the least bit interested in that, as I remember it, which struck me as odd. Bearing in mind we were the last people to speak to him besides his colleagues and family, and I had a significant conversation with him, I would have thought they'd have treated that as something of a priority, but they didn't. The police told me they were in no doubt Dr Kelly had taken his own life.

When making his statement, Mr Dabbs held firm to his voluntary promise to Dr Kelly not to repeat the contents of their conversation. Even if the police could have compelled him to tell them anything, they did not try to do so. 'They did say at the time that we might be asked to appear [at the Hutton Inquiry] but that never happened,' Mr Dabbs added.

The failure even to mention in passing the role played by Mr and Mrs Dabbs underlines one of many major oversights in the Hutton Inquiry process. Not only was Mr Dabbs one of the last people to speak to Dr Kelly in a social context, just five days before he disappeared, but he was also truly independent in that he had never met Dr Kelly before. Mr Dabbs or his wife could potentially have provided vital testimony about Dr Kelly's state of mind, about his mood and behaviour, and about the conversational areas they covered. But for reasons best known to himself, Hutton decided not to call them.

Added to this, questions must again be asked about James Dingemans's examination of Janice Kelly. The idea that she had forgotten about her two-hour visit to the Dabbses' house, or that Dingemans was unaware of it, is hard to believe. Dingemans did ask her what else she and Dr Kelly had done that day but was apparently content for her not to mention her visit to the Dabbses. All in all, this was odd. Apart from anything else, she saw Mr and Mrs Dabbs on two further occasions during the time she was in Cornwall. Yet, bizarrely, all contact was expunged from her account.

Not only that, but Mr Dabbs also told me that Mrs Kelly rang him at about 6 a.m. on Friday, 18 July – some fifteen hours after she had last seen her husband alive – to tell him that Dr Kelly was missing. She wanted to know whether, by any chance, her husband had returned to Cornwall for some reason and was staying with the Dabbses. Tragically, he was nowhere near Cornwall at that time, of course, but lying dead on Harrowdown Hill. This does suggest, however, that Mr and Mrs Dabbs were at the front of Mrs Kelly's mind throughout this time.

No reasonable, objective examiner of the circumstances leading up to Dr Kelly's death could deny that Mr and Mrs Dabbs unwittingly played a small but important role during his last week alive. They showed him friendship and listened to his problems at a time when, according to his own wife, he was near his wits' end. They also supported Mrs Kelly, whose trust in them appears to have been absolute. And yet, for reasons unknown, they were essentially written out of the script by Janice Kelly and, by extension, Hutton.

When Mrs Kelly was questioned about the events of Saturday, 12 July by Dingemans, his main concern appeared to be to get her to paint the bleakest possible picture of her husband's depressed mood and negative physical appearance. Re-reading the transcript of their exchange, anyone would think that Dingemans's aim was somehow to prove that Dr Kelly had likely been on the brink of suicide in the days leading up to his death. Securing from Mrs Kelly such descriptions of her husband's mood as he did was apparently crucial to Dingemans in a way that asking her about the visit to Mr and Mrs Dabbs was not. The evidence of Mr Dabbs might easily have contradicted the impression of Dr Kelly that Dingemans was apparently at pains to create.

Could it be that Mr Dabbs's own suspicions about Dr Kelly's death were considered inconvenient to a narrative the Hutton Inquiry might have been trying to advance? Did somebody associated with the Hutton Inquiry recognize

Mr Dabbs as a 'tricky' witness? After all, he has told me that he firmly believes there should have been a coroner's inquest into Dr Kelly's death many years ago and remains troubled that there has never been one, given the number of outstanding questions surrounding the case. Mr Dabbs's own exclusion from the Hutton Inquiry is arguably, of course, one of those unanswered questions.

A CURIOUS LACK OF CURIOSITY

It is not clear who in the Kelly family took the decision on the night of 17 July 2003 to wait almost nine hours to ring the police to report as missing a man who had gone out for a thirty-minute walk. Such details were, seemingly, of no interest to the Hutton Inquiry. Neither did Hutton establish which of the two Kelly daughters rang the police to report their father missing, Mrs Kelly having said that she could not recall who had done so. Furthermore, in his official report, Hutton recorded the time the call was made to the police as being 00.20 – some forty minutes later than Mrs Kelly had said. It is therefore still unknown which time is more accurate – one of a catalogue of basic errors for which Hutton is responsible and which have caused so many questions to be raised about his inquiry.

Sgt Simon Morris of Thames Valley Police would have been perfectly placed to shed some light on these and many other unclarified matters. Morris took the lead role at the very beginning of the search for Dr Kelly, and spent a significant amount of time with the Kelly family that night. Bizarrely, however, Hutton decided not to call him as a witness. Although seven other Thames Valley Police officers were required to give evidence in person, Morris's duties were not even considered worthy of inclusion in the form of a written witness statement on the Hutton Inquiry website. His precise thoughts and actions as the officer who anchored the start of the search remain unknown.

Then again, perhaps Morris's absence from the Hutton Inquiry should not come as such a surprise. For in an equally odd oversight, the officer who was eventually put in charge of Thames Valley Police's overall investigation into Dr Kelly's death, Chief Inspector Alan Young, was not called to give evidence either. Is it any wonder that the Hutton Inquiry is widely considered to have lacked stringency?

By way of example, one consequence of Hutton's decision not to ask Morris for any evidence concerns the two communications masts erected by the police outside the Kellys' house shortly after he was reported missing on the night of 17 July. It was Mrs Kelly, in her evidence, who first mentioned these masts during the Hutton Inquiry and who, somewhat absurdly, was then asked by Dingemans to explain their purpose. Of course, she should not have been expected to answer this technical question, even if she had been qualified to do so. A police officer should have done so – not least since Thames Valley Police began giving evidence to the inquiry the day after Mrs Kelly. Yet, surprisingly, no police officer was asked about the masts, so the exact time that they were installed, their precise purpose and the individual who requested them remain unknown.

The first mast that arrived was thirty-five feet tall but was found not to be strong enough, so it was soon replaced by an eighty-five-foot mast whose strength was significantly greater. It has long been speculated that the bigger mast would have been powerful enough to communicate with an aeroplane and might therefore have allowed contact with either Tony Blair or with Alastair Campbell, returning to London from Washington. This was not an area Hutton felt any need to explore.

Having decided that Morris should not give evidence to his inquiry, Hutton instead chose to rely on the testimony of another senior officer involved in the search for Dr Kelly, ACC Michael Page. He appeared on two separate occasions and both times was examined by Dingemans.

As another example of just how ill advised Hutton was in excluding Morris, Page incorrectly informed the inquiry that the helicopter ordered by Morris to search for Dr Kelly came from RAF Benson, close to where Dr Kelly lived. In fact it came from Luton. Morris had called the helicopter in the first place, and would therefore have known this. But a far more urgent question remains unanswered.

Virtually nothing else was said by anybody throughout

the Hutton Inquiry about the helicopter's activity that night – and yet it turns out to have been an important piece of the jigsaw if, as the official account has it, Dr Kelly really did take his own life on Harrowdown Hill sometime between 4.15 p.m. on Thursday, 17 July and 1.15 a.m. on Friday, 18 July.

By 3.20 a.m. the Eurocopter EC 135 was on the scene. Police on the ground outside the Kellys' house switched on their cars' emergency flashing lights to guide it to the place from where Dr Kelly began his walk and indicate the start of the search area. Records confirm that the three people on board, a pilot and two observers, spent forty-five minutes flying over the land surrounding Southmoor and Kingston Bagpuize. The task report shows that the areas searched included bridle paths from Longworth north to the River Thames; that it then flew east to Newbridge; and then went south back to Kingston Bagpuize.

The Longworth to River Thames leg of the sortie meant that the helicopter flew directly over Harrowdown Hill, where Dr Kelly's body was found less than six hours later – but despite its perfect position and specialist heat-seeking equipment, it did not detect him. All of its devices were working properly at that time, according to the latest check which had been carried out three weeks earlier. The police have said that the FLIR LEO II thermal-imaging device, manufactured by American defence company Tecna Corporation, is so powerful it would have been 'capable of reading a car number plate three-quarters of a mile away from a height of 1,000 feet'.

While thermal-imaging equipment cannot penetrate water or buildings, it is capable of penetrating a tree canopy and detecting a body lying under it – a body which must still have been warm at the time the helicopter flew overhead. For when Dr Kelly's body temperature was taken by the forensic pathologist, Dr Nicholas Hunt, some fourteen hours later, at 7.15 p.m. on Friday, 18 July, to help determine what time he died, it was still found to be 24 Celsius, or 75 Fahrenheit.

To put this in perspective, by 7.15 p.m. on 18 July it was estimated that Dr Kelly may have been dead for as long as twenty-seven hours, yet his body easily remained warm enough potentially to be picked up by the helicopter's heat-seeking device. Still, despite its high-grade equipment, it detected nothing. (This basic discrepancy was not even mentioned at the Hutton Inquiry. It only came to light in 2008 thanks to a Freedom of Information request submitted by journalist Garrick Alder.) Does this mean that the body might not have been on Harrowdown Hill when the helicopter flew over the scene between 3.20 a.m. and 4.05 a.m.?

Considering the significant police search operation which had been launched by sunrise on 18 July, it is also worth pointing out that, strangely, there was no mention that anybody had been trying to contact Dr Kelly by mobile phone, although it is known that Dr Kelly's MoD colleagues did try to ring it the afternoon before. Since Hutton didn't go to any lengths to establish mobile phone use either, it has been left to others to fill in the blanks.

What is known, according to Dominic Grieve's official review of Dr Kelly's death in 2010–11, is that Thames Valley Police tried to carry out checks on Dr Kelly's mobile phone from about 5 a.m. In 2003, technology existed which would allow details of a person's whereabouts to be found by searching a central mobile phone database called the Home Location Register. This shows a wide range of data, including the geographical position of the phone when it was switched off or ran out of battery, plus the time it was last used. But in the case of Dr Kelly, whose mobile was in his coat pocket when his body was discovered, these details were never established because, the police said, it was switched off.

Under the Freedom of Information Act Thames Valley Police have provided what facts they know about Dr Kelly's phone, including the time at which it was last working and whether it was switched off deliberately or damaged by a third party. They initially refused to answer these questions, forcing the FoI watchdog, the Information Commissioner's Office (ICO), to intervene. Perhaps explaining their reluctance to disclose the relevant information when they first had the chance, officers admitted that they could not state where the weapons inspector was when his phone was switched off because they 'do not hold information as to when Dr Kelly's phone was last operating'.

They were also asked to state the time and location of the last call made from the mobile, and when and where a call was last received. They were able to provide times but not locations, which also suggests they carried out only a partial inquiry. They said there were 'no signs of damage' to the phone.

According to their records, Dr Kelly last answered his phone to receive a call at 7.18 p.m. on Wednesday, 16 July and last made a call from it at 12.58 p.m. on Thursday, 17 July, roughly two hours before he was last seen alive. It is known that Dr Kelly's phone was functioning because while the Hutton Inquiry was under way, on 17 September 2003, the police took it to Harrowdown Hill to check whether it had a signal there. They found it to be in perfect working order at that location.

A BODY DISTURBED

It is clear that, as far as some aspects of Dr Kelly's death are concerned such as his whereabouts on the evening of 9 July and the morning of 10 July, the public has effectively been asked to accept at least two different stories at the same time. It's not surprising, therefore, that their confidence in the Hutton Inquiry has been undermined.

Nowhere is this more evident than in the discovery of Dr Kelly's body on Friday, 18 July 2003 – in particular its position when found, whether it might have been moved subsequently, and how much blood was visible on and around it.

Louise Holmes, the volunteer searcher who, officially, first found Dr Kelly's body at 9.20 a.m. on Friday, 18 July, told the Hutton Inquiry that, when she went within a few feet of his body: 'He was at the base of the tree with almost his head and his shoulders just slumped back against the tree… His legs were straight in front of him. His right arm was to the side of him. His left arm had a lot of blood on it and was bent back in a funny position.' And yet at 1 p.m. on the same day as Ms Holmes's gruesome discovery – almost four hours later – Thames Valley Police released a public statement saying that the body at Harrowdown Hill was lying 'face down' when found. Both accounts cannot be correct. But who can possibly know which story to believe?

When recalling at the Hutton Inquiry what she first encountered in the wood at Harrowdown Hill, Ms Holmes told Dingemans, who examined her: 'I could see a body slumped against the bottom of a tree, so I turned around and shouted to Paul [Chapman, her co-searcher] to ring Control and tell them that we had found something and then went closer to just see whether there was any first aid that I needed to administer.'

Holmes said she went within 'a few feet' of the body

211

and noticed it slumped back against the tree. She has certainly never said anything about it being 'face down'. Indeed, whenever I have spoken to Ms Holmes about her discovery that morning, she has been absolutely certain that she would not change a word of the evidence she gave to the Hutton Inquiry.

Ms Holmes told the inquiry she saw no blood anywhere else other than on Dr Kelly's left arm, but because the body looked like that of Dr Kelly she concentrated on getting help. She made no mention of seeing any other items – such as the knife and water bottle later found – nor was she asked about them.

Paul Chapman also stated at the Hutton Inquiry, where he too was examined by Dingemans, that when he got to within thirty or forty feet of the scene he saw 'the body of a gentleman sitting up against a tree'. So, like Holmes, his view was also that Dr Kelly's body was touching the tree. And, like Holmes, Chapman said nothing to the inquiry about having seen a knife or water bottle beside Dr Kelly's body.

THE THIRD MAN

After the discovery of Dr Kelly's body Holmes and Chapman were asked to stay in the Harrowdown Hill area and told that some officers would meet them at Holmes's car, about a ten-minute walk away. The two officers who had been formally asked by senior Thames Valley Police personnel to meet Chapman and Holmes were PCs Franklin and Sawyer.

Chapman and Holmes, however, both told the Hutton Inquiry that they first encountered three different police officers: DC Graham Coe, who was in plain clothes; his colleague DC Colin Shields; and a third man whose identity the police and Lord Hutton have ensured has always remained secret. Of these three, only Coe was required to give evidence to the inquiry.

Paul Chapman said the trio told him they were CID officers, though at the Hutton Inquiry Coe was never asked – and did not volunteer – the name of his department, leading some to ponder whether he was in fact a Special Branch officer and therefore essentially working in conjunction with the security services.

Coe had apparently been making house-to-house inquiries in the villages of Southmoor and Longworth on the morning of 18 July. This was not necessarily the kind of work expected of an officer of his senior rank, immediately posing the question of why he was drafted in to do it.

In his evidence to Hutton, Coe related that he and a 'colleague' – singular – had knocked on Ruth Absalom's door that morning. This was certainly a lucky break, given that Mrs Absalom was the last person known to have seen Dr Kelly alive, at about 3.30 p.m. the previous afternoon.

According to Coe, she apparently told him of her brief meeting with Dr Kelly, though, interestingly, during her evidence to Hutton – two weeks before Coe gave his – Mrs Absalom said nothing of this chat and was not asked about it.

After Coe saw Mrs Absalom, he and the 'colleague' to whom he referred in his evidence decided to walk to the river near Harrowdown Hill. Why they chose this route is not clear, since Dr Kelly had last been seen by Mrs Absalom walking east towards the Appleton Road, not north towards Harrowdown Hill. It would not be unreasonable to believe that Mrs Absalom told Coe of this, so why did he head in the opposite direction? The helicopter had searched there overnight and found nothing, and Chapman and Holmes had already been sent to the area by Thames Valley Police that morning.

Coe told the Hutton Inquiry that he spoke to Chapman and Holmes as soon as he bumped into them. At this point he apparently had no idea that they had just found a body. He also specifically stated to the Hutton Inquiry when asked that he was with just one other police colleague at the time, DC Shields.

Coe said that Chapman led him to the wood and showed him to where the body was and then returned to Holmes. Coe's testimony on at least one point was faulty. Both Chapman and Holmes said that Coe had been with two other officers, yet he categorically told Hutton that he was with only one man – DC Shields. Coe was never asked to explain this discrepancy, even though he gave evidence to the Hutton Inquiry two weeks after the searchers, on 16 September 2003.

In 2010, seven years later and safely in retirement, Coe admitted to *The Mail on Sunday*, after being called on at his house without invitation by a reporter, that he had been accompanied by another man as well as Shields that morning, but he refused to name him. He claimed that the 'third man' was a PC who had not yet completed his two-year probation period and who was at the time on secondment to the CID team.

There is no way of testing the truth of this, though shortly after Coe had given his interview Bruce Hay, an Oxfordshire businessman who described himself as a 'distant friend' of Dr Kelly, wrote to me out of the blue because of the number of news stories about Dr Kelly I had published in the *Daily Mail*. He confirmed Coe's story, saying that he personally knew the 'third man' well. In his letter, Mr Hay said the young man was a 'probationary constable' with the initials 'S. B.' who believed the scene where Dr Kelly's body was found to be 'extraordinarily contrived', saying it looked as though Dr Kelly's body had been 'propped' against the tree. Mr Hay made no further communication with me and died in the spring of 2015. The 'third man' is understood to have left the police force.

Why Coe did not reveal the seemingly innocuous fact that he was accompanied by a third person is itself a mystery coloured by whether, as Mr Hay claimed, the 'third man' really did have suspicions about the scene. Whenever I have rung Coe he has put down the phone, depriving me of the chance to discuss this with him.

And so the question remains: who was the 'third man'? If the observations attributed to him by the late Bruce Hay are correct, and the scene where Dr Kelly's body was found really was 'extraordinarily contrived', it seems even more unfortunate that he was not available to speak publicly about this during the inquiry, because Coe was never asked by Hutton to explain the discrepancy between his account of the number of police officers at the scene and that of Chapman and Holmes.

After Coe had been led to the wood, he said he elected to stand guard, alone, over Dr Kelly's body until a back-up team arrived. He stayed there for about twenty-five minutes but has always insisted that during this time he did not touch the body. He told the Hutton Inquiry that he saw 'a knife, like a pruning knife, and a watch' beside the body, making him the first person to have noticed these items. That they turned out to have no fingerprints on them when they were analysed is of great potential significance, as we shall see – a significance not addressed in Coe's evidence. Dr Kelly was not wearing gloves on the July day his life ended, and no gloves were found with his body.

The other important admission Coe made during his 2010 *Mail on Sunday* interview related to the amount of blood he observed at the scene during the time he was there alone. He volunteered: 'I certainly didn't see a lot of blood anywhere. There was some on his left wrist but it wasn't on his clothes. On the ground, there wasn't much blood about, if any.'

Given the wrist injury which is said to have been the primary cause of Dr Kelly's death, and the large volume of blood – 'arterial rain' – which slashed wrists usually produce, this was a comment which one would have expected Coe to have shared during the Hutton Inquiry, seven years earlier than he did. What prevented him from taking this opportunity? He did mention blood twice during his evidence, though only in passing. But he could only respond to questions and was not asked explicitly when examined by Peter Knox, junior counsel to the inquiry, how much blood he saw at the scene.

THE BODY: A THIRD RECOLLECTION

When ACC Page heard of Chapman's and Holmes's discovery at Harrowdown Hill, he told colleagues that the case should be treated as a potential murder inquiry, even if it was not one officially. Page instructed the Metropolitan

Police Special Branch officers who had already carried out searches for Dr Kelly in three government offices in London earlier that morning to return to them and remove anything they deemed to be 'relevant'. Page also appointed the aforementioned Chief Inspector Alan Young to formally open a case file on the official investigation into Dr Kelly's death – Operation Mason.

PCs Franklin and Sawyer arrived at Harrowdown Hill at about 10 a.m. to meet the searchers, who had waited there as requested in order to lead them to the wood where Dr Kelly's body lay. As previously noted, Sawyer was specially trained to search major crime and murder scenes. Franklin and Sawyer were with Sgt Alan Dadd, an officer with the Thames Valley Police protection unit, based at Reading. They had expected to be the first policemen at the scene so were surprised to find that DC Coe had beaten them to it. PC Franklin still sounded annoyed by this when he gave evidence to the Hutton Inquiry several weeks later, saying: 'I had no idea what he [Coe] was doing there or why he was there. He was just at the scene when PC Sawyer and I arrived.'

Coe led them to the body, whereupon PC Sawyer began photographing it with a digital camera. Sawyer was aware that he had only a few moments to capture the scene untouched before paramedic Vanessa Hunt and ambulance technician David Bartlett, who had been rung at about 9.45 a.m., arrived and, inevitably, disturbed it when checking for signs of life, which they had to do as a matter of routine. These photos remain under embargo so have never been seen by any member of the public.

On entering the wood Hunt and Bartlett soon saw Dr Kelly's body. Significantly, Ms Hunt said she saw 'a male on his back', in contrast to the earlier descriptions of Chapman and Holmes, who described Dr Kelly as lying with his head and shoulders against a tree, and she noticed 'dry blood on his left arm, which was outstretched to his left'.

Hunt and Bartlett stood behind Franklin and Sawyer while Sawyer continued to take photographs of the body. When he had finished, Bartlett and Hunt examined Dr Kelly's body to see if he was alive. This included placing heart monitor paddles onto his chest over the top of his shirt to check for signs of life. Hunt then wanted to put four electrode pads directly onto Dr Kelly's chest. The police, mindful of securing images of the body before it was disturbed even more, apparently took additional pictures.

Bartlett unbuttoned Dr Kelly's shirt and Hunt placed the four electrodes onto his chest, two on the upper part and two underneath the ribcage area, before connecting them to a heart monitor which showed a flat line. The paramedics declared Dr Kelly dead at 10.07 a.m. They were asked by the policemen to leave the pads on Dr Kelly's chest and to leave the shirt unbuttoned, which they did.

By this point they were aware of the items found next to the body: a watch; a knife; and a 500ml bottle of Evian water. Curiously, the bottle was positioned upright, parallel with Dr Kelly's head, and still contained some water. Its lid had been removed.

All three items were on the left side of Dr Kelly's body. The paramedics also noticed a pouch clipped to the belt holding up Dr Kelly's jeans which looked as though it would hold a mobile phone. It was empty.

Ms Hunt told the Hutton Inquiry: 'The only part of the body we moved was Dr Kelly's right arm, which was over the chest, to facilitate us to place the fourth lead onto the chest. It was just lifted slightly from the body.' Ms Hunt also told the inquiry she observed that

> the amount of blood that was around the scene seemed relatively minimal and there was a small patch on his right knee, but no obvious arterial bleeding. There was no spraying of blood or huge blood loss or any obvious loss on the clothing… I could see some [blood] on – there were some stinging nettles to the left of the body. As to on the ground, I do not remember seeing a sort of huge puddle or anything like that. There was dried blood on the left wrist. His jacket was pulled to sort of mid-forearm area and from that area down towards the hand there was dried blood, but no obvious sign of a wound or anything, it was just dried blood… as I say, there was dried blood from the edge of the jacket down

towards the hand but no gaping wound or anything obvious that I could see from the position I was in.

Troublingly, Bartlett, the other member of the ambulance crew, has speculated that, based on the account of Dr Kelly's body position given by Chapman and Holmes – namely that it was touching the tree – the body could have been moved between the time Chapman and Holmes first saw it and when he and his colleague Ms Hunt arrived at the scene.

Bartlett has often told friends – and once said to me over the phone when I spoke to him about the case – that the body was sufficiently far from the tree, perhaps as much as two feet, for him to be able to stand behind it. He has also said that he even suspected initially that the body had fallen out of the tree, such was the gap between the two.

Consider the major difference between Bartlett's and Hunt's recollection of the body position and those of the others who saw it at that time. Louise Holmes told the Hutton Inquiry he was 'at the base of the tree with almost his head on his shoulders, just slumped back against the tree'. Her co-searcher Paul Chapman said he saw 'the body of a gentleman sitting up against a tree'. He added: 'He was sitting with his back up against a tree.' The next person to see it – DC Coe – told the inquiry: 'The body was laying on its back by a large tree, the head towards the trunk of the tree.' And the next two people to see it, PCs Franklin and Sawyer, both said that when they arrived – just before the paramedics and after DC Coe had guarded the body alone – Dr Kelly was on his back. Sawyer also said: 'His jeans... were pulled up slightly, exposing the lower half of his leg or his ankle. It looked as if he had slid down and his trousers had ridden up.' This could, of course, be consistent with his having been moved by a third party from an upright position to a lying position.

Thames Valley Police were the last to comment on the body position. As previously mentioned, their statement on the day Dr Kelly's body was found was that it was lying 'face down'.

Despite these discrepancies, none of the three police officers was asked at the inquiry whether they touched or moved the body, although DC Coe did deny doing so in his 2010 *Mail on Sunday* interview. Hutton made no mention of the contradictory evidence in his report's conclusions. It was therefore left to Attorney General Dominic Grieve's 2011 review of the case to try to settle this vexed question – and Grieve failed to do so. He said: 'As to the issue of the position of the body, Lord Hutton commented on the fact that in his wide experience – indeed the experience of any individual with even a slight acquaintance with court processes – witnesses may recall events differently.'

A forensic pathologist called Dr Richard Shepherd was commissioned by Grieve in 2011 to review certain aspects of the evidence. Shepherd wrote in his report: 'It is quite clear from consideration of the photographs of the scene that, at the time they were taken, the body of David Kelly lay with his feet pointing away from the tree and that there was a significant gap between the base of the tree and the top of the head.' This conflicted with Ms Holmes's recollection of the scene and that of the paramedics. When asked about this at the time, Grieve's office refused to acknowledge any disparity. And, as with so many other aspects of the case, there the matter has remained.

Because Hutton secretly recommended in January 2004 that all photographs of Dr Kelly's body be classified for seventy years, along with all medical and scientific evidence, it is not likely that anybody alive today with an interest in the case will ever see the photographs and establish the truth about the body position.

The significance of these lingering questions is twofold. Firstly, they point once again to a lack of rigour at the Hutton Inquiry. Secondly, such undoubted discrepancies raise the possibility that the body might have been moved. But why?

DR MALCOLM WARNER

One man who would surely have known Dr Kelly well was his GP, Dr Malcolm Warner. In this context it is worth mentioning a little-known recollection by Robert Jackson, who in 2003 was Dr Kelly's MP.

In 2010, I rang Jackson to speak to him about the case. Towards the end of our twenty-five-minute conversation, he said to me almost in passing that he believed Dr Kelly had taken his own life because Dr Warner had seen his corpse on the day it was found. Jackson explained that he knew this because, during a routine appointment which he, Jackson, had had with Dr Warner at his surgery some weeks after Dr Kelly's death, it was made clear to him by the GP personally.

Jackson told me: 'As it happens my doctor, my local GP, was his [Dr Kelly's] GP and shortly after all this happened I happened to go and see him, and he was called to look at the body and his view was completely compatible with the story which was eventually adopted by Hutton, and I think that's important first-hand evidence from a chap who was on the scene right at the beginning and who was an experienced medical man.'

Jackson went on: 'He [Dr Warner] was his doctor... I remember I asked him about it because there were already these kinds of suspicions and stories going around and he thought it was all complete balls.'

Jackson then said: 'You may well find he's [Warner] not prepared to talk about it... I shouldn't perhaps have told you about it..., but of course I was the local MP. I think he was actually called to the body.' Jackson cannot be criticized for his candour. After all, why should he have hidden this information, or had any qualms about sharing it? Perhaps he believed it to be of some significance.

When asked to clarify if Warner was called to the scene in the wood to see the body Jackson said 'Yup.' When asked who called Warner to the scene Jackson said: 'Well the police, I suppose. I didn't go into the details of it. But it would have made sense. When they found the body he had to be examined before he was moved. They would have asked, you know, he was a doctor, and he was the local doctor. I mean, you know, Jan Kelly would have given his name. I think he actually saw the body at the site.'

Warner, who did give evidence to the Hutton Inquiry during its first phase, on 2 September, made no mention of any unofficial identification when he was examined by Peter Knox – nor was he asked about it. In the mere seventy-seven words he spoke at the inquiry, he said little more than that he had known Dr Kelly for twenty-five years and confirmed that Dr Kelly would have undergone medical checks as a Civil Service employee. He was asked whether, as far as he was aware, Dr Kelly had ever shown signs of depression and answered 'No'. He agreed that he had not prescribed him medication since 1994 and had never prescribed him co-proxamol. He said he was unaware of any 'serious condition' from which Dr Kelly suffered. He confirmed that the MoD health check which Dr Kelly had undergone on 8 July had been sent to him.

When asked if it said anything significant, Warner replied 'No.' He was asked if he was aware of anything else which might have contributed to Dr Kelly's death and answered 'No'. He was also asked if there was anything else which he would like to tell the inquiry and said 'No.'

Another question put to him related to when he had last seen Dr Kelly. His short response was '1999'. Technically, of course, this could have been true, if he meant that the last time he saw him as a *patient* was in 1999. But it does not exclude the possibility, however remote, that he saw him dead on 18 July 2003.

When I approached Warner, now retired, shortly after my chat with Robert Jackson, who has also retired as an MP, he was defensive, saying to me by phone: 'I'm not prepared to make any comment about my patients to the press and I'm sure there are ways in which you could find out whether that was so. I'm terribly sorry. I'm not prepared to make any comment under any circumstances.'

When I rang him a second time he was so reluctant to speak to me that he hung up. Then, in response to an email which I wrote to him, he replied in rather lawyerly language, denying having been called to the scene where Dr Kelly's body was found, saying: 'You are correct in thinking that I did not attend the scene where Dr Kelly's body was found and that this is compatible with the evidence that I gave to the Hutton Inquiry. As I said to you on the telephone I have nothing further to add and

I would be grateful if you would refrain from contacting me again.'

Since Warner was never asked at the Hutton Inquiry about seeing or identifying Dr Kelly's dead body, there is no suggestion that he misled anybody about this. On a closer examination of the wording of his email to me, however, it is plain to see that Dr Warner's chance to rebut Robert Jackson's story, apparently told to him in the privacy of Dr Warner's surgery, was not taken by the GP.

He did not actually deny having seen the body. I later asked Warner for a response as to whether he saw Dr Kelly's body by some other means – via a video recording, for example – but he never replied. Re-reading his evidence in this light, it could be argued that he was among the least illuminating witnesses to appear before the Hutton Inquiry. But why?

The official review of the Dr Kelly case in 2011 carried out by Dominic Grieve also neatly side-stepped the suggestion that Warner ever saw Dr Kelly's body that day. In it, Grieve stated: 'Thames Valley Police has confirmed that there is no record of Dr Warner having seen the body of Dr Kelly. There is a difference between formal identification and recognizing that the body found was that of Dr Kelly.'

This, of course, leaves open the possibility that Warner *unofficially* identified Dr Kelly remotely. Thames Valley Police has confirmed its officers had a video camera at the scene on the morning Dr Kelly's body was found. Just because the police have no record of an identification taking place, it doesn't mean that one didn't occur.

Grieve's document contained one further nugget of new information, namely that Warner 'was visited by officers from the investigation team to view his [Dr Kelly's] medical records'. Though Grieve did not mention the time of day this took place, it is reasonable to wonder why Warner was not asked about it during the Hutton Inquiry – and to express surprise at why he did not volunteer the information. It seems entirely logical that the police should have visited Warner during their search for Dr Kelly to establish some basic facts about him.

It naturally follows that, as an upstanding member of the community who had known Dr Kelly for twenty-five years, Warner would have been perfectly placed to identify him – even unofficially – when the body was found at Harrowdown Hill. And yet at no point during the Hutton Inquiry did anybody refer to the police having visited Warner that day. It was only a slip of the tongue by Robert Jackson, years later, that advanced the possibility – which Warner has never definitively denied.

There is no doubt that Warner was certainly considered an important Hutton Inquiry witness. Firstly, he submitted sixteen separate written documents to the inquiry, none of which has ever been made public. These comprised thirteen doctor's letters stretching back to 1979, two letters to the coroner's office written after Dr Kelly's death, plus a police witness statement.

Furthermore, a notebook belonging to Dr Kelly and recovered by police after his death contained a hand-written note of Warner's name and contact details. The notebook was one which Dr Kelly used immediately before his death, proving that for some unknown reason the GP was at the front of Dr Kelly's mind at the very end of his life. This can be stated with near-certainty because the relevant entry in the notebook was made by Dr Kelly on a page subsequent to some notes which he wrote in preparation for the ISC hearing on 16 July.

On the page in question, below two short headings about Andrew Gilligan, Dr Kelly wrote: 'Dr MD Warner' followed by what looks like an address and, perhaps, a telephone number. The police redacted the latter details with a bold marker pen, but there is little doubt that they relate to Dr Warner, who gave his full name at the Hutton Inquiry as 'Malcolm David Warner'.

Four years later Jackson repeated exactly the same story about Dr Warner which he told me in 2010 to some-one else with an interest in the case, proving that he had not changed his mind about it, nor forgotten these details. He even said that, if asked about it in court under oath, he would have to stick to this story, for it was the truth as he saw it.

And yet despite Warner's seemingly important place in

any inquiry into Dr Kelly's death, during his appearance at the Hutton Inquiry he spoke very few words, many of them single-syllable answers, making him one of Hutton's least forthcoming witnesses. It is not just that Warner seems to have been a concise witness, but also that he was not even asked to address some basic points by Hutton and his team.

Bearing in mind the speed with which Tony Blair was able to set up the Hutton Inquiry without, as far as what is in the public domain reveals, having any idea how Dr Kelly had died – or indeed knowing that the body found was definitely that of Dr Kelly – the question remains: if Robert Jackson is wrong, and Warner didn't in fact tell him shortly after Dr Kelly's death that he personally saw Dr Kelly's body immediately after it was found, did someone else help to identify the body unofficially at an early stage?

ACC PAGE AND
THE DENTAL RECORDS

The weekend immediately following Dr Kelly's death was a particularly odd one for his dentist, Dr Bozena Kanas.

As revealed earlier, Dr Kanas arrived for work at the Ock Street dental practice in Abingdon on the Friday morning when it was announced that Dr Kelly was missing, and before midday on that day made the bizarre discovery that his dental notes were missing.

Very little has ever been known about this alleged theft, mainly because Dr Kanas refuses to discuss it because of her professional commitment to patient confidentiality, but with the help of Freedom of Information requests made to Thames Valley Police, plus the recollections of former staff who wish to remain anonymous, I have been able to piece together some of the puzzle.

I visited the practice unannounced in 2013 following a tip-off and spoke to its manager, Nick Barnes. He was happy enough to chat to me but refused to confirm or deny whether his was the surgery in question. A reliable source later came forward to tell me that they knew that Dr Kelly had been a patient at this practice, which was fairly close to his house in Southmoor.

The first that anybody heard about the disappearance of Dr Kelly's dental records was at the Hutton Inquiry itself. On 23 September 2003, on one of the final hearing days, Hutton recalled ACC Michael Page to give evidence for a second time.

Page began by telling the inquiry that he had ruled out the possibility that Dr Kelly was murdered, either at Harrowdown Hill or elsewhere. He said confidently that this left only the possibility that Dr Kelly had killed himself and he believed there was no 'criminal dimension' to his death.

A series of questions were then put to Page about loose ends relating to Dr Kelly's death which he had not been able to tie up during his previous visit to the inquiry, on 3 September. During this questioning he was asked the following, out of the blue and apropos of nothing, by Dingemans: 'Were you ever contacted by Dr Kelly's dentist?'

Page explained that Thames Valley Police had indeed been rung by Dr Kelly's dentist – he was unable to specify on what date – because of worries she had about the whereabouts of his dental records. Asked what he did about this, Page said: 'We carried out a full examination of the surgery and, in particular, one window which the dentist was concerned may not have been secure. We found no trace of anything untoward either in the surgery or on the window.'

He was asked by Dingemans whether any further examinations of the surgery were conducted. He said that the police had received a second call from Dr Kelly's dentist on Sunday, 20 July informing them that the records 'had reappeared on the Sunday in the place in the filing cabinet where they should have been'. He added that the records were forensically examined and he stated that the laboratory where this had taken place 'could find no evidence of extraneous fingerprints or whatever on that file'.

Page then volunteered: 'However, upon hearing about this, and again I stress because I am a police officer and probably inherently suspicious, because dental records are a means of identification it did prompt me to take the extra precaution of having DNA checks carried out to confirm that the body we had was the body of Dr Kelly, notwithstanding the fact that that had been identified by his family.' Page said the DNA tests confirmed it was indeed the body of Dr Kelly.

In total, Page was asked only four questions about the mysterious matter of Dr Kelly's dental records and the suggestion of a break-in at the surgery where they were kept. Dr Kanas's name was not revealed. Nothing more was said about this peculiarity and hardly anything was picked up in news reports. The matter was therefore effectively opened and closed within a couple of minutes.

This was a most unsatisfactory way of leaving things, however. While it is not immediately clear why anybody would have wanted to steal or borrow Dr Kelly's dental records around the time of his death, it appeared very much as though this is what had happened. Before examining what purpose the records could have served to a thief, it is vital to ask the questions which Hutton, for whatever reason, did not.

On Monday, 21 July, all surgery staff, plus the builders, had their fingerprints taken by police. The only identified prints left on the records belonged to Dr Kelly's hygienist. Despite the fact that Dr Kanas believed the records had been missing, and despite there being six unidentified prints on the records, the police concluded there was no sign of a break-in at the surgery.

In April 2011 I lodged a Freedom of Information request with Thames Valley Police, despite not knowing at the time who Dr Kelly's dentist was or where her surgery was. The police responded openly, stating that Dr Kelly's dentist, whom they did not name, had rung them once – not twice, as ACC Page claimed at the Hutton Inquiry.

In effect, therefore, Dr Kanas rang the police to report a non-crime: she told police she had been under the impression that Dr Kelly's records were missing on the Friday and Saturday, but that they had turned up in the filing cabinet where they should have been all along on the Sunday. And yet the fact that she rang them so late on the Sunday night suggests she felt distinctly uneasy about the situation and saw its potential urgency – otherwise she could presumably have waited until the Monday morning to report this matter.

Nevertheless, if ACC Page's testimony at the Hutton Inquiry is to be accepted as given, we are asked to believe that on the basis of this non-event the police examined the surgery, interviewed and fingerprinted the staff and builders, and went as far as to conduct a DNA test on Dr Kelly's body – all on the strength of Dr Kelly's dentist contacting them to alert them to something that may or may not have happened.

It is a certainty that Dr Kanas was relieved at having

found the records, because she was responsible for their safekeeping. But it follows that, as their custodian, she would have been extremely concerned about where the records had been. Dr Kanas was therefore being candid and honest with the police – as early as possible – because she clearly thought this apparent theft was significant to the police investigation into Dr Kelly's death. Plus, there were professional considerations: if the records had indeed been taken and perhaps tampered with, it would have been important for her to inform the police because they themselves might need to see the records at some future point. For these reasons, Dr Kanas presumably knew she had to be as proactive as possible.

In their response to my questions, the police cast more light on the situation than ACC Page had been able to do at the Hutton Inquiry. They said that Dr Kelly's records were examined for fingerprints, as were the covers of the records positioned either side of his. These tests took place between 15 and 18 August 2003 – two weeks before Page's first appearance at the Hutton Inquiry and five weeks before his second appearance. In other words, on both occasions when he gave evidence to the Hutton Inquiry, the tests had been completed. The police told me:

A total of fifteen marks were revealed for photography. Two marks were revealed on the outside cover of an adjacent set of patient records; neither of these marks was of a usable quality. No marks were revealed on the adjacent cover. The remaining thirteen marks all came from Dr Kelly's record's [sic] folder and contents. Five of these were unusable and two were eliminated to a member of staff. The remaining six marks were of sufficient quality to be checked against elimination prints. These were all negative. None of the six marks were of sufficient quality to be permanently loaded onto the national database. All six marks were filed.

The police therefore confirmed that contrary to what Page told the Hutton Inquiry, there were six unidentified prints on Dr Kelly's dental records. Why had Page told the Hutton Inquiry that there were no 'extraneous' marks? Indeed, why was the word 'extraneous' used by Page at all? Its meaning is defined as 'irrelevant', 'immaterial', or 'inconsequential'. And yet, on the basis that it had carefully conducted these checks and then filed away the results, the police clearly did not regard them as being any of these things.

A month after the police had replied to my Freedom of Information request, in June 2011, former Attorney General Dominic Grieve's review of the David Kelly affair yielded more results. Thames Valley Police revealed to Grieve – and in turn Grieve revealed to the public – that Dr Kanas returned to her surgery on the afternoon of

Sunday, 20 July because she was still concerned that she could not find Dr Kelly's notes. The records were in their rightful place.

But Dr Kanas waited several hours before reporting her find to the police. It now seems likely that not only was she upset about her friend's death, but also that she was wrestling with the situation. Had she imagined the apparent disappearance? Had losing the records – if they had been stolen – made her appear unprofessional? Would there be consequences for her? She had to weigh these questions against her belief that the records had been removed by somebody other than herself.

Most likely a debate lasting some hours took place between her and the practice manager, her boyfriend Nick Barnes. How else to explain her finding the records on the Sunday afternoon but waiting until almost 10.30 on the Sunday night to alert the police to her concerns?

The police surmised that there were four possible explanations. The notes were either in the filing cabinet all the time; or they were misfiled and then refiled; or a member of staff took the notes for an unknown reason and then replaced them when it was noticed they were missing; or the surgery was broken into, the notes were stolen, and then returned. The police admitted to Grieve that they had not been able to solve the mystery.

A former member of staff who was willing to share some memories said there was no burglar alarm at the surgery at that time, meaning that it would have been perfectly possible for someone to have accessed the building and removed the records without attracting attention.

Some might say that the matter of the dental files needn't have been raised at Hutton at all, and the fact it was shows it was an open and honest inquiry. But the disclosure at the inquiry of the apparent theft of the dental records certainly had an effect. It had not been revealed by anybody else – such as a member of staff, or one of the builders, or perhaps a police officer – through speaking to a journalist, for example. The impact was to neutralize this information by volunteering it in a controlled environment.

So Page opened up the dentist story at the prompting of Dingemans, but no sooner had he done so than he closed it down again by saying that nothing untoward had happened. His subsequent assertion that, because he was 'inherently suspicious', he ordered DNA tests to confirm the identity of the body could be read as a deliberate over-reaction, diverting attention away from an apparent theft and on to the rather more dramatic matter of having DNA checks carried out on Dr Kelly's body. If so, the tactic seems to have worked, for nobody ever asked any further questions about the apparent break-in at Dr Kelly's dentist. But even if leaving an 'extraneous' fingerprint – or six – on some dental records is not what a proficient thief does, how come Page was unaware of their existence?

Why might anybody have wanted Dr Kelly's dental

records? It is conceivable that they may have provided information about his medical history which was useful to somebody with an interest in him, such as whether he took a particular medicine or had a health condition. As it is not possible to photograph X-rays of teeth without using specialist equipment in the best possible conditions, it was also perhaps considered necessary for some reason to 'borrow' the records for several hours. Was Dr Kelly known to be dead far earlier than 9.20 a.m. on 18 July and did somebody need his records to identify him? Alternatively, did somebody take the records to prevent another person from identifying him, and then perhaps changed their mind? Another possibility is that Dr Kelly's records were replaced with somebody else's for a reason which has not yet come to light.

What is clear is that a very thorough search of the dental surgery was made during the weekend after Dr Kelly's death by Dr Kanas and her staff and they found no trace of them. Surely it would have been vital for Hutton to consider this in open court and to get to the bottom of what had happened? Apparently not. In his June 2011 review, Grieve wrote: 'Lord Hutton was fully aware of the evidence that could be given by Kelly's dentist but did not consider it took the matter any further.'

It is thanks only to the conscientiousness of Dr Bozena Kanas that anybody knows anything about this inexplicable mystery. For professional reasons, she has never spoken publicly about this event nor confirmed it to me directly or indirectly. Neither has she ever privately revealed anything about it, to the best of my knowledge. While this is unhelpful to anybody with an interest in the matter, it is understandable when considering Dr Kanas's own professional reputation and responsibilities.

AN UNUSUAL LETTER

Mrs Kelly may have maintained a public silence on the matter of her husband's death since speaking to Judith Miller of *The New York Times* on the day her husband's body was found, but in private she has been more forthcoming on at least one occasion.

Less than a year after the event, on 10 June 2004, she wrote a surprisingly candid personal letter to Rowena Thursby, whom she has never met but who at the time was campaigning publicly for a full inquest into Dr Kelly's death. Thursby, then in her forties, worked in the publishing industry and, as nothing more than a laywoman with no specialist scientific or legal background, took it upon herself to devote scores of hours to scrutinizing the circumstances surrounding Dr Kelly's death and the investigation into it. She remains convinced that the truth about how, where and when Dr Kelly died has been withheld from the public.

In late 2003 she formed the Kelly Investigation Group, a loose coalition of doctors and lawyers dedicated to establishing the truth and pointing out the deficiencies of the Hutton Inquiry. Their efforts to persuade the Oxford-shire Coroner, Nicholas Gardiner, to reconvene his inquest included writing to him twice in 2003. Gardiner did not respond to either petition.

The letter which Thursby received from Mrs Kelly in June 2004, typed and written on two and a half sides of A4, was in response to one which she had sent to Mrs Kelly that month. At the time, she and five senior doctors were attempting to secure a judicial review of Gardiner's decision not to hold a full coroner's inquest into Dr Kelly's death. It was in this context that Thursby wrote to Mrs Kelly.

Somewhat oddly, on the day that Thursby opened Janice Kelly's letter, she also took a phone call from her asking her to return it. During the call, Mrs Kelly apparently explained to Thursby that she had sat up late into the night writing the letter and had left it in an envelope, addressed and stamped, on her kitchen table before going to bed. She claimed to Thursby that, early the next morning before she got up, her cleaner had posted the letter without Mrs Kelly's knowledge, and that she had been upset by this because, having thought about it over-night, she had decided not to send it. Thursby agreed to return the letter but, since it was legally her property, she made a copy of it, an excerpt of which she shared with some of the Kelly Investigation Group. This excerpt has never been published before.

The letter says that Mrs Kelly is in no doubt that her husband killed himself and the reason he did so was because 'his life's work was at an end'. She says she would have been 'at the forefront of the movement to declare foul play' if she suspected otherwise. She then says: 'It is hardly surprising that when individuals came to recall what happened that night [17 July 2003] and in the morning [18 July] it was hard to be clear. Our own uncertainty had rubbed off on the search teams and what had come of our own muddle-headedness would persist for a very long time.'

It is not immediately apparent to whom Mrs Kelly refers when she mentions 'individuals', though it is probably the police. From the subsequent sentence, however, it is difficult to avoid the idea that she credits herself and her family with influencing the police investigation by having been confused while her husband was missing. How else to explain what she meant by 'muddle-headedness'?

She goes on: 'James Dingemans' questioning of me was based almost solely on a police witness statement made a few days after David's death when I was in deep shock and therefore contained little of my later thoughts and considerations. In retrospect, I could have made clear my overpowering belief that David took his own life.'

Mrs Kelly gave her evidence to the Hutton Inquiry on 1 September, about six weeks after her police witness statement and forty-five days after telling *The New York Times* of her belief that Dr Kelly had killed himself. Given that she had already told that newspaper – and therefore its millions of readers – on the day that her husband's body was found of her belief that he had committed suicide, it is hard to know how much clearer she could have been about this subsequently. Furthermore, no matter how painful, there was nothing preventing her from repeating her opinion at the Hutton Inquiry. But she chose not to do so.

In the letter she writes that she and Dr Kelly 'were both utterly traumatized' during the last week of his life, adding: 'He needed no outside agency to end his life. He could use his own means and his own timing. The fact that he chose to end his life at the first available opportunity after he'd completed what was demanded of him speaks volumes. This was the first moment he could decide what next. He could face nothing else. He could see his wife was ill because of what was happening to him.'

Why Mrs Kelly wrote of herself in the third person in this last sentence we do not know. But she showed that she was prepared to acknowledge the oddities surrounding her husband's death by what she wrote next:

I am aware that the evidence presented by the physical circumstances surrounding David's death may not give a complete and well-rounded verdict of the suicide itself... this has made it hard for some to accept that his death was indeed suicide... Conspiracy theory is relatively easy to put together, possibly much easier than the accepted fact of suicide. It's often said that the truth is stranger than fiction. It is often much, much more mundane in our view. I cannot give you chapter and verse of what happened on the day David killed himself. I will never get over David's death or the manner of his death. I will not ask you to desist from your group's work. I would only say that, had you known David well, you would agree that he committed suicide. I've had a large volume of conspiracy theory letters and I've had a long time to consider and reconsider... I've gone over and over the hours before David's death and I remain utterly certain that he committed suicide. If only it were different.

To have written such an honest letter, but also such an emotional one, apparently late into the night to a person she did not know is unarguably indicative of Mrs Kelly's anguish and pain. And yet this letter is also rather troubling. It would have made more sense if Mrs Kelly had asked Thursby to cease her self-appointed investigation into Dr Kelly's death – and yet she did no such thing, saying specifically that she would not ask Thursby to drop it.

Furthermore, one is inclined to ask why Mrs Kelly was so adamant that Thursby would share her view that Dr Kelly committed suicide had she known him. Having used the word 'suicide' so bluntly at least five times in her letter, it was peculiar that Mrs Kelly should then have asked for it back after sending it, perhaps suggesting some loss of confidence in its contents on her part.

PART 3

A CALLING TO ACCOUNT

KEY FINDINGS CONTESTED

The forensic pathologist Dr Nicholas Hunt completed his autopsy on Dr Kelly's body in the early hours of Saturday, 19 July. Two days later, when Nicholas Gardiner opened his inquest into Dr Kelly's death, Hunt told the coroner that in his view, based on his post-mortem, the cause of death was likely to have been haemorrhage as a result of the wounds on Dr Kelly's left wrist. Six days later, on 25 July, the toxicology tests had been completed and Hunt widened his opinion to incorporate two further contributory causes of death: co-proxamol ingestion and coronary artery atherosclerosis, or heart disease. Gardiner was, quite rightly, made aware of all this.

When Hutton published his report in January 2004

he concluded that the principal cause of Dr Kelly's death was 'bleeding from incised wounds to the left wrist which Dr Kelly inflicted on himself with the knife found beside his body'. More specifically, the official story is that Dr Kelly severed his left ulnar artery, which is buried within the wrist on the little-finger side. Hutton added that it was 'probable that the ingestion of an excess amount of co-proxamol tablets coupled with apparently clinically silent coronary artery disease would both have played a part in bringing about death more certainly and more rapidly than would have otherwise been the case'. In other words, Hutton echoed Hunt's findings precisely.

Yet there has been a strong degree of doubt among some medical professionals as to whether Dr Kelly, a learned man of science whose work meant he was essentially an expert in death, really did intend to end his own life in this way. Having studied the available evidence, they say that this method of death would have been slow, painful and uncertain, and they have questioned it publicly ever since.

The Hutton Inquiry itself is partly to blame for such scepticism. Granted, there will always be a minority who disbelieve the official account of any controversial topic, let alone one involving the death of a government employee who was privy to some of the world's most sensitive secrets; but doubts about Dr Kelly's death are shared by many people other than 'conspiracy theorists', as certain commentators lazily label those who question the official account. The point is that many people lack confidence in the way in which the Hutton Inquiry was set up and run, as well as in its findings.

Nor do these sceptics understand why the coroner's inquest, which was opened as a matter of routine three days after Dr Kelly's body was found, was quickly suspended on the order of Lord Falconer, and replaced by a government-appointed investigation which was less rigorous. There was no reason why the Hutton Inquiry and the coroner's inquest into Dr Kelly's death could not have run in tandem. After all, as has already been established, ultimately they were investigations with rather different aims and powers: the coroner's job was to find out how, when and where Dr Kelly died, while Hutton's remit was to conduct a more general inquiry into the circumstances of his death. In terms of satisfying the public as to how Dr Kelly died, it now looks very much as if Tony Blair made a monumental miscalculation in instructing Falconer to establish the Hutton Inquiry.

On 16 March 2004, seven weeks after Hutton published his report, Nicholas Gardiner, the Oxfordshire Coroner, did hold a further hearing at the Old Assize Court in Oxford to see whether there was any reason why he should resume the inquest into Dr Kelly's death. Gardiner did this in keeping with the law, having been prevailed upon by the government to halt temporarily the inquest which he had begun the previous July. He had the option to continue with his inquest in March 2004 if he believed there was an 'exceptional' reason to do so. But over the course of a mere fourteen minutes, Gardiner told the court he agreed with the Lord Chancellor, Lord Falconer, that the issue had been properly examined. Effectively, the inquest was suspended in perpetuity.

According to newspaper accounts at the time, Gardiner said he had reached his decision after reading an 'excellent report' from DCI Alan Young of Thames Valley Police, who led the police investigation into Dr Kelly's death (but who did not give evidence to the Hutton Inquiry). He said he had also seen photographs, records, transcripts, statements and 'a great deal else'.

Gardiner acknowledged receiving representations from sceptical members of the public who had pointed out, for example, that the Hutton Inquiry did not have the same powers as a coroner's inquest – in particular that no evidence was heard under oath – and he accepted that the burden of proof would have been higher in a coroner's court than it was at the Hutton Inquiry. Yet these concerns were not, apparently, made by anyone who would be classed by a coroner as an 'interested person' usually a relative or perhaps a colleague – allowing Gardiner to overlook them.

Jeremy Gompertz QC, representing the Kelly family, said at the hearing that Mrs Kelly and her three daughters also accepted Hutton's suicide finding and did not want the inquest resumed. But he added they were 'disappointed that Lord Hutton did not consider more fully the extent to which the state of mind in which Dr Kelly took his own life was induced by the Ministry of Defence in the exercise of the duty of care owed to him as his employer.'

It is noteworthy that Gardiner appears to have based his decision not to reconvene his inquest in part on the family's wishes, for coroners are not supposed to hold inquests according to the opinion of the family of the deceased. Rather, they are required by law to investigate any violent or unnatural death in their jurisdiction. Indeed, a 1994 Court of Appeal review of coronial law stated: 'It is the duty of the coroner as the public official responsible for the conduct of inquests, whether he is sitting with a jury or without, to ensure that the relevant facts are fully, fairly and fearlessly investigated...He must ensure that the relevant facts are exposed to public scrutiny, particularly if there is evidence of foul play, abuse or inhumanity. He fails in his duty if his investigation is superficial, slipshod or perfunctory.'

Whether Gardiner was ever able fearlessly to investigate Dr Kelly's death is an open question but, extraordinarily, even the forensic pathologist who conducted the post-mortem on Dr Kelly's body, Dr Nicholas Hunt, told Channel 4 News that month that he would be 'more comfortable' with a full inquest.

Perhaps the coroner's position was hardly surprising, though, since Hutton had already delivered his report and findings into this most high-profile matter, and Falconer's office had made it abundantly clear to Gardiner the previous summer that it did not believe it was necessary for Dr Kelly's death to be the subject of a full coroner's inquest.

For copious reasons – medical, legal, scientific and practical – doctors, lawyers and other parties had doubts about the Hutton Inquiry shortly after it was set up, and when the Hutton Report was published in January 2004 their concerns intensified. Not only was it felt that Hutton was a bad choice of Chairman because of his complete lack of coronial experience, but none of the five barristers who appeared at his inquiry had any qualifications for questioning any witness on the forensic elements of Dr Kelly's death. People giving evidence were not cross-examined, they were merely walked through prepared evidence.

Among those airing such concerns was David Halpin, a retired orthopaedic and trauma surgeon whose efforts have been crucial in keeping the Dr Kelly affair in the public eye.

Halpin first wrote a letter to the *Morning Star* raising questions about Dr Kelly's death which was published on 15 December 2003 – six weeks before the Hutton Report was released. This marked perhaps the first time that a respected medical professional had publicly voiced doubts about the probability that Dr Kelly had died as a result of cutting his ulnar artery, as the police had been so quick to suggest on the day Dr Kelly's body was found.

Halpin wrote to the newspaper:

> We have been told that he died from a cut wrist and that he had non-lethal levels of an analgesic in his blood. As a past trauma and orthopaedic surgeon I cannot easily accept that even the deepest cut into one wrist would cause such exsanguination that death resulted. The [ulnar artery is] of matchstick size and would have quickly shut down and clotted. Furthermore we have a man who was expert in lethal substances and who apparently chose a most uncertain method of suicide. The picture fits more with 'a cry for help'.

The point that Halpin raised was – and is – key. His experience told him that the primary cause of death could not have been haemorrhage – the explanation of Dr Nicholas Hunt, which was given first to Nicholas Gardiner and then to Hutton in oral evidence.

In Halpin's professional opinion it is virtually impossible to bleed to death by severing an ulnar artery. Halpin's opinion is consistent with the lack of blood reported by many people who attended the scene where Dr Kelly's body was found. Given the fact that no tests were done to establish exactly how much blood Dr Kelly's body lost, and none were conducted on the soil in the wood where his body was found in order to see how much blood might have seeped into the ground, Halpin's opinion can hardly be dismissed. Not only that, but Halpin has always questioned whether the knife found with Dr Kelly could have killed him anyway.

Based on Hunt's description of the wound, each of the cuts was made *across* Dr Kelly's wrist. Yet those truly intent on taking their life with a knife or sharp object usually ensure the cuts run *upwards* towards the body – in other words, moving from the wrist area up towards the elbow – because this has a higher guarantee of fatal blood loss. It seems inconceivable that Dr Kelly, a man of science, would not have been aware of this.

The knife which Dr Kelly allegedly used has never been seen in public and its sharpness never tested. All that is known of it is that he had owned it since boyhood. As an orthopaedic surgeon, Halpin has extensive professional experience of amputating limbs. He has said publicly many times that the knife attributed to Dr Kelly's death was about the worst possible for cutting tough tissues. Mr Halpin told me: 'As someone who made numerous incisions into skin, tendon and nerve – the latter I trimmed with a fresh razor blade because nerves are tough, tendon more so – I believe this firmly. The knife which Dr Kelly allegedly used had a concave blade. Not only is there a certain amount of difficulty in sharpening such an object, it would also be very painful to cut one's own skin with. The crushing, notching and maceration probably reflected its use – but with force.'

Many medical experts, including Halpin, believe that this artery is too small to have caused sufficient blood loss to kill Dr Kelly. In their opinion, it would also have clotted and closed down quickly for several reasons, including the trauma used to sever the artery repeatedly.

Furthermore, Dr Kelly was right-handed, as his eldest daughter, Sian, was required to confirm in a sworn statement to the police. If a right-handed person were to deliberately wound their left wrist, however, they would likely do so by revolving their left hand so that the palm faced upwards, giving them easy access to it. If moving in a horizontal direction, the natural inclination would probably then be to slice the wrist from the far side, below the thumb, towards the near side, below the little finger – in other words, from left to right. Yet Dr Kelly's wounds are believed to have begun to have been made in the opposite direction, from the little finger side to the thumb side – from right to left – requiring the knife to have been held at an awkward angle. If Dr Hunt found this in any way unusual, he kept his thoughts to himself.

In his book on the death of Dr David Kelly, the former Liberal Democrat MP Norman Baker was able to go further by quoting official figures. He noted that those truly intent on taking their own life by cutting a wrist – a notoriously unreliable form of suicide in any case – would make a lengthwise cut along the arm rather than cutting across the wrist. He also stated that Karen Dunnell, at that time the Head of the Office for National Statistics, had confirmed to him that only six people in Britain had died from an injury to the ulnar artery between 1997 and 2004. Baker reported: 'Only one such death occurred in 2003, the year of Dr Kelly's death.' That lonely statistic must have been Dr Kelly himself.

From early 2004 onwards, after the publication of the Hutton Report, Halpin and a group of other doctors, including Dr Stephen Frost, Dr Chris Burns-Cox, Dr Andrew Rouse and vascular surgeons Martin Birnstingl and John Scurr, together with the coronial expert Dr Michael Powers QC, built a case contesting Hutton's findings and pointed out a series of inconsistencies arising from his inquiry which they published in letters to the *Guardian*. Central to their challenge was that, in their experience, cutting through skin and tendons is hard work best done with surgical equipment or a razor blade.

MAI PEDERSON

Later a new, and arguably more powerful, voice echoed those of the doctors in querying the official story that Dr Kelly bled to death having cut his left wrist. That voice belonged to Mai Pederson, a linguist and member of the US military who was assigned to work as a UN translator in Iraq in 1998. While in Iraq she met Dr Kelly, and they formed a close friendship which culminated in him joining her to become a member of the Bahá'í Faith, the spiritual movement founded in nineteenth-century Persia. Pederson, who was sixteen years younger than Dr Kelly, counselled him during his conversion but has always insisted he was nothing more than a 'big brother' figure in her life.

While many have viewed Dr Kelly's conversion from his Welsh Protestantism to the Bahá'í faith – coupled with his intense friendship with the unmarried Sgt Pederson – as surprising, it is not as though these developments in his personal life were kept entirely secret from Janice Kelly. When asked at the Hutton Inquiry about her husband's conversion to Bahá'í, she admitted that she knew only 'a little' about it as he kept it 'very privately to himself'. But she went on to say that it dated back 'five or six years'. She said he had begun to read the Koran, 'and he was becoming perhaps gentler in his ways, in some ways'. She went on: 'It really was a spiritual revelation for him. He read widely on the subject and met a number of people.' She then singled out his interpreter, Pederson, and said she 'later became a family friend, who was quite influential there'.

It is quite possible that Pederson's work in American

intelligence prevented Mrs Kelly from elaborating at the Hutton Inquiry, but others were willing to go further. Midway through the inquiry *The Times* carried a report on Pederson quoting Marilyn VonBerg, who was at the time secretary of the local Bahá'í assembly in Monterey, California, where Dr Kelly converted in 1999.

Mrs VonBerg told the paper that Pederson was 'very close' to Dr Kelly's family and had visited them some time before his death. She said: 'He and Mai were friends because she had taught him the faith. She is high-security so we never asked them questions. But I am sure she was his translator at one point.' Mrs VonBerg also revealed that she and her husband, John, received a telephone call from Pederson shortly after Dr Kelly's death, telling them he had died. Of it, John VonBerg recounted: 'All she [Pederson] said is: "Don't believe what you read in the newspapers."' He added: 'I do not know which direction she was coming from. It's very mysterious to us.'

Nothing more was heard of the twice-divorced Pederson in either the American or British press until she gave an interview to *The Mail on Sunday* in August 2008. In it, she explained in the clearest terms why she disputed Hutton's official finding. She said that during the five years she knew Dr Kelly, she observed that he was unable to use his right hand to perform tasks requiring basic strength such as carrying a briefcase or opening a door. Pederson told the newspaper:

David would have had to have been a contortionist
to kill himself the way they claim. When he embraced
friends at the beginning and end of Bahá'í meetings, it was his left arm that you felt hugging you
and you could tell his right arm hurt him because
he rubbed the elbow a lot. I didn't want to pry but he
finally told me the reason in the spring of 2003.
It was the last time I saw him before he died. He
was visiting America on business and we went out
to dinner. He ordered steak and he was holding
his knife very oddly in the palm of his right hand,
with his wrist crooked, trying to cut the meat. He
told me that some time ago he had broken his right
elbow and it was never fixed properly, so he had real
problems with it. It was painful and it never regained
its strength.

Pederson's astonishing insights did not end there. She
also had information about the very knife which she
assumed Hutton believed Dr Kelly had used to injure his
wrist. She said:

I just don't see how he could have used his right
hand to cut through the nerves and tendons of his
left wrist – especially as the knife he supposedly
used had a dull blade. He always wore a Barbour
jacket and he kept a knife in his pocket. It had a

folding blade and I remember him telling me he couldn't sharpen it because his right hand didn't have the strength to hold a sharpener. It would have taken him a long time to reach the artery that was severed and it would have been very painful. As a scientist, David had no need to kill himself that way. I don't understand why the British Government isn't thoroughly investigating this. Logically, he cannot have committed suicide.

And there was more. Pederson also mentioned something never previously realized: Dr Kelly's great difficulty in swallowing pills. As a result of this, he never did so if, say, he had a headache – a fact confirmed by Mrs Kelly during the official review of the Kelly case in 2011. Would he really have chosen to swallow twenty-nine tablets to bring about his own death? This point is especially relevant in view of a Freedom of Information response provided by Thames Valley Police in 2010. It confirmed that 111ml of water remained in the 500ml bottle found with Dr Kelly at Harrowdown Hill. This means that he apparently drank only 389ml of water – about half a pint – to help swallow twenty-nine pills while bleeding to death, a state which immediately triggers thirst. Shouldn't Hutton have established publicly how much water remained in the bottle, and asked the relevant witnesses about Dr Kelly's inability to swallow pills? If the thought ever crossed his mind, he didn't bother reacting to it. It is also unclear where this bottle of water came from. The last person to see him alive, Ruth Absalom, did not mention having seen him holding it. Did he buy it somewhere? Did he take it from home? Again, Hutton did not ascertain this.

Many will wonder why Hutton made no mention of any of Pederson's testimony in his report. The simple answer is that he didn't have to refer to it because he did not call Pederson as a witness to his inquiry.

Pederson revealed that in August 2003, shortly after Dr Kelly's death, Thames Valley Police officers flew to America and questioned her over a period of two days. During this time she told them of her concerns, as she explained to *The Mail on Sunday*: 'The facts just don't add up. The more I have heard about this, the more I have thought about the significance of his weak right hand. I told the police about it when they interviewed me. I said, "How could David have cut his left wrist using a dull knife with his weak right hand?" They said, "It wasn't a straight cut. It was jagged."'

The ten-page statement which Thames Valley Police attributed to Pederson was completed on 1 September 2003 – some three and a half weeks before Hutton concluded the hearings relating to his inquiry. The concerns she aired with officers in the summer of 2003 were the same ones she raised with *The Mail on Sunday* five years later.

The police have always implied that Pederson did not give her permission for her statement to be used at the Hutton Inquiry. But in fact, with the help of her lawyer, Mark Zaid, she stipulated to the police following her conversation with them: 'If specific information [in the statement] is deemed relevant to the coroner's inquiry into the death of David Kelly, I am willing for Thames Valley Police to reveal the information in a non-attributable way.'

Hutton said his inquiry took the place of a coroner's inquest, so he might have interpreted Pederson's statement as something to which he could refer if he wished. Yet the contents of her statement were never formally lodged with the inquiry team and therefore never quoted from during the inquiry. Hutton has confirmed that he was well aware of what Pederson told the police, so nothing would have prevented him from publicly exploring Pederson's points about the arm injury with one of the medical professionals whom he did call to his inquiry, not mentioning Pederson by name. Indeed, as already discussed, one witness gave evidence to the Hutton Inquiry from another room while using a pseudonym – Rod Godfrey, who appeared at the Hutton Inquiry as 'Mr A'; Pederson's statement could therefore easily have been referred to while calling her 'Miss B', for example. But Hutton, apparently, was having none of it.

On 23 September 2003, during his second and final evidence session at the Hutton Inquiry, ACC Michael Page was asked by Dingemans about Pederson's contact with the police regarding Dr Kelly. With what now appears to be astonishing insouciance, Page said: 'We interviewed Mai Pederson. She declined to give a statement as such but I have a record of the interviews that took place... The conversation with Mai Pederson added nothing that was of relevance to my inquiry at all.'

Did Page, whose evidence to Hutton regarding Dr Kelly's dentist was, at the least, incomplete, seriously believe that Pederson's opinion of Dr Kelly's arm injury was irrelevant? Did Page honestly believe that Pederson's knowledge of his swallowing difficulty was not worthy of public comment? Undeniably, Pederson's recollections about Dr Kelly's arm injury could be seen as unhelpful in that they interrupted the official account that was being advanced.

It has subsequently been revealed via Dominic Grieve's 2011 review of the Dr Kelly affair that Hutton's belief was that Pederson's statement offered nothing 'that could not be adduced from [Dr Kelly's] family members'. This is not exactly a fair reflection of the facts either. For none of Dr Kelly's family mentioned anything in their verbal evidence about his arm injury or the alleged bluntness of the knife he supposedly used or his difficulty swallowing pills – nor were they asked about any of these points at the Hutton Inquiry.

So how did Dr Kelly injure his right elbow? In 2011 it emerged that the fracture apparently occurred in December

1991 while Dr Kelly was riding a horse. Dr Kelly's friend and colleague Dr Andrew Shuttleworth expanded on the extent of the injury on 30 April 2010 in an unsolicited letter to the then Labour Attorney General, Baroness Scotland. Shuttleworth said the injury to Dr Kelly's right elbow 'led to a severe fracture and residual weakness'. Was the 'residual weakness' in Dr Kelly's right arm so severe that it raised questions about his ability to cut into his own wrist? Regardless, the Hutton Inquiry did not even bother to investigate this key point.

And what of the knife Dr Kelly supposedly used? At the Hutton Inquiry it was described as a Sandvik knife which Dr Kelly had owned since boyhood, so had perhaps been in his possession for about fifty years. Mai Pederson said he always carried a knife with him in his Barbour – something she might have remembered, having visited him and Mrs Kelly at home in Oxfordshire on occasion – whereas Hutton deduced that the knife was kept in Dr Kelly's desk drawer at home along with some other penknives. Crucially, the knife found next to his body was never physically shown to his family or presented at the Hutton Inquiry. Rather, a photo of it was shown by Thames Valley Police to two of his daughters for identification purposes. Who, therefore, knows for certain where the knife came from?

The knife was described by the police as being 'a stainless steel pen-knife' with a single, curved 7.5cm blade.

Its sharpness, however, was never debated or discussed at the Hutton Inquiry. Furthermore, tests conducted on it after Dr Kelly's death by the forensic biologist Roy Green, whose results were revealed only in 2011, showed the presence of twelve animal hairs on the blade. Green decided these were probably rabbit hairs. Yet Dr Kelly was not a man known to go around skinning rabbits, or indeed any animal. If anybody associated with the Hutton Inquiry was remotely interested in finding out why these animal hairs were there, they never said so publicly. Some have speculated that, the knife found with Dr Kelly having been blunt, Dr Kelly or somebody else may have first attempted to cut the skin of a dead rabbit or another small creature in order to test its sharpness and therefore its suitability for cutting Dr Kelly's wrist. Green said he also found what he concluded were six human hairs which, in his opinion, 'could' have come from Dr Kelly's wrist. On this basis, he determined that the knife found beside Dr Kelly's body was used to cut his wrist. DNA tests showed his blood on its blade and handle.

Taking all of this into account, it can be summarized that Dr Kelly had an injury to his right arm that was apparently painful enough to prevent him from cutting a steak shortly before his death, though this injury was not disclosed at the Hutton Inquiry; he used a knife which highly experienced surgeons believe would have been too blunt to cut through the skin and tendons in his wrist, yet whose sharpness was never discussed at the Hutton Inquiry; and he managed to sever an artery in his wrist which, being hidden, is so difficult to locate that according to official statistics he was the only person in Britain to die of such an injury in the year 2003.

Despite the validity of these points, Hutton never raised them at his inquiry, and maintained that Dr Kelly bled to death having severed the ulnar artery in his left wrist.

BLOOD AND PILLS

It is noteworthy that the two paramedics who attended Harrowdown Hill about thirty minutes after the volunteer searchers found Dr Kelly's body on 18 July have always been extremely concerned about the small amount of blood they observed there. Their views must be taken seriously, given that they had worked together for fifteen years and during that time had attended many suicide attempts involving wrist-slashing, only one of which, incidentally, had been successful and which they recalled had generated so much blood it was like a 'slaughterhouse'.

In her evidence to Hutton, during which she was examined by Dingemans, paramedic Vanessa Hunt was offered the chance to make any observations she wanted to about the circumstances of Dr Kelly's death. She said:

'Only that the amount of blood that was around the scene [at Harrowdown Hill] seemed relatively minimal and there was a small patch on his right knee, but no obvious arterial bleeding. There was no spraying of blood or huge blood loss or any obvious loss on the clothing... There was dried blood on the left wrist... but no obvious sign of a wound or anything, there was just dried blood.'

To this, Dingemans seemed to react a little testily. He said: 'One of the police officers or someone this morning said there appeared to be some blood on the ground. Did you see that?' Ms Hunt replied: 'As to on the ground, I do not remember seeing a sort of huge puddle or anything like that. There was dried blood on the left wrist. His jacket was pulled to sort of mid-forearm area and from that area down towards the hand there was dried blood, but no obvious sign of a wound or anything, it was just dried blood.'

Dingemans pressed the paramedic: 'You did not see the wound?' She replied: 'I did not see the wound, no.' He went on: 'You were not looking at the wound, then?' To this, Ms Hunt responded: 'The hand – from what I remember, his arm – left arm was outstretched to the left of the body... Palm up or slightly on the side and, as I say, there was dried blood from the edge of the jacket down towards the hand but no gaping wound or anything obvious that I could see from the position I was in.' She said she had not examined Dr Kelly's wrist. Dingemans then asked: 'And were you examining the ground for blood or blood loss?' Ms Hunt replied: 'No.'

Vanessa Hunt's colleague, David Bartlett, was asked for his observations and he said he noticed no stains on Dr Kelly's clothes other than a bloodstain about a quarter of an inch across on the right knee of Dr Kelly's jeans. At the end of his evidence he was asked if he would like to make any other comments and he volunteered that he and Ms Hunt were both 'surprised there was not more blood on the body if it was an arterial bleed'.

Bartlett and Hunt have given several newspaper interviews since Dr Kelly's death in which they have again expressed doubts about the lack of blood at the scene. In December 2004 the pair spoke to *The Observer*. In this interview Bartlett remarked: 'I remember saying to one of the policemen [at Harrowdown Hill] it didn't look like he died from that [the wrist wound] and suggesting he must have taken an overdose or something else.'

As has been noted, the forensic biologist Roy Green, in contrast to Hunt and Bartlett, told Hutton that he observed 'arterial rain' at Harrowdown Hill, and that some nettles beside Dr Kelly's body were covered in such droplets. He also said he believed that the stain on the knee of Dr Kelly's jeans had been caused by him kneeling down and coming into contact with a pool of blood. But there was no mention of blood on, for example, Dr Kelly's hair, as might have been expected as a result of arterial rain.

The forensic pathologist Dr Nicholas Hunt stated at the Hutton Inquiry that Dr Kelly had showed signs of what he termed a 'vital reaction', described as a reddening and swelling around the area of injury. Hunt took this as proof that the cuts were inflicted 'over a reasonable period of time, minutes, though, rather than seconds or many hours before death'. Hunt therefore believed that Dr Kelly bled so profusely as a result of the cut to his ulnar artery that he died quickly – all of which sits uncomfortably with the paramedics' observation that there was little blood at the scene and the sceptical doctors' insistence that it is not possible to bleed to death by severing the ulnar artery.

The pills which are said to have contributed to Dr Kelly's death are also the subject of much debate for solid practical, medical and scientific reasons. Co-proxamol was, as we have seen, a prescription-only painkiller whose product licence in Britain was withdrawn in 2007 because it was considered too toxic for the open market.

It has been noted already that three blister packs of co-proxamol were found in Dr Kelly's Barbour pocket when his body was discovered. (Incidentally, would a dying man really go to the trouble of carefully replacing all three packets in his coat pocket instead of merely discarding them?) Each pack held ten pills. Two packs were empty. The third had only one tablet remaining. The immediate assumption was that Dr Kelly had swallowed twenty-nine of the thirty tablets he apparently took with him on his final walk.

Yet although it was known that Janice Kelly took these pills for her arthritis, it was never established properly that the pills found with Dr Kelly came from his wife's supply. She kept hers in the kitchen and bedroom and had last replenished her stock eight weeks earlier, thanks to her GP – also Dr Kelly's GP – Dr Malcolm Warner. He had most recently given her a prescription on 20 May 2003.

When the Kellys' house was searched on 18 July 2003, a drawer in Mrs Kelly's bedroom revealed a box with four packets of co-proxamol remaining out of a possible ten packs. In the kitchen was a full box of ten packets. Therefore, Mrs Kelly had fourteen packets left out of a possible twenty.

The manufacturer of the pills found with Dr Kelly's body was later asked by Thames Valley Police if it would be possible to trace the packs found with the body, to match them with Mrs Kelly's supply. The police were told that each batch release in Britain amounted to a total of 1.6 million packets, and could end up at any chemist in the country, making the task extremely difficult.

Despite this, it was taken as read at the Hutton Inquiry that Dr Kelly had stolen his wife's painkillers – medication which, remember, he never normally took because of his aversion to swallowing tablets. Surprisingly, Mrs Kelly was not asked at the Hutton Inquiry whether the pills belonged to her, whether she noticed any missing from her supply, or how often she took them. The closest anybody came to discussing this with her was when Dingemans asked if she took any medicine and she said she took co-proxamol for her arthritis. Dingemans then said to her: 'I think we are also going to hear that appears to be the source of the co-proxamol that was used.' Mrs Kelly replied: 'I had assumed that. I keep a small store in a kitchen drawer and the rest in my bedside table.' But since Dingemans did not follow up on this by asking her about quantities, his line of inquiry led nowhere.

Dr Kelly's GP, Dr Warner, was asked whether he prescribed co-proxamol to Dr Kelly. His one-word answer was 'No.'

Why was the Hutton Inquiry so reluctant to enter into a straightforward discussion with Mrs Kelly about the sensitive matter of her pills? It seems incredible – in the truest sense of the word – that nobody sought some sort of proof that Dr Kelly had appropriated some of his wife's supply. As a result, there is no evidence that the co-proxamol found with Dr Kelly was his wife's, or that it was Dr Kelly who removed it from the Kellys' house. This leaves open the possibility that the pills were removed from the Kellys' house by a third party, or may even have come from another source altogether.

As for how many pills Dr Kelly allegedly swallowed, this was never established either, though some will wonder why a man apparently intent on killing himself did not swallow every tablet supposedly available to him. Medical tests carried out on 19 July 2003 to detect the presence of alcohol or drugs in Dr Kelly's body revealed that in his stomach was the equivalent of just a fifth of one co-proxamol pill – perhaps not so surprising considering his known dislike of swallowing pills.

The forensic toxicologist who worked on the Dr Kelly case and then gave evidence to the Hutton Inquiry, Alexander Allan, stated that he found one active ingredient, paracetamol, at a concentration of 97mcg per millilitre of blood; and another, dextropropoxyphene, at a concentration of 1.0mcg per millilitre of blood. Allan told the inquiry that these levels were 'much higher than therapeutic use… They clearly represent an overdose.' Appearing to contradict himself, however, he added: 'But they are somewhat lower than what I would normally expect to encounter in cases of death due to an overdose of co-proxamol.'

He then said he would expect there to be 'two, three, four times as much paracetamol and two, three, four times as much dextropropoxyphene in the average overdose case which results in fatalities'. He added that it was not possible to determine how many pills Dr Kelly allegedly took, 'because of the complex nature of the behaviour of the drugs in the body'. He remarked that his test results were 'consistent with, say, twenty-nine or thirty tablets but [they] could be consistent with other scenarios as well'.

This seems a very long-winded way of saying that he could make his tests comply with the notion that Dr Kelly had swallowed twenty-nine pills, but that his results were not as conclusive as they might have seemed – at the very least were open to interpretation – and that it was in fact debatable as to how many pills Dr Kelly had actually swallowed. Ergo, Dr Kelly might very well *not* have swallowed twenty-nine pills as assumed – or, indeed, even just nine pills. But the most significant point Allan did confirm was that neither dose alone would necessarily have been enough to kill him.

Further undermining Allan's ability to nail down solid facts was that when Dr Kelly was found, vomit trails ran down either side of his face from the corner of his mouth to his ear, as Nicholas Hunt had noted. Bearing in mind the reliance which Hutton placed on Dr Hunt's view that Dr Kelly had died partly as a result of swallowing twenty-nine co-proxamol tablets, it was a woeful oversight on Hunt's part not to have insisted this 'vomit' be analysed. Its content remains unknown.

Anyone who took co-proxamol when it was on the market was warned that one of its side effects was of drowsiness. Again, it must be asked: is it likely that Dr Kelly took twenty-nine pills, left one pill because he was drowsy, but then found the strength to start or continue cutting into his wrist – potentially, given that he may have died as late as 1.15 a.m., when it was pitch-black?

THE DOCTORS VERSUS
THE ATTORNEY GENERAL

In July 2009 the group of senior doctors mentioned earlier, which included David Halpin, Stephen Frost, Chris Burns-Cox, Martin Birnstingl and Andrew Rouse, produced a twelve-page dossier which drew on their collective expertise in human anatomy. Again focusing on the ulnar artery, it was a comprehensive rejection of Hutton's conclusion that Dr Kelly bled to death and was written to underscore their legal attempt to demand a coroner's inquest. They retained the pro-bono services of London law firm Leigh Day and received advice from Richard Hermer QC to argue in detail that a wound to this artery could not have resulted in enough blood loss to cause his death. The doctors wrote: 'This artery has the width of a matchstick in its constricted state. It is not easily felt on the little finger side of the wrist... on the contrary, the radial artery pulse is easily felt beneath the skin on the opposite side of the wrist. It is thus more difficult to cut the ulnar artery.'

They also argued that, according to the evidence given by Dr Hunt to the Hutton Inquiry, Dr Kelly's blood would have quickly clotted, therefore stemming the flow and preventing his death. They stated:

> Dr Hunt describes complete severance of this artery,
> i.e. transection. This means the elasticity of the artery

would have caused it to retract within its sheath. Contraction of the circular smooth muscle within the arterial wall would have narrowed the artery, thus reducing or stopping blood flow. Blood clots would have formed in the wound, but also within the narrowed artery. That clotting within the artery would have happened more speedily because the cutting was done with considerable trauma, thus causing more damage to the lining membrane, the intima. Damage to the cells of the intima causes aggregation of blood platelets, thus hastening clotting within the vessel.

In January 2010, the same doctors told me of their discovery of Hutton's secret recommendation that all medical and scientific reports relating to Dr Kelly's death should be classified for seventy years – a 'recommendation' which was obediently followed by the government. This information came to light in a letter from a legal officer working for Oxfordshire County Council while the doctors were gathering evidence in support of their case. Undeniably, details of this secret sealing reignited the Dr Kelly affair. Within twenty-four hours of my publishing that story in *The Mail on Sunday*, Hutton released a statement explaining his decision and revealing that he had written to the Ministry of Justice making it clear that he was, after all, happy for the doctors to see the post-mortem papers. This amounted to the lifting of the embargo on this one document.

In his statement, Hutton said:

> At the conclusion of my inquiry into the death of Dr David Kelly, I requested that the post-mortem report relating to his death should not be disclosed for 70 years as I was concerned that the publication of that report in newspapers, books and magazines would cause his daughters and his wife further and unnecessary distress. Much of the material in the post-mortem report had been given in oral evidence in public at the inquiry and substantial parts of that evidence had been set out in my report. However, I consider that the disclosure of the report to doctors and their legal advisers for the purposes of legal proceedings would not undermine the protection which I wished to give to Dr Kelly's family, provided that conditions were imposed restricting the use and publication of the report to such proceedings, and I have written to the Ministry of Justice to this effect.

In other words, Hutton sought to distance himself from the idea that there was anything secret about his embargo. But if he had had nothing to hide in the first place, it remains unclear why he did not simply state in his report that he had made the seventy-year recommendation.

In March 2010, one of the group, Dr Michael Powers QC, wrote on an informal basis to then Shadow Justice Secretary and Tory MP Dominic Grieve, seeking his opinion on the Dr Kelly matter. Powers did this in the knowledge that Grieve was likely to be appointed to a senior legal post in any future Tory government and would therefore potentially be involved in overseeing the group's attempt at achieving a full coroner's inquest.

Grieve wrote back to Powers on 16 March 2010 to say that he recognized the public 'have not been reassured' by the official verdict that Dr Kelly had killed himself. Grieve wrote: 'I am aware of the work of the doctors' group on challenging Lord Hutton's findings. They have made an impressive and cogent case.' Grieve added: 'This is something I would review if in Government as I am conscious this is a matter where the public have not been reassured that the Hutton Inquiry satisfactorily resolved the matter.'

Two months later, in May 2010, Grieve was appointed Attorney General in the new Conservative/Liberal Democrat coalition government, making him its chief law officer. Believing that he looked favourably upon their case, the doctors began preparing a formal submission known as a 'memorial', a petition in which they set out the reasons why they felt Dr Kelly's death should be subject to a full coroner's inquest. As Attorney General, Grieve had the power, having considered the case, to apply to the High Court in London for an inquest to be held.

Quite independently of this, in June 2010 Mark Zaid, the Washington-based lawyer representing Mai Pederson, wrote to Grieve on behalf of his client. In this letter Zaid said: 'Given the absence of a coroner's inquest and the perpetual secrecy surrounding the post-mortem examination, it is painfully obvious that this matter continues to cry out for a formal, independent and complete review. Ms Pederson fully supports and adds her voice to such an effort.'

Zaid then confirmed that Pederson had agreed to give testimony to the Hutton Inquiry but had been denied the opportunity because the 'reasonable privacy protections' she requested as an active member of the US military at the time were not afforded to her. He added:

> Ms Pederson has publicly raised several concerns, few if any of which appear to have been accorded due consideration by the Hutton Inquiry, based on her personal knowledge of Dr Kelly and contemporaneous events at the time that further call into question the final verdict. These include important observations, such as Dr Kelly's difficulty in swallowing pills and an injury that would have hampered if not prohibited his ability to slash his own wrist (indeed, he had difficulty cutting his own steak), which contradict the official verdict of suicide.

Zaid's letter also pointed out that it was 'the government's responsibility to ascertain the full truth, whatever that might be'. He concluded: 'The accusation that Dr Kelly committed suicide, if untrue, maligns the good character and reputation of a well-respected and honourable person. Not only is the public entitled to be assured of the truth, but Dr Kelly deserves it.'

It was the second time in twelve months that Zaid had written to a British Attorney General about Dr Kelly, having also done so in 2009 when Baroness Scotland was in post. It is clear that Mai Pederson felt it a great injustice and a personal frustration that she had effectively been barred from giving evidence to Hutton about her friend, whom she did not believe would have taken his own life.

In August 2010 a different group of doctors – save Dr Michael Powers QC, who was associated with both groups – wrote a powerful letter to *The Times*, also calling for a coroner's inquest and basing their argument on the same point, namely an insufficient amount of blood to back up the official cause of death. Alongside Powers the distinguished signatories included Julian Bion, a Professor of Intensive Care Medicine at the Queen Elizabeth Hospital, Birmingham; Dr Margaret Bloom, a barrister and former GP and Deputy Coroner; Dr Neville Davis, Consultant Forensic Physician; Dr Elizabeth Driver, a solicitor and Fellow of the Royal College of Pathologists; Sir Barry Jackson, former President of the British Academy of Forensic Sciences; Dr Jason Payne-James, a Consultant Forensic Physician and Honorary Senior Lecturer, Cameron Forensic Medical Sciences, Barts and the London School of Medicine and Dentistry; Professor John Francis Nunn; and Denis Wilkins, a retired Consultant Vascular Surgeon. The letter read:

> Amid the continuing interest surrounding the death of the government weapons inspector, the late Dr David Kelly, we wish to express our concern about the conclusion as to the cause of death in the light of the information now in the public domain. It is extremely unlikely, from a medical perspective, that the primary cause of death would or could have been haemorrhage from a severed ulnar artery in one wrist without any evidence of a blood clotting deficiency. This small artery, deeper in the wrist than the larger radial artery used to palpate the pulse, would have retracted on being severed and within a short time blood loss would be expected to have ceased. Insufficient blood would have been lost to threaten life. Absent a quantitative assessment of the blood lost and of the blood remaining in the great vessels, the conclusion that death occurred as a consequence of haemorrhage is unsafe. The inquiry by Lord Hutton was unsatisfactory with regard to the causation of death. A detailed investigation of all

the medical circumstances is now required and we support the call for a proper inquest into the cause of Dr Kelly's death.

At about the same time a leading suicide expert, Colin Pritchard, Emeritus Professor at Southampton University's School of Medicine, told me that in his opinion there was nothing in the evidence given to the Hutton Inquiry to suggest Dr Kelly had any 'intent' to commit suicide, meaning that in his opinion a coroner would not return such a finding. Intent was an area that Hutton had not even mentioned. Professor Pritchard told me:

David Kelly had planned to see his daughter on the evening of his death so the timing is very odd. Secondly, on the morning of the day of his death he had some positive – what you might call optimistic – emails. When you read the available evidence it states categorically that Dr Kelly was not or had not previously been mentally ill. A major factor in suicide is mental illness. The crucial thing for me is that if you read the Hutton Inquiry there is not a sliver of evidence to suggest he intended to kill himself. There was nothing in the psychiatric evidence to indicate intent. I believe if a coroner's inquest was taken the likelihood would be an open verdict.

The Hutton Inquiry had taken evidence on two separate occasions from a Professor of Psychiatry at Oxford University, Keith Hawton, regarding Dr Kelly's mental state in the run-up to his death. But on neither occasion did Hutton ask Professor Hawton a simple but vital question – whether, in his 'expert opinion', he thought Dr Kelly had killed himself, meaning that Hawton was never required to deliver a formal opinion to Hutton in the way he might have had to do in a coroner's court. Hawton said he believed Dr Kelly suffered from 'severe loss of self-esteem' at the time of his death but not depression, adding: 'There is certainly no evidence that he had significant mental illness, either at the time of his death or previously.' Was this not an oversight on Hutton's part? Shouldn't he have asked for an expert opinion? The eminent Professor Pritchard certainly believes so.

At the Hutton Inquiry seven years previously, Dingemans had picked up on the fact that Dr Kelly had left no note of intent and raised this with Professor Hawton, asking him to provide the type of evidence of planning he would expect to see in an older person considering suicide. Hawton said: 'Well, evidence of planning would be, for example, saving up medication to carry out an act, deliberately going and obtaining a specific method for the act, obviously seeking out a place to carry out the act, where one is least likely to be disturbed, and things such as a person putting their affairs in order, changing their will and so on.'

Dr Kelly's will was drawn up in November 1998 and he did not change it before he died. Neither did he take any medication. Therefore, Dingemans carried on with this line of questioning. He said to Professor Hawton: 'And do you always have to communicate your intention to commit suicide? Is there always a note left?' Hawton said: 'Not at all, no. In recent studies from the United Kingdom, somewhere between 40 and 50 per cent of people who die leave a suicide note or a suicide message, it is not always a note.' Dingemans responded: 'So the majority do not leave a note?' He was told: 'That is correct.'

This could be interpreted as another instance when Dingemans' questions were effectively underlining the premise that Dr Kelly took his own life. The clear inference on Dingemans's part was that because the majority of older people who commit suicide do not leave a note, there was nothing strange about Dr Kelly failing to do so. This was a sweeping generalization.

Was it not incumbent upon Dingemans to dig a little and ask Hawton to talk more about suicide in older people? Perhaps the majority of those he was describing were isolated figures with no family, or those serving life prison sentences, or ex-offenders, rather than people like Dr Kelly, aged fifty-nine, whose much-loved, soon-to-be-married daughter he had arranged to meet on the evening he went missing. Would he really have killed himself while knowing that she was finishing work and expecting to see him? Indeed, they were to have met close to the spot where, we are to believe, he had perhaps already taken his life.

Surely Hawton knew that no two suicides are the same. Was it not down to him, as a Hutton Inquiry expert, to probe a little deeper and talk about Dr Kelly's case specifically, in as much as he could do so, rather than rely upon mere statistics whose application without qualification appears to have been misleading, at best? Yet again it is almost as if it was somehow important to Dingemans that he should secure support from a third party which backed up the suicide finding, rather than viewing the situation objectively.

Because it is a commonly held belief that suicide can run in families, it is important, though obviously poignant, also to bear in mind that at the Hutton Inquiry Hawton chose to dismiss the possibility that Dr Kelly would have been suicidal as a result of his mother apparently taking her own life on the eve of his twentieth birthday in 1964. Dr Kelly was a student at Leeds University at the time. Interestingly, although Dr Kelly told his wife that he believed his mother, Margaret, had taken an overdose, the coroner who investigated her death recorded an open verdict, attributing the death to bronchopneumonia, a chest infection as a result of barbiturate poison.

In August 2010 Dr Kelly's distant cousin, a former nurse called Wendy Wearmouth, also expressed her scepticism of the official finding. She told me: 'Whether David was my cousin or not I would never imagine that a man with his background, his knowledge, would slash his wrists, take painkillers. This is what teenage girls do. This is not what eminent scientists do. If you knew the man it's totally against his whole way of being. He doesn't fall into a category of someone who would commit suicide.'

Ms Wearmouth was merely echoing what Mai Pederson had said in 2008 about the suggestion that Dr Kelly took his own life. For at that time Pederson said she knew he had been 'upset' by the Gilligan episode but he was not devastated: 'He said he was misquoted and his words were twisted and taken out of context. He wasn't depressed. He was upset. I have taken courses on suicide prevention and he exhibited none of the signs. He was planning for his retirement. He wanted to make more money to provide for his family and he'd had job offers in the States as well as Europe. Also, he was excited that one of his daughters [Rachel] was getting married. He said, "The controversy will blow over."'

Pederson said he had much to look forward to in life and, as his own mother had in Dr Kelly's own view killed herself when he was young, he would never have inflicted the same thing on his own family – not least because his new religion, the Bahá'í faith, expressly forbids suicide:

All the facts suggest that David did not kill himself.
It is against our Bahá'í faith. But for David there

were also personal reasons – he believed his mother's death was suicide. Research shows that suicide runs in families and I asked him if he would ever do that. I said, 'Hypothetically, if you are ever at your wits' end, promise me that you will seek help.' He said, 'I don't see the relevance. I would never take any life, let alone my own.' He finally did say that if he was ever desperate, he would get help. That's important because he was a man of his word. He could never hurt his wife and daughters the way that he was hurt by his mother's death.

It is worth adding that no witness to the Hutton Inquiry ever suggested that Dr Kelly had any history of committing acts of self-harm, making suicide attempts, abusing drugs or alcohol, reckless or risky behaviour, financial worries or psychiatric disorders of any description – in short, anything suggesting a predisposition to taking his own life.

With public scepticism mounting, a cross-party group of politicians decided to speak out in favour of a coroner's inquest. Lord Howard of Lympne QC – the former Tory leader, Michael Howard, who was in charge of his party in January 2004 when the Hutton Report was published – led the way. He told *The Mail on Sunday*: 'In view of the growing number of relevant questions that have arisen and cast doubt on the conclusions reached by Lord Hutton, I believe it would now be appropriate for a full inquest to be held. Recent evidence by the first police officer on the scene, together with new statements by doctors, raise serious questions which should be considered. This has been on my mind for quite a while and recent events have crystallised my view.'

That same day, retired pathologist Dr Jennifer Dyson told *The Independent on Sunday* that she believed that Dr Kelly had suffered a heart attack due to the stress he was under, adding that no coroner would have found his death to be a suicide and would instead have been much more likely to record an open verdict. She said it was 'silly' that Lord Hutton, rather than a trained coroner, had been appointed to pronounce upon Dr Kelly's death.

Yet it now appears that some kind of pro-Hutton fight-back was under way. Who was conducting this rearguard action is unclear, but on 16 August 2010, the day after Howard's view was published, a vascular surgeon called Michael Gaunt, who had never previously been publicly associated with the Dr Kelly affair, gave an interview to the BBC Radio 4 *PM* programme in which he stated he had reviewed 'the transcripts of the Hutton Inquiry and the post-mortem report'. It cannot be established how Gaunt came to be invited to comment on the case by the BBC, but he told the programme's interviewer that he was happy with the official finding.

Neither is it known how Gaunt obtained a copy of the post-mortem report – at that time it was still a restricted document which was not in the public domain, despite Hutton having said seven months previously that he would be happy for the group of campaigning doctors to see it. Indeed, the doctors had still not been granted access to it at this point. Gaunt would not have been allowed to see it without the authorization of the coroner, Nicholas Gardiner. He has told friends that he was sent a copy by a national newspaper. But who was responsible for handing out this sensitive information to a newspaper? And why was this newspaper happy to be used, essentially, as the mouthpiece of those who wanted to bolster the idea that Dr Kelly had killed himself?

What is clear is that Gaunt seemed happy to take to the airwaves at this time to reinforce the official version of events in what appears to have been nothing more than a crude public relations exercise to try to silence the doctors.

It did not end there. On 22 August 2010 Dr Nicholas Hunt then confronted the growing criticism of the findings of his autopsy on Dr Kelly, which had proved so influential in leading Hutton to his conclusion. Hunt gave an interview to *The Sunday Times* in which he referred to Dr Kelly's death as a 'textbook' case of suicide and graphically explained that he had found 'big, thick clots of blood inside [his] sleeve, which came down over the wrist, and a lot of blood soaked into the ground'.

It was unorthodox of Hunt to discuss his post-mortem of Dr Kelly with a newspaper reporter. Official guidelines at the time made clear that a Home Office pathologist "must preserve confidentiality unless he has been explicitly authorized by a relevant person or body to disclose information." According to the Royal College of Pathologists, Hunt would have been expected to obtain official permission from the Oxfordshire Coroner, Nicholas Gardiner, before discussing Dr Kelly's case publicly. Gardiner confirmed to me at the time that he had no prior knowledge of Hunt's interview.

Furthermore, Hunt had made no mention of these clots at the Hutton Inquiry or in his post-mortem report, which merely stated that there was 'heavy bloodstaining over the left arm, including that part which was over the jacket sleeve'.

Why was he bringing this new information to light in such an unusual way? Hunt also told the paper that two of Dr Kelly's main coronary arteries were 70 to 80 per cent narrower than normal – a figure not included in his post-mortem report – and that his heart disease was so severe that he could have 'dropped dead' at any minute. He said: 'If you have narrower arteries, your ability to withstand blood loss falls dramatically. Your heart also becomes more vulnerable to anything that could cause it to become unstable, such as stress – which I have no doubt he was under massively.'

Again, if true, and as already mentioned, it was peculiar that this condition, known as atherosclerosis, had not been picked up nine days before Dr Kelly's death, when he underwent a medical check at the behest of the MoD ahead of his planned trip to Iraq. Hunt seemed to use his *Sunday Times* interview to make more of Dr Kelly's heart condition than he had done either in his post-mortem report or during the evidence he gave to the Hutton Inquiry. In any case, it appears that when Hunt gave his evidence, he was unable to get everything off his chest that he might have wanted to. During his examination by Knox, he was asked to confirm whether there was 'any sign of third party involvement in Dr Kelly's death'. His perplexing answer to this straightforward question was: 'No, there was no pathological evidence to indicate the involvement of a third party in Dr Kelly's death. Rather, the features are quite typical, I would say, of self-inflicted injury if one ignores all the other features of the case.' Whatever those 'other features' were, neither Knox nor Hutton wanted to know because they didn't ask him to expand on whatever point he was trying to make.

Soon after Hunt had spoken to *The Sunday Times*, I discovered that his professional judgement was at that time also in doubt. He was serving an official GMC five-year warning for showing to members of the public photographs of the mutilated bodies of three Royal Military Police who had been killed in Iraq in June 2003. Hunt did this at a seminar in Lincolnshire in 2004 on how to set up temporary mortuaries in disaster zones.

It was attended by travel agents, council officials and public-service workers – none of whom had the right to see the sensitive photographs. The GMC had imposed the penalty on Dr Hunt in July 2006 for breaching confidentiality. It expired in 2011.

The warning, which was available to read on the GMC website, stated:

> "In future, when using details or photographs from post-mortems for teaching, research or seminars, he should respect patient privacy and dignity and consider the feelings of any families, gaining consent where necessary. In the absence of consent, he should not use any information (photographs or otherwise), which may identify the subjects, or present such information in such a way that may identify the subjects. He must adhere to GMC guidance including Good Medical Practice, 'Confidentiality: Protecting and Providing Information' (April 2004), and 'Making and Using Visual and Audio Recordings of patients' (May 2002).

The renewed interest in whether Dr Kelly's death had been investigated sufficiently at his inquiry clearly bothered Lord Hutton. Indeed, in what now appears to have been a pre-emptive strike, on 3 September 2010 he wrote a letter to the Attorney General, Dominic Grieve, headed 'The death of Dr Kelly', stating that he had 'asked to have a meeting with the Lord Chancellor [Kenneth Clarke] on his return from holiday'. Why Hutton wished to meet Clarke is not known, but he had obviously already prepared for it, for he had written fairly extensive notes covering what he thought were the eight key points addressing the perceived failures of his inquiry. The purpose of the letter was to share these points with Grieve as well. He quoted extensively from witnesses' testimony to his inquiry as a way of trying to explain how he had reached his conclusion that Dr Kelly had died by his own hand.

In September 2010 the doctors submitted their afore-mentioned memorial to Dominic Grieve. It said there was 'serious doubt' that sufficient evidence was available at the time of the 'hastily conducted' Hutton Inquiry to reach the conclusion that Dr Kelly deliberately killed himself by cutting his wrist and swallowing some painkillers, as his death certificate suggests, and described scrutiny of the medical evidence as 'unacceptably limp'. Nicholas Hunt's unwarranted *Sunday Times* interview was also criticized as being inconsistent with the evidence he gave to Hutton. The doctors further used the memorial to query from where Dr Kelly had got the co-proxamol he had apparently taken, why his blood and stomach contained a non-lethal amount of the painkiller, why the police helicopter failed to locate his body on the night it searched for him and why no fingerprints were found on the knife apparently used to slit his wrist. Falconer's dual role in ordering the inquiry as Secretary of State for Constitutional Affairs and then as Lord Chancellor, declaring himself satisfied with its findings, was also raised as a concern, as was the fact that Hutton, a man with no previous coronial experience, was appointed to pronounce on Dr Kelly's death. The memorial read:

> The Hutton Inquiry was manifestly relatively power-less and lacking investigative bite when compared to its statutory equivalent or coronial proceedings. The evidence provided by witnesses was not tested in the normal way through cross-examination by the representatives of other properly interested persons to the proceedings. Evidence was accepted, with minor clarifications only, at face value and without challenge – just one flaw in the procedural framework of the Hutton Inquiry which had the consequence of rendering the Inquiry insufficient in its breadth, reach and thoroughness.

It concluded: 'It is necessary and desirable in the interests of justice for there to be a fresh, full inquest into Dr Kelly's death before a different coroner.' It also requested that the doctors be allowed to view the post-mortem and toxicology reports in private and in the strictest of confidence.

By the time Grieve received this document, he had already begun to gather information from those parties he considered relevant to the question of whether Dr Kelly's death had been properly investigated in accordance with the law.

While he did so, in October 2010 the government decided to publish Dr Kelly's post-mortem report and the toxicology reports into his death. This was a curious decision – and, arguably, a convenient smokescreen. By appearing to release into the public domain more information – some of it highly personal about Dr Kelly in a physical sense – than had initially been requested by the doctors, it allowed the government to say it had gone above and beyond the call of duty in being as transparent and thorough as possible. This looked very much like an attempt to silence the clamour for an inquest.

In actual fact, the publication of the post-mortem still left some key questions unanswered. Furthermore, this course of action did nothing to quell the doctors' desire for a proper inquest to take place. For example, the reports offered no more insight into the direction of the cuts on Dr Kelly's wrist; there was no evidence that Dr Kelly's body had been tested for more exotic drugs like ricin or saxitoxin; there was no independent verification of the blood test results; and Dr Allan's analysis of Dr Kelly's blood had been confined to just one site sampling – the heart blood – even though four other site samples were available. In short, the doctors found what they regarded as numerous holes in the post-mortem and toxicology reports.

In December 2010, three months after submitting their memorial to Dominic Grieve but having had no answer from him, the doctors published it. By then, Grieve had launched what amounted to a private, behind-closed-doors mini-inquiry of his own, though it is not at all obvious on what legal basis he did this, since his own legal adviser, Kevin McGinty, stated in an email to one of the doctors, Stephen Frost, dated 19 July 2010, that the Attorney General 'cannot investigate matters himself'.

At a time when Grieve's inquiry was still active, five months later in May 2011 it was announced that the Metropolitan Police were to review the case of missing child Madeleine McCann, who had vanished during a family holiday in Portugal in 2007. At Prime Minister's Questions on 18 May 2011, the surprising figure of the Tory MP Sir Peter Tapsell – then the Father of the House – put the following tricky question to David Cameron: 'Now that there is to be a full investigation into the abduction or murder of Madeleine McCann, is there not a much stronger case for a full investigation into the suicide or murder of Dr David Kelly?'

Cameron replied, saying: 'My hon. Friend is raising two issues. First, on the issue of Madeleine McCann, it is welcome that the Metropolitan Police has decided to review the case and the paperwork. On the issue of Dr David Kelly, I thought the results of the inquest that was carried out and the report into it were fairly clear, and I do not think it is necessary to take that case forward.'

Cameron was wrong, of course. There has never been a full inquest into Dr Kelly's death, and this is precisely the crux of the problem. Was the Prime Minister being deliberately dim in order to get himself out of an uncomfortable situation? Whether his erroneous statement was intentional or not, because Grieve's review was ongoing at the time it looked very much as though Cameron had pre-judged it by being so dismissive. Had Cameron let the cat out of the bag? Had it been decided already that there would be no inquest? What is almost certain is that from that point on, Grieve was very unlikely to go against the view of his Prime Minister by bowing to the wishes of the doctors campaigning for an inquest.

Within a few weeks, Grieve's review had been completed. Grieve was to deliver his findings in the Commons on 9 June 2011. By coincidence, that morning Tony Blair was interviewed on the BBC One *Breakfast* programme on an unrelated matter. At the end of the interview he was asked whether he would welcome a new inquiry into Dr Kelly's death. Appearing uncomfortable at being bowled this googly, Blair answered: 'There was an inquiry which went for six months, headed by a senior Law Lord... maybe he [Grieve] has different information, but frankly

I doubt it... [the Hutton Inquiry] was one of the most detailed inquiries that has taken place on an issue like that.'

A few hours later, Grieve announced in the House of Commons that he had turned down the doctors' request for an inquest into Dr Kelly's death, saying that in his opinion the evidence that he killed himself was 'overwhelming' and rejecting claims there had been a 'cover-up'. The Cabinet Minister was careful to use the term 'conspiracy' twice during his statement, perhaps subtly smearing those who believed – and believe – that Dr Kelly has been failed by successive British governments which have refused to allow his death to be examined in full by a coroner. Looked at in one way, however, Grieve's decision changed nothing.

Grieve had appointed two medical professionals – Professor Richard Shepherd, a forensic pathologist, and Professor Robert Flanagan, a toxicologist – to review the evidence that was present in the post-mortem and toxicology reports. It is noteworthy that neither Shepherd nor Flanagan conducted further forensic tests themselves; they merely gave opinions based on information already in the public domain by re-reading the relevant records. Having done so, they reached conclusions which nobody was allowed to cross-examine. Furthermore, many of the questions raised by the doctors in their petition for an inquest either were not answered or, if they were, were not answered in the way they would have been at a coroner's inquest.

An example of this relates to the question of Dr Kelly's weight, which could have had a bearing on calculating what time he died, as has already been observed. Hunt's autopsy report states that Dr Kelly weighed fifty-nine kilos, or nine stone and four pounds. Yet at a medical check-up nine days before his disappearance, Dr Kelly's weight was recorded as being seventy-four kilos, or eleven stone and six pounds. In Grieve's review of the case in 2011, he dismissed Hunt's error as a 'moot' point. Indeed, Richard Shepherd sought to blame Dr Hunt's miscalculation on faulty hospital scales, as though that was somehow acceptable. As Dr Kelly's body was naked when it was weighed at the post-mortem, Shepherd also tried to suggest that Dr Kelly might have been clothed when he was weighed during his Ministry of Defence medical. Clothing, Shepherd reasoned, would have made him seem heavier.

Shepherd further speculated that the loss of blood he suffered could account for the missing fifteen kilos, or two stone and three pounds. On any logical basis this appears to stretch credulity too far, given that fifteen kilos represented 20 per cent of Dr Kelly's total body weight. Therefore, the public is being asked to believe that Dr Kelly lost more than two stone during the last nine days of his life. If this were true – because stress can trigger severe weight loss – why didn't Shepherd just say so instead of introducing complicated and unconvincing explanations?

The doctors felt – and feel – very much that the issues they raised ought to have been explored in court proceedings, not under the umbrella of the Attorney General's office. Grieve's private investigation had strong parallels with Hutton's own inquiry in that, while appearing open, it was in fact completely closed. Once again the question had to be asked: why was there such reluctance to stage a full coroner's inquest into Dr Kelly's death? What had the authorities to fear from every relevant fact and every available witness being scrutinized under oath?

What is certain is that Grieve, the only MP who has ever reassessed the Dr Kelly case on anything approaching a formal basis – and who believed in Opposition in 2010 that it merited further scrutiny to reassure the public – was content in 2011 when in government to let the matter drop. (Interestingly, he was removed as Attorney General in a 2014 Cabinet reshuffle and the following year appointed to the sensitive post of Chairman of the ISC, where he is considered a safe pair of hands.)

Later in June 2011, some of the doctors gathered at the London offices of the law firm Leigh Day, which had represented them throughout, to discuss what to do in light of Grieve's decision. Among those present were the retired orthopaedic and trauma surgeon David Halpin, Dr Stephen Frost, Dr Chris Burns-Cox and Dr Michael Powers QC. (Their eminent colleague Martin Birnstingl had died six months previously, his *Daily Telegraph* obituary noting that he 'never accepted the verdict of suicide'). Solicitor Frances Swaine chaired the meeting. Ultimately, a collective decision was taken that afternoon to press pause on the case, but the event was recorded onto a CD and later sent to each doctor so that everybody present could reflect on what had been said. There followed a strange and possibly sinister episode in which a franked Jiffy bag clearly bearing the name of Leigh Day and containing a copy of the CD was sent by recorded delivery to David Halpin's house in Devon on 29 June. It failed to arrive. Eight days later, on 7 July, a note was put through Halpin's door by the Royal Mail asking him to pick up a parcel from the local sorting office which had an outstanding fee of £2.35 to pay on it. Halpin was away at the time. When he collected it on 9 July he realized straight away that the envelope had been opened. At his request, the secretary at Leigh Day responsible for sending it to him and the other doctors checked her records and was satisfied that she had successfully paid the necessary recorded delivery fee in full, leaving open the possibility that somebody had managed to intercept Halpin's post and perhaps listened to the CD for some reason. Needless to say, Halpin took the precaution of reporting his suspicions to the police, despite knowing they could do nothing other than record this incident.

Undeterred, soon afterwards Halpin made a public plea for help in seeking permission at the High Court to launch a judicial review of Grieve's decision not to grant an inquest. In the space of six weeks, 830 donors from all over the world, including the spread-betting tycoon Stuart Wheeler, gave £40,000 to Halpin's fund to cover the cost of his legal fees, reflecting the public's strong interest in the case. Many of these donors were members of the public who had followed the case for years and who gave sums of just £5 or £10. Margaret Hindle, a retired NHS employee, volunteered to oversee the campaign, called the Dr David Kelly Inquest Fund, when she discovered that no other independent person was willing to do so. Halpin's legal challenge, launched at considerable financial risk to himself, was not intended to review the facts relating to Dr Kelly's death or the inconsistencies surrounding it. It was, in essence, the only potential route left open to sustain the possibility of an inquest taking place.

Eight and a half years after Dr Kelly's death, it was again being discussed at the Royal Courts of Justice, this time in Court 3, not Court 73 where the Hutton Inquiry was held. A few days before Christmas in December 2011 Mr Justice Nicol denied Halpin's request. The judge said he believed that Grieve had acted appropriately in turning down the original request for an inquest brought about by the memorial. Legally, at least, the matter had come to a full stop.

In Court 3 there were cries of 'Shame!' and 'This is not justice!' as Nicol gave his decision. Speaking outside the

High Court afterwards on a wet and gloomy afternoon, Halpin said: 'Today's result does not alter the fact that there has been no inquest into Dr Kelly's death, neither does it change the fact that I and many others believe it highly improbable that he died in the manner officially found.'

He may have been right, but he was still ordered to pay £5,568 towards Grieve's legal costs.

CONCLUSION

The timeline of events associated with the death of Dr David Kelly is so strange as to be almost unbelievable. From an aeroplane thousands of miles away from Oxfordshire Tony Blair ordered Lord Falconer to set up a public inquiry into his 'suspected suicide' when, officially, neither man had any accurate knowledge as to how he had died. The public has never been told on what basis Blair made this unprecedented decision. Given the direct consequence it had in removing the Oxfordshire coroner from any conclusive involvement in the matter, however, it is not unreasonable to consider the idea that Blair acted on something other than a mere hunch.

It is also distinctly odd that Thames Valley Police invested so many resources and such significant manpower looking for Dr Kelly within minutes of hearing of his disappearance. Officially, nothing more tangible than his failure to return home suggested that anything untoward had happened to him. And yet somebody ensured that the force went to very great lengths, as soon as he was reported missing, to carry out a full-scale search. It seems hard to believe that any other fifty-nine-year-old man's disappearance would have been accorded the same importance so quickly. In this regard, Hutton's decision not to hear evidence at his inquiry from Sgt Simon Morris, who led the initial hunt for Dr Kelly, remains profoundly surprising.

As a result of Tony Blair's decision to set up the Hutton Inquiry, the British public is required to accept that Dr Kelly took his own life. But, based on the available evidence, there are too many inconsistencies attached to the official finding of suicide to accept it wholeheartedly. On that basis, I cannot do so. I find it equally unlikely that, after a full examination of the evidence heard under oath, any coroner would conclude that Dr Kelly left his house on the afternoon of 17 July 2003 with the sole intention of taking his own life and then did so. For what man of science, with a sound working knowledge of human anatomy, would choose one of the least effective methods of killing himself if he truly wanted to do so?

Add to these points the dispute over how much blood Dr Kelly lost, and the confusion over how many pills he allegedly swallowed, plus the fact that it was unsatisfactorily concluded only that he died sometime between 4.15 p.m. on 17 July and 1.15 a.m. on 18 July, and the official account looks even shakier.

Had any government acted responsibly, and indeed been willing to do the right thing by Dr Kelly, a coroner's inquest would have been held by now and there would probably be no need to re-examine this case. That is not to say that all coroners are infallible: there are well-known examples of some who failed badly in their duties. But it is overwhelmingly likely that if the Oxfordshire Coroner, Nicholas Gardiner, had been allowed to continue with his original inquest into the death of Dr Kelly, instead of being instructed by the government to suspend it, he would have been meticulous in investigating every relevant aspect – in sharp contrast to the approach the Hutton Inquiry was able to take as a result of its less stringent terms of reference.

By extension, it is quite probable that Gardiner would have been unable to determine exactly how Dr Kelly died or what his true intentions were, prompting him to reach an open verdict, in circumstances where a cause of death cannot be established. The uncertainty presented by such a verdict would have been the government's worst nightmare, of course, which could explain why Gardiner was pragmatically set aside and replaced by Hutton, whose inquiry was able to reach a definite conclusion, even if it has been disputed ever since.

Because the evidence that Dr Kelly took his own life

at Harrowdown Hill in the manner officially found is so subject to scepticism, scores of people will continue to wonder what else could have happened to him on the day he disappeared. If conjecture is considered unhelpful by those who say Dr Kelly did kill himself, my view is that because the Establishment has gone out of its way to maintain a sense of control and secrecy over the Dr Kelly affair, such speculation is also inevitable. After all, why should the public be expected to have complete confidence in the opinion of Lord Hutton when his inquiry has turned out to be so unreliable in so many ways?

If Dr Kelly did not die by his own hand, this leaves only three other possibilities. Either he was murdered and the scene where his body was found was set up to look as if he had taken his own life there; or he died of a natural cause like a seizure or heart attack – perhaps during an official meeting or interrogation of some sort – and the 'suicide scene' at Harrowdown Hill was then created; or he did not die at all, but was 'disappeared' and went to live elsewhere under a new identity. It is not the aim of this book, however, to back one of these theories. Instead, the objective is to drive forward the case for a full coroner's inquest.

It is a reality that truths in public life are often obscured. One need only recall that Alastair Campbell and his colleagues pretended that the 'dodgy dossier' produced in February 2003 was the product of their own hard work. It is also worth remembering the 2012 investigation into the 1989 Hillsborough disaster, in which ninety-six football supporters died. It proved that police officers are capable of masking the facts of an extremely serious situation if they wish to, or are told to do so by senior colleagues. The shocking evidence of a police cover-up which emerged from this investigation triggered new inquests into the deaths, heard over a period of 279 days between 2015 and 2016 by Sir John Goldring. He concluded that all ninety-six had been unlawfully killed, overturning the original findings. The same cover-up charge can be laid at the door of the BBC, some of whose employees were aware of Jimmy Savile's criminal activities both during his life and after he died but were ignored or even obstructed when they tried to raise the alarm. And the same applies to those senior politicians who knew that the late Cyril Smith sexually abused children while an MP.

The Kelly family has never spoken publicly about Dr Kelly's death. Latterly, journalists who have been required to seek a statement from them have had to do so through Peter Jacobsen of the London law firm Bircham, Dyson, Bell – the same firm, incidentally, used by Tony Blair after he left Downing Street. Mr Jacobsen died in April 2016. Was it just a coincidence that the Kellys and Blair became clients of the same firm?

Five further peculiarities concerning the Dr Kelly affair are notable enough to warrant comment. The first of these relates to journalist Andrew Rawnsley's book *The End of the Party*. In it, he stated that Geoff Hoon – the Defence Secretary who oversaw the MoD's treatment of Dr Kelly shortly before his death – was so furious about being removed by Tony Blair as Leader of the House of Commons in May 2006 that he wrote out a resignation statement. Rawnsley said that Hoon 'planned to make a speech about the Kelly affair that he told friends could trigger the instant downfall of the Prime Minister'. If nothing else, this suggests that some of Blair's former colleagues still know things about the case which could compromise the former Prime Minister's reputation – or worse.

The second point is that, as Norman Baker revealed in his book on the Dr Kelly affair, in 2006 Hutton attended the retirement dinner of the aforementioned ACC Michael Page of Thames Valley Police. Indeed, he gave a speech in his honour. Given that these two men are understood not to have known each other before the Hutton Inquiry began, and were of contrasting backgrounds and ages, Hutton's presence at this event, which he has admitted, certainly surprised some there enough to tip off Baker about it. Hutton boasted that he used the occasion to tell an Irish joke to guests, but he has never elaborated further. ACC Page's strange evidence to the Hutton Inquiry concerning Dr Kelly's dentist, as examined in this book, is not easy to forget. He was asked about the apparent theft of Dr Kelly's dental records – apropos of nothing – during the second of his two appearances at the inquiry; he claimed Dr Kelly's dentist had rung the police about this matter twice when she only rang them once; and he stated that forensics tests conducted on the records when they were eventually found showed there were 'no extraneous' fingerprints on them when in fact there were six unidentified prints. All of this was known to the police at the time of Page's first evidence session to Hutton's inquiry but it was not mentioned publicly until his second appearance.

The third oddity relates to Carne Ross, a former British diplomat and friend of Dr Kelly. Mr Ross was the UK's Iraq expert at the UN Security Council between 1998 and 2002 and got to know Dr Kelly well during this time. He had lunch with him in New York shortly before his death. Mr Ross told me that when he gave verbal evidence to the Iraq Inquiry, chaired by Sir John Chilcot, in July 2010 he was warned by a senior civil servant overseeing it that if he mentioned Dr Kelly by name he would be asked to leave. 'I was taken into the room where witnesses sat and shortly before I was to testify an official came in and said: "You are not to speak about Dr Kelly."' Mr Ross added: 'Chilcot was incredibly tense. Clearly he feared I was going to say something.' Quite why this level of paranoia existed is not clear, but it shows, if nothing else, that Dr Kelly continues to haunt those who patrol the corridors of power.

The fourth point to note is altogether more bizarre.

It relates to a semi-literate email disclosed to the Hutton Inquiry by Thames Valley Police. The force apparently received it shortly after Dr Kelly's death. Dated 31 July 2003, it would appear to be the work of a crank or parodist because it was written using a strange typeface of varying sizes more commonly associated with a poison-pen letter, some characters being highlighted in bold. The heavily redacted message alleged there was a link between Dr Kelly's death and what it described as 'The World's Worst Paedophile Ring', some members of which, it claimed, were present at the 'murder' of Dr Kelly. The author emphasized that Dr Kelly was not a member of this group and requested that anyone wanting further information should 'consult the Federal Bureau of Investigation in China, Asia'. In his book on the Dr Kelly affair, Norman Baker speculated not on the document itself, which can almost certainly be dismissed as nonsense or a code which would require specific instructions to crack, but on the reason why it was made public at all. Of the thousands of documents on the Hutton Inquiry website, it appears to be the only one which strays into anything approaching such absurd, conspiratorial territory. What on earth was it doing there? Who decided it should be submitted and made public – particularly when so many documents on the site have been redacted? Baker writes: 'Naturally, documents like this, aided perhaps by the internet, produce all sorts of wild rumours. One, actually repeated to me in all seriousness by a very senior BBC executive, was that a leading figure in the Hutton inquiry process was known by the government to have had a paedophile past in a part of the United Kingdom well away from London. Was the inclusion of this particular document a way of reminding him to "do his duty"?' Baker's research went no further, and for now his fascinating question remains hanging in the air.

The last peculiarity involves Alastair Campbell and Cherie Blair. In May 2006 the pair decided to autograph a copy of the Hutton Report which was subsequently sold for £400 at a Labour Party fundraising evening held at the Arts Club in Mayfair to raise money for the constituency of the Labour MP turned BBC executive James Purnell. It is hard to escape the conclusion that the signatures of Campbell and Mrs Blair were committed to that copy of the report with a sense of triumph and perhaps glee. What other reason could there have been for this obnoxious act – tantamount to dancing on Dr Kelly's grave – than to indicate their joy that the Labour government had scraped through the Dr Kelly affair? Neither Campbell nor Mrs Blair has ever tried to justify their actions – presumably because they never expected the public to find out. Their behaviour came to light only because somebody who was at the auction that night was so disgusted by what they saw that they rang me the next morning and told me about it. I was able to note it in the *Evening Standard*'s diary column, where I worked at the time. The following week Tony Blair was challenged over this crass incident in the House of Commons. He delivered a few mealy-mouthed words of explanation, saying that no offence had been intended. As far as I can ascertain, neither Cherie Blair nor Campbell has ever apologized publicly.

We must decide for ourselves whether Campbell and Mrs Blair showed a woeful lack of judgement, demonstrated appalling taste or, from a psychological viewpoint, displayed something far stranger altogether. Mrs Blair's link to this tawdry stunt is all the more remarkable given that in 2004 she and her husband invited Mrs Kelly and her three daughters to the Prime Minister's country residence, Chequers. She even explained in her memoir, published four years after the autograph incident, that she and her husband asked the Kelly family there in order 'to say personally how very sorry we were about what had happened [to Dr Kelly]'. For his part, Campbell would now far rather people forget his behaviour – both before and after Dr Kelly's death. Six years after autographing the Hutton Report, in 2012, he published yet another volume of his expletive-ridden diaries in which he wrote:

> I never met David Kelly, but I think about him often, and whether I could have done anything differently that might have stopped him from taking his own life.

With the exception of the deaths of family and close friends, the day his body was found was perhaps the worst of my life, certainly the worst of my time with TB... The feelings I had then are among the reasons why, despite staying involved, and going back to help in two general elections, I have never really wanted to return to a full-time position in the front line of politics.

Here Campbell could be interpreted as saying that the Dr Kelly affair continues to haunt him. Certainly anybody who watched an edition of BBC One's *Andrew Marr Show*, first broadcast in February 2011, would accept this possibility: Campbell suffered from sudden shortness of breath live on air while attempting to explain to Marr how the 'intelligence' surrounding WMD had come about and had to temporarily halt the interview. Whatever caused Dr Kelly's tragic death, there are many reasons why Campbell should continue to feel regret over it.

In life, Dr Kelly was betrayed by those officials who saw to it that he was publicly humiliated by being named as Andrew Gilligan's source, a charge which Dr Kelly always denied. In death, Dr Kelly was again betrayed, this time by Blair, Falconer and Hutton. This trio set up and ran the slipshod public inquiry which was such a poor substitute for a coroner's inquest and which in reality investigated his death with only the lightest of touches. Its lack of thoroughness failed to establish so many crucial facts that it is now clear that a full coroner's inquest is vital.

One cold Saturday morning in January 2010, I went to see the Oxfordshire Coroner, Nicholas Gardiner, at his house near Blenheim Palace. I had not been invited. Standing on the doorstep, I asked him why, in his opinion, Hutton had recommended in 2003 that all of the records relating to Dr Kelly's death, including the photographs of his body, should have been secretly classified for seventy years. Under the terms of the Public Records Act 1958, which covers records created by government departments, only the most sensitive documents usually remain closed for more than thirty years. Examples include murder files, which stay hidden until the victim's youngest child is aged 100, in order to protect them from exposure to distressing information. Gardiner said: 'They're Lord Hutton's records, not mine. You'd have to ask him.' I persisted with my question, mindful not only that Dr Kelly's youngest children were aged thirty when he died, and would therefore be 100 when the remaining records and photographs can be disclosed; but also that the records will not be available to view until 2073, when everybody with a clear memory of the Dr Kelly affair will most likely be dead themselves. Gardiner looked at me and, without hesitation, replied: 'As you said, anybody concerned will be dead by then, and that's quite clearly Lord Hutton's intention.'

POSTSCRIPT

In early August 2017 I was contacted by Gerrard Jonas, the Oxfordshire garage owner mentioned in the Introduction, who had been warned in 2014 by a civil servant in the Ministry of Justice to stop visiting Dr Kelly's grave. Mr Jonas told me that he had been alerted by some local friends to the fact that Dr Kelly's remains had recently been exhumed in the dead of night from the churchyard of St Mary's, Longworth. Dr Kelly's headstone had also been removed. This had happened exactly fourteen years to the month after his death.

Once I had verified this baffling development independently, I tried to find out more about its circumstances. In the absence of any announcement that a police force had been involved in the course of a criminal investigation, it seemed most likely from a legal perspective that Dr Kelly's family had been responsible. But why take such a radical step?

Firstly, the question of whether Dr Kelly had been buried or cremated in 2003 had to be solved. I knew from a check I had made in 2015 that his name did not show up in available records at the two crematoria nearest to where his grave was situated, suggesting that he was buried. The handwritten register of St Mary's Church to which I then gained access confirmed that his funeral had taken place there on 6 August 2003, but the word 'Ashes'

– which was written next to the names of some deceased – was also absent, again strongly suggesting that he had originally been buried.

In late October 2017 Mr Jonas rang me again, this time to say that to his amazement he had been contacted for comment by Andrew Gilligan, now a *Sunday Times* reporter. Having learned of the exhumation, Gilligan had been told by a source that Mr Jonas had upset the Kelly family, thanks to the interest shown in Dr Kelly's grave by his campaign group, Justice For Kelly. Knowing that Gilligan's article was going to be published imminently, I filed my own report about the exhumation for another newspaper. Our stories about this extraordinary situation therefore appeared simultaneously. Missing from my account, however, was Gilligan's suggestion in his front-page piece that Dr Kelly's remains had been cremated, having been dug up.

It is not clear how Gilligan can have known of this apparent cremation unless he had been in touch with someone with first-hand knowledge of it, or, as unlikely as it seems, a member of the Kelly family. This can be stated with confidence because no authority that I have contacted – St Mary's Parish Church, the Ministry of Justice, the Oxfordshire Coroner, the nearest crematorium or the Diocese of Oxford – was prepared to comment on it. Each said only that the exhumation had been a private family matter. To everybody bar Gilligan, it seems, an official cloak of secrecy was therefore thrown over this aspect of what had happened to Dr Kelly's remains.

As well as noting that Mr Jonas's group had once placed a placard by Dr Kelly's grave, Gilligan's report carried the alarming detail that Jonas and his fellow 'conspiracy theorists' had 'threatened to remove his remains'. It had also been suggested to Gilligan by 'family sources' that the Justice For Kelly group had 'desecrated' Dr Kelly's grave, contributing to the decision to exhume his remains.

I asked Mr Jonas about this. He confirmed that he had written to the present Oxfordshire Coroner, Darren Salter, in 2016 and 2017 suggesting that he might apply to have Dr Kelly's remains exhumed. While this is not a move that anybody I know who has ever supported the campaign for an inquest would be prepared to endorse without some sort of cast-iron proof of its necessity, it is not illegal per se to make such an application. Mr Jonas also said that he had visited Dr Kelly's grave about forty times in 2015, a similar number of times in 2016, and about five times in 2017. On none of these occasions had he left anything on Dr Kelly's grave, he said, only flowers near to it. Again, while the frequency of his visits shows a level of interest in Dr Kelly's grave which many will find hard to comprehend, does it count as 'desecration'?

Mr Jonas explained that he would stop at the grave on his way home from work sometimes, simply to pay his respects to a man he believed had been treated unjustly.

On occasion his octogenarian mother would join him and weed the grave. She did so, he said, because it looked as though it had been forgotten and was in an uncared-for state. All of this had, apparently, led to the decision to exhume Dr Kelly's body. Mr Jonas said he had done nothing illegal at the grave, nor would he dream of doing so.

If, as Gilligan has claimed, Dr Kelly's remains were cremated in 2017, it is worth raising three points. Firstly, the form which must be completed before a licence to exhume human remains can be issued specifically asks the applicant: 'Do you know of any person (relative or otherwise) who may object to the proposal to remove the remains or is likely to do so?' If this question is answered affirmatively, the details of the objector must be listed. We must assume that this question would have been answered; however, it has been confirmed to me that the public is not allowed to know how, or what consideration was given to it by the Diocese of Oxford, the Church of England's administrative office for Oxfordshire, which oversaw the exhumation. The Deputy Registrar of the diocese, Darren Oliver, wrote to me in November 2017 stating that it had been decided that 'it would not be in the public interest' for copies of the exhumation application to be disclosed. I was invited by the diocese to embark on a legal application to see the forms, but this would cost money and time and would offer no guarantee of a positive response.

Secondly, it is clear that there are a great many people who would have objected to the cremation of Dr Kelly's remains, if that is what happened to them; for with their destruction, the opportunity to carry out any future forensic tests has been lost.

Thirdly, on an altogether more personal note, as has already been noted, Dr Kelly converted to the Bahá'í faith a few years before his death – a faith which not only opposes suicide, but strongly encourages its adherents to be buried and not cremated. The uncomfortable question must therefore be asked: did Dr Kelly's family go against his (assumed) beliefs by exhuming his remains and disposing of them in the way Andrew Gilligan reported?

In November 2017, *Private Eye* quoted in its 'Street of Shame' column the words of a *Sunday Times* colleague of Gilligan who thought it should be known how enthusiastic Gilligan had been to have his name on the story of Dr Kelly's exhumation, which, incidentally, conveniently overlooked his own wider involvement in the Dr Kelly case. 'It was bizarre,' the anonymous journalist told the magazine; although there was much hand-wringing in the *Sunday Times* offices about whether it was sensible for Gilligan to be bylined on the story, 'he very much wanted it'.

And so, fourteen years after the instrumental part Gilligan played in the unmasking of Dr Kelly, he assumed a further key role in reporting that his remains had been disposed of in extraordinary circumstances. He did so, however, in such a way that nobody has yet been willing or able to verify.

As a result of the exhumation, I had a conversation with somebody who told me that they spoke to David Kelly at length during the month he was found dead, a fact I have been able to confirm independently. This person, who wishes to remain anonymous, explained to me that they have carried with them what they call a 'burden' ever since. They said that in July 2003 Dr Kelly told them something about his work, rather than his personal life, which had shocked them so profoundly that they believed they should have gone straight to the police to report his claim. They never did so, for reasons best known to themselves, but they remain reluctant to let go of the likelihood that what he told them has some link to his death. At the time of going to press, the person concerned would not elaborate other than to say they believed there must be a coroner's inquest into Dr Kelly's death. They accepted that they would probably be called as a witness if an inquest were held and they would have to give evidence on oath. Whatever it was that Dr Kelly admitted to them immediately before he died, I still believe for a multitude of reasons – including this one – that a coroner's inquest is the only way that the full truth about his death will ever be known.

APPENDIX 1

HUTTON INQUIRY WITNESSES AND THE DATES ON WHICH THEY WERE CALLED

DATE	WITNESS
First phase of the inquiry	
Friday, *1 August 2003*	• Lord Hutton's opening statement and application for the proceedings to be televised
Monday, *11 August 2003*	• Terence Taylor, President and Executive Director for the International Institute of Strategic Studies (US) • Richard Hatfield, Personnel Director, MoD • Martin Howard, Deputy Chief of Defence Intelligence, MoD • Patrick Lamb, Deputy Head of the Counter-proliferation Department, FCO • Julian Miller, Chief of the Assessment Staff, Cabinet Office

Tuesday, 12 *August* 2003	◆ Andrew Gilligan, BBC reporter ◆ Susan Watts, BBC reporter
Wednesday, 13 *August* 2003	◆ Susan Watts, BBC reporter ◆ Gavin Hewitt, BBC reporter ◆ Richard Sambrook, Head of News, BBC
Thursday, 14 *August* 2003	◆ Dr Bryan Wells, Director of Counter-proliferation and Arms Control, MoD ◆ Patrick Lamb, Deputy Head of the Counter-proliferation Department, FCO ◆ Martin Howard, Deputy Chief of Defence Intelligence, MoD ◆ John Williams, Director of Communications, FCO
Monday, 18 *August* 2003	◆ Pam Teare, Director of News, MoD ◆ Jonathan Powell, Prime Minister's Chief of Staff ◆ Sir David Manning, former Foreign Policy Adviser to the Prime Minister, and Head of the Overseas and Defence Secretariat in the Cabinet Office
Tuesday, 19 *August* 2003	◆ Alastair Campbell, Prime Minister's Director of Communications

Wednesday,
20 August 2003
	• Sir Kevin Tebbit, Permanent
	  Secretary, MoD
	• Godric Smith, Prime Minister's
	  Official Spokesman
	• Tom Kelly, Prime Minister's
	  Official Spokesman

Thursday,
21 August 2003
	• Donald Anderson MP, Foreign
	  Affairs select committee
	• Nick Rufford –
	  The Sunday Times, journalist
	• James Blitz –
	  Financial Times, journalist
	• Richard Norton-Taylor,
	  Guardian, journalist
	• Peter Beaumont,
	  The Observer, journalist
	• Tom Baldwin,
	  The Times, journalist
	• Michael Evans,
	  The Times, journalist
	• David Broucher, Diplomatic
	  Service and Permanent
	  Representative to the Conference
	  on Disarmament in Geneva,
	  Foreign and Commonwealth
	  Office
	• Lee Hughes, Hutton Inquiry
	  Secretariat

Tuesday,
26 August 2003
	• Andrew Mackinlay MP, Foreign
	  Affairs select committee
	• John Scarlett, Chairman of the
	  Joint Intelligence Committee
	• Sir David Omand, Cabinet Office

Wednesday, *27 August 2003*	• Geoff Hoon MP, Secretary of State for Defence • Wing Commander John Clark, Proliferation and Arms Control Secretariat, MoD • James Harrison, Deputy Director of Counter-proliferation and Arms Control, MoD • Ann Taylor MP, Chair of Intelligence and Security Committee
Thursday, *28 August 2003*	• Tony Blair MP, Prime Minister • Gavyn Davies, Chairman of the Board of Governors, BBC
Monday, *1 September 2003*	• Mrs Kelly, family • Sarah Pape, family • Rachel Kelly, family • Professor Roger Avery, friend • David Wilkins, family
Tuesday, *2 September 2003*	• Ruth Absalom, neighbour • Dr Malcolm Warner, GP • Louise Holmes, search team • Paul Chapman, search team • PC Andrew Franklin, Thames Valley Police • PC Martyn Sawyer, Thames Valley Police • Sgt Geoffrey Webb, Thames Valley Police • PC Jonathan Martyn, Thames Valley Police • Vanessa Hunt, ambulance • David Bartlett, ambulance • Barney Leith, Bahá'í faith • Professor Hawton, psychiatrist

Wednesday, *3 September 2003*	• Alexander Allan, toxicologist • ACC Page, Thames Valley Police • Steven Macdonald, Assistant Director on the Central Budget, Security and Safety, MoD • Dr Brian Jones, former branch head in the Scientific and Technical Directorate of the Defence Intelligence Analysis Staff • Mr A, casually employed civil servant with the Counter-proliferation Arms Control Department, MoD • Mr Green, forensic biologist • Patrick Lamb, Deputy Head of the Counter-proliferation Department, FCO
Thursday, *4 September 2003*	• Olivia Bosch, colleague • Leigh Potter, neighbour • Tom Mangold, journalist • Richard Taylor, Special Adviser to Secretary of State for Defence

Second phase of the inquiry

Monday, *15 September 2003*	• Counsel's opening statement • Tony Cragg, Former Deputy Chief of Defence Intelligence • Air Marshal J. French, Former Chief of Defence Intelligence • Sir Richard Dearlove, Chief of the Secret Intelligence Service • Dr Richard Scott, Director, Defence Science and Technology Laboratory • Greg Dyke, Director-General, BBC

Tuesday, *16 September 2003*	• DC Graham Coe, police officer, Thames Valley Police • Dr Nicholas Hunt, forensic pathologist • Martin Howard, Deputy Chief of Defence Intelligence • Dr Shuttleworth, Defence, Science and Technology Laboratory • Kate Wilson – Chief Press Officer, MoD
Wednesday, *17 September 2003*	• Andrew Gilligan, reporter, BBC • Richard Sambrook, Head of News, BBC • Richard Hatfield, Director of Personnel, MoD
Thursday, *18 September 2003*	• Richard Hatfield, Personnel Director, MoD • Pamela Teare, Director of News, MoD • Edward Wilding, computer investigator • Professor A. J. Sammes, Professor of Computer Science and Director of the Centre for Forensic Computing, Cranfield University • Andrew Gilligan, reporter, BBC
Monday, *22 September 2003*	• Geoffrey Hoon MP, Secretary of State for Defence • Lee Hughes, Secretary to the Inquiry • Alastair Campbell, Prime Minister's Director of Communications

Tuesday, *23 September 2003*	• Tom Kelly, Prime Minister's Official Spokesman • Godric Smith, Prime Minister's Official Spokesman • John Scarlett, Chairman of the Joint Intelligence Committee

Wednesday, *24 September 2003*	• Gavyn Davies, Chairman of the BBC Board of Governors • Patrick Lamb, Deputy Head of the Counter-proliferation Department, FCO • Dr Bryan Wells, Director of Counter-proliferation and Arms Control, MoD • James Harrison, Deputy Director of Counter-proliferation and Arms Control, MoD • Wing Commander John Clark, Proliferation and Arms Control Secretariat, MoD • Nick Rufford, *Sunday Times*, journalist • Professor Keith Hawton, psychiatrist • Richard Hatfield, Personnel Director, MoD

Thursday,
25 September 2003
	Closing Statements:
	• Jeremy Gompertz QC,
	  counsel for the Kelly family
	• Jonathan Sumption QC,
	  counsel for the government
	• Andrew Caldecott QC,
	  counsel for the BBC
	• Heather Rogers QC,
	  counsel for Andrew Gilligan
	• James Dingemans QC,
	  counsel for the inquiry
	• Closing statement by Lord Hutton

Monday, *13 October 2003*	• Sir Kevin Tebbit, Permanent Secretary, MoD

APPENDIX 2

KEY WITNESSES WHO DID NOT APPEAR AT THE HUTTON INQUIRY AND THE REASONS THEY SHOULD HAVE DONE SO

A) **Mai Pederson:** The (now retired) American Air Force officer who served as translator with Dr Kelly's inspection team in Iraq in the 1990s. Through her lawyer, Mark Zaid, she has urged two Attorneys General – Baroness Scotland and Dominic Grieve – to reopen the inquest into Dr Kelly's death. She told Thames Valley Police that an injury Dr Kelly sustained to his right elbow in a 1991 horse-riding accident meant that his right hand was so weak he even 'had difficulty cutting his own steak' when they had lunch in a Washington restaurant in spring 2003, a couple of months before his death. She therefore has deep reservations that he could have taken a blunt pruning knife to his wrist. She also revealed that Dr Kelly had great difficulty swallowing pills. Pederson was initially asked to give evidence to the Hutton Inquiry in 2003 and agreed to do so but was not called. This was because, it is claimed, the inquiry would not allow her to testify in private. But one of Dr Kelly's other MoD colleagues – who we now know was Rod Godfrey, but at the Hutton Inquiry was referred to only as 'Mr A' – was allowed to give evidence anonymously due to the sensitive nature of his work. Since Godfrey was accorded this special treatment, why not Ms Pederson?

B) **John and Pamela Dabbs:** the married couple whom the Kellys saw in Cornwall over the last weekend of Dr Kelly's life. The Kellys spent two hours at the Dabbses' house on Saturday, 12 July 2003, but Mr Dabbs refused to disclose what they discussed and told me he would never tell the police either. Mr Dabbs also told me that Mrs Kelly rang him at about 6 a.m. on 18 July – the day Dr Kelly's body was found – to ask if Dr Kelly had returned to his house. Mr Dabbs is crucial in helping to define Dr Kelly's mood as he neared the end of his life. Both gave witness statements to Thames Valley Police.

C) **The 'boat people':** This trio or quartet were on the River Thames beside Harrowdown Hill overnight between 17 and 18 July 2003. Were they traced and interviewed by Thames Valley Police? What did they see? This was never made public. They were the witnesses closest to Harrowdown Hill at this pivotal time but, bizarrely, they didn't appear at the Hutton Inquiry.

D) **Dr Bozena Kanas:** Dr Kelly's dentist who, on 20 July 2003, alerted police to an apparent break-in at her dental surgery which must have occurred before it opened at 8 a.m. on 18 July 2003, the day Dr Kelly's body was found. It appears that Dr Kelly's dental records were removed in the break-in and were then replaced within forty-eight hours of Dr Kanas discovering this. Although fingerprint tests showed six unidentified prints on the file holding the records, ACC Page of Thames Valley Police told the Hutton Inquiry that 'no extraneous fingerprints' were found.

E) **The helicopter pilot and crew:** After Dr Kelly disappeared a police search helicopter with thermal-imaging equipment flew over the exact spot where his body was found less than six hours later but detected nothing. The forensic pathologist determined that the latest Kelly could have died was 1.15 a.m., meaning that his body would still have been warm when the helicopter was looking for him. This key detail was only established through the Freedom of Information

Act six years after the Hutton Inquiry. It was never raised at Hutton.

F) **Sgt Simon Morris:** One of three Thames Valley Police officers who arrived at Mrs Kelly's house just before midnight on 17 July 2003 in response to a missing person call. Morris anchored the initial search of the Kellys' house and the operation to find Dr Kelly. Despite his key role that night, he was not required to submit a written statement to Hutton and did not give oral evidence either.

G) **Steve Ward and the Hinds Head cribbage players:** Dr Kelly apparently played cribbage with friends including Pat Forster in the Hinds Head pub a mile from his house on the evening of 9 July 2003. Landlord Steve Ward told Thames Valley Police of this by email. Yet Janice Kelly claims Dr Kelly was driving her to Weston-Super-Mare at exactly the same time. Who is telling the truth about this seemingly innocuous matter and why were assertions regarding Dr Kelly's possible alternative activities withheld from the Hutton Inquiry?

H) **The radio mast operator:** The person operating the eighty-five-foot mast parked outside the Kellys' house on the night of his disappearance should be asked for a full account of their role. Was this standard police equipment? Was it used to communicate with either of the planes on which Tony Blair and Alastair Campbell were travelling at the time? Was Charles Falconer contacted by this means?

I) **DC Shields:** Why did DC Shields and his colleague DC Coe suddenly head northwards to search for Dr Kelly on the morning of 18 July 2003 when Ruth Absalom, Dr Kelly's neighbour and the last person known to have seen him alive on the day he disappeared, the 17th, suggested that Dr Kelly had walked eastwards? What can DC Shields recall about the position of Dr Kelly's body when found?

J) **The 'third man':** apparently a probationary constable with Thames Valley Police at the time of Dr Kelly's death, this individual was with DC Coe and DC Shields at Harrowdown Hill within a few minutes of Dr Kelly's body being found. Coe 'forgot to mention' this person at the Hutton Inquiry but seven years later admitted his existence to *The Mail on Sunday*. The late Bruce Hay wrote to me revealing that the third man's initials are 'S. B.'. Mr Hay said S. B. found the scene at Harrowdown Hill to be 'extraordinarily contrived'. Who is S. B.? What did he see? Why was he erased from the official account?

K) **Judith Miller:** American journalist, formerly with *The New York Times*, and friend of Dr Kelly to whom he wrote an email on the day he vanished saying that there were 'many dark actors playing games'. What did this mean? And what else do the notes of Miller's peculiar interview of Janice Kelly, conducted on 18 July 2003, show?

L) **Alan Young:** As Chief Inspector of Thames Valley Police he was the senior investigating officer who oversaw the investigation into Dr Kelly's disappearance on 17 July 2003. His high status surely warranted his being called.

M) **Sgt Paul Wood:** Thames Valley Police officer who gave PCs Franklin and Sawyer a briefing on 18 July 2003, the morning of the search for Dr Kelly.

N) **Neil Knight:** Berkshire Search and Rescue control manager who told Louise Holmes and Paul Chapman, the two volunteer searchers who found Dr Kelly's body, to go to the area of Harrowdown Hill. Given that the police had already looked there for Dr Kelly using a helicopter, and presumably eliminated it from their inquiries, why were they told to return there?

O) **Sgt Alan Dadd:** Senior Thames Valley Police officer who accompanied PCs Franklin and Sawyer to Harrow-down Hill and was therefore one of the first people to see Dr Kelly's body.

P) **David T. McGee:** Official Thames Valley Police photographer. His memories of the scene at Harrowdown Hill are crucial, bearing in mind the ongoing dispute over the position of Dr Kelly's body. Hutton's 2004 report states: 'I have seen a photograph of Dr Kelly's body in the wood which shows that most of his body was lying on the ground but that his head was slumped against the base of the tree.' Yet pathologist Dr Richard Shepherd, commissioned by the Attorney General in 2011 to review key evidence, wrote in his report: 'It is quite clear from consideration of the photographs of the scene that, at the time they were taken, the body of David Kelly lay with his feet pointing away from the tree and that there was a significant gap between the base of the tree and the top of the head.' When asked, the Attorney General's office refused to acknowledge any disparity. Which version is true?

Q) **The ten people present at Dr Kelly's autopsy:** It has always been considered irregular that so many people attended this post-mortem, considering that Dr Kelly's death was immediately labelled a simple case of suicide. Mark Schollar, John Sharpley, Andrew Hodgson,

Katie Langford, Michelle Sapwell, Charles Boshell, Sally Hunt, Paul Kingsley, Mark Bray and Alan Young should all be asked to account for their presence.

R) **Dr Eileen Hickey:** The forensic biologist who accompanied forensic scientist Mr Green to Harrowdown Hill on the day Dr Kelly's body was found. Her testimony could be crucial in examining theories of a lack of blood at the scene where Dr Kelly apparently bled to death.

S) **Robert Jackson:** The former MP claims he was told by Dr Kelly's GP, Dr Malcolm Warner, that Warner identified Dr Kelly's body – perhaps unofficially. Is this true?

T) **Nigel Cox:** Long-standing friend of Dr Kelly for whom, during the week of his death, an answerphone message was left by Dr Kelly, arranging to meet him on 23 July. Mr Cox was on holiday at the time and returned on 19 July. He told me that Thames Valley Police didn't ever listen to the message despite his offering it to them. The Attorney General later claimed in his review of the case that the police did listen to the message. Yet, according to a Freedom of Information response, the police have 'no information' about having listened to the message. What is the truth?

U) **Unnamed MoD doctor:** This person performed Dr Kelly's medical check in early July 2003 and would potentially be able to resolve questions about Dr Kelly's disputed weight during the month he died. They might also have an opinion on the health of Dr Kelly's heart.

V) **Carne Ross:** Former British diplomat and friend of Dr Kelly who had lunch with him in New York shortly before his death and who was an occasional confidant of Dr Kelly. Mr Ross was subsequently ordered by an official not to mention Dr Kelly when giving oral evidence to the Iraq Inquiry conducted by Sir John Chilcot.

W) **Paul Weaving:** Oxfordshire farmer who knew Dr Kelly for twenty years. Some believe he saw Dr Kelly on the day he was last seen alive. He also took part in a search for him along with another neighbour from Dr Kelly's village, John Melling.

AFTERWORD

Forty-eight hours after *An Inconvenient Death* was published in April 2018, it was attacked in the books pages of *The Times*. 'It stinks, really, does this waste of publisher's, purchaser's and reviewer's time and money,' the author of the piece growled as he accused me of 'cashing in' on a 'conspiracy theory'.

Initially, I was rather stunned by this torpedo. I've always thought journalists were at least open-minded enough to allow other journalists to ask awkward questions without lambasting them in print for having done so. Yet on re-reading this 'review', I realized it was factually inaccurate and, far from being a standard critique, was largely self-justificatory in tone. Not being familiar with the output of the *Times* journalist in question, I then learned that he is the author of a book ridiculing what he sees as conspiracy theories, and a chapter of his book is devoted to the David Kelly affair. When I read it, I realized that he thinks anybody who has a single doubt about Lord Hutton's assessment of the circumstances of Dr Kelly's death, or is in favour of a full coroner's inquest into it, is a fantasist.

Two things occurred to me. Firstly, I was struck by the irony that, of the two of us, it was only the *Times* reviewer who had in fact 'cashed in' by writing a book about conspiracy theories. The second thing immediately obvious to me was that, having written his book buttressing the official story on Dr Kelly, this person himself had a position to defend. Otherwise, why should he even bother writing a review of a book which, according to him, is so bad it 'stinks'?

I was advised by those who know the journalist in question that he is a forceful personality, so his hostile interpretation of my book was even easier to comprehend. I can well imagine an impressionable young commissioning editor being blind to this critic's distinct lack of objectivity in the matter of Dr David Kelly when presented with his assessment of *An Inconvenient Death*.

Several people who read both *The Times* review and then my book later contacted me to point out that one of the directors of Times Newspapers Limited is Sir John Scarlett. As I state in Chapter Three, in July 2003 Scarlett was the Chairman of the Joint Intelligence Committee and the government's chief intelligence adviser. He is also the man who said, ten days before Dr Kelly disappeared, that he thought Dr Kelly should be subjected to a 'proper security-style interview' to see if he really was Andrew Gilligan's source. This course of action surely placed Scarlett in an awkward position regarding the Dr Kelly affair. Yet after the Hutton Inquiry, Scarlett was elevated to the post of director-general of MI6 before retiring and joining *The Times* board in December 2010, where he styles himself a 'business adviser'.

I had never before considered that there might be a link between *The Times*'s questionable review of this book and Scarlett's presence on the newspaper's payroll. Indeed, it seems to me to be verging on the conspiratorial to give this connection too much credibility. But of all the newspaper reviews, *The Times* alone savaged *An Inconvenient Death*. *The Daily Mail*, *The Mail on Sunday* and the *Observer* were unanimous in their opinion that it raises serious questions about the Kelly affair, which are no less relevant now than they were in 2003. *The Daily Telegraph* also described it positively, selecting it as one of its recommended books of the year. It is heartening to know that this investigation was, overwhelmingly, given fair consideration in the national press.

Since the hardback edition of this book was published there have been some developments worth reporting.

I was contacted during the summer of 2018 by John Scurr, a vascular surgeon who, as mentioned in Part 3, was aligned with the group of doctors who campaigned for an inquest to be held into Dr Kelly's death shortly after it occurred. Having read the book, Scurr told me an intriguing story which I believe adds to the sense of unease surrounding this tragic episode.

He explained that Dr Kelly's half-sister, Sarah Pape, contacted him months after Hutton published his report in January 2004 to say she didn't believe he took his own life.

Scurr said: 'Sarah Pape clearly had concerns about whether Dr Kelly could have died from slashing his wrist. We had an in-depth conversation about it. She took the trouble to contact me after the Hutton Inquiry finished to discuss whether one could actually die from slashing the ulnar artery. She is a plastic surgeon and has considerable medical knowledge.'

Scurr's claim is significant not only because Dr Kelly's family has remained almost entirely silent since he died, but also because Ms Pape, a consultant plastic surgeon at the Royal Victoria Hospital in Newcastle, gave evidence to the Hutton Inquiry but did not admit her doubts on that occasion.

Scurr said he and Ms Pape, who is almost fifteen years his junior, were previously colleagues at University College Hospital in London. She apparently contacted him having seen his name in a newspaper report alongside the other doctors who had voiced concerns about the circumstances of Dr Kelly's death. She and Scurr had not worked together for very long and had not known each other well, making her decision to contact him out of the blue all the more meaningful. He told me:

> The reason she rang me was I don't think she believed he had died by slashing his wrist. She doubted whether he could have done that on a personal and a medical level. During the discussion I expressed my doubts about whether he actually committed suicide and my concerns about why his wife would accept that he had committed suicide when there was no good medical evidence that he could have died from slashing his wrist.

Scurr, whose specialism in arteries and veins gives him a great deal of credibility in questioning the medical aspect of Dr Kelly's death, added:

> I don't believe it's possible to die from simply cutting your ulnar artery. It is a very small artery and even with a tourniquet loosely applied to the arm it is still unlikely that you could lose enough blood to cause cardiac arrest and death. It is much more likely that he died from another cause. One possibility is a heart attack caused by whatever reason and this was an attempt to mask that. The relative absence of blood at the scene and the fact that a rather blunt knife was

used are significant. If one were to cut the wrist holding the knife in the right hand the artery that would be cut is not the ulnar artery, which is on the inside of the hand, but the radial artery on the outside of the hand. It seems more probable that somebody else took the knife and actually slashed the wrist taking the stroke across the ulnar artery.

He went on:

There were many other parts of this story which were never fully explained. My own feeling at the time was, and remains, that a full coroner's inquest with evidence taken under oath would have provided us with a proper understanding. It is pure speculation as to what happened to Dr Kelly and until a proper explanation is obtained then I think we will go on with the speculative claims that are currently abounding.

Scurr wrote to Ms Pape on several occasions in the summer of 2018 to try to encourage her to speak to him again, but she did not respond. Her conversation with Scurr supplements her testimony to the Hutton Inquiry. It could be argued that a note of doubt seemed present in her voice when she spoke about the idea that her half-brother had taken his own life. It is worth repeating what she told Hutton. She said:

Believe me, I have lain awake many nights since, going over in my mind whether I missed anything significant. In my line of work I do deal with people who may have suicidal thoughts and I ought to be able to spot those, even in a telephone conversation... He certainly did not convey to me that he was feeling depressed; and absolutely nothing that would have alerted me to the fact that he might have been considering suicide.

Another reader, Peter Mulvihill, wrote to me to point out what he considered a peculiarity concerning the amount of blood Dr Kelly is said to have lost. Mr Mulvihill is a wildlife enthusiast and for more than twenty years has observed and fed foxes near his Northamptonshire house. He said that if Dr Kelly really did haemorrhage a significant amount of blood, as officially claimed, and if his body was lying on Harrowdown Hill for up to eighteen hours, it is striking that no fox or other wild animal in this semi-rural Oxfordshire location was attracted by the scent. Mr Mulvihill acknowledged that this is not a pleasant thought, and it is only his view as a countryman, but he was moved to comment on how strange it is to him that there appears to be no record in the post mortem report of any interference with the blood on and around Dr Kelly's body, despite it having been exposed to the elements for a maximum of eighteen hours between the afternoon of

17 July, when he was last seen alive, and the morning of 18 July, when his body was found. He said this runs counter to his experience of monitoring foxes' feeding habits, whereby they will 'lick clean' anything containing blood. This is an undeniably interesting observation, albeit one without any scientific basis.

It also leads on to a point regarding Dr Kelly's clothing when his body was found. In August 2018, I submitted a Freedom of Information request to Thames Valley Police seeking full details of any tests conducted on his clothes, including what kinds of tests were carried out; by whom they were carried out; where they were carried out; and on what date they were carried out. I also asked to see the test results. A force spokesman wrote to me a month after receiving my request to say that a further month was needed in order to consider their answer. In October 2018, the force duly wrote to me again with a final response. It was, regrettably, less comprehensive than I had hoped.

I was told that tests were indeed carried out on Dr Kelly's clothes but the police refused to confirm what types of tests these were. They were happy to confirm that the forensic biologist Roy Green and toxicologist Alexander Allan, both of the Oxfordshire-based company Forensic Alliance Ltd, had conducted the tests but they did not know on what date. As to the results, I was advised that these must also remain confidential. The reasons given by the police for withholding so much information were that 'current and future investigations would be compromised' if they told me too much about them. I was also told: 'The force is firmly of the view that the family members of Dr Kelly would be negatively affected by the generation of any publicity if this information were disclosed into the public domain under FOI. The test results are extremely detailed and provide very personal information, regarded as special category data.' And, furthermore, the police response stated that 'the fact that the case is now closed and over ten years old, reduces significantly any public interest in disclosure.'

All of this sits rather uncomfortably with me. Not only has Thames Valley Police been happy to furnish me and others with all sorts of information relating to the Dr Kelly case in the past, including sharing test results, but I am also perplexed by what 'very personal information' it feared divulging by telling me about tests carried out merely on his clothes – understood to be a pair of jeans, a shirt, a Barbour jacket, a cap, and his shoes and socks.

In this context, it should not be forgotten that in October 2010 the government decided to publish Dr Kelly's post mortem report. It really *did* contain highly personal information about the sorts of tests carried out on his body, plus a full description of an intimate body part. It is striking that the police were not able to be so transparent in response to my Freedom of Information request. Lastly, it is also profoundly unsatisfactory that the force should have used the passing of time as an excuse for claiming the public interest in this matter has somehow decreased. This was an entirely subjective piece of thinking on the part of Thames Valley Police.

Since Roy Green and Alexander Allan were responsible for testing Dr Kelly's clothes, I was prompted to look again at their evidence to the Hutton Inquiry. Interestingly, Allan was not asked – and did not volunteer – anything about Dr Kelly's clothes when he appeared on the morning of 3 September 2003. Neither did Green, who appeared that afternoon. But Green did explain on that day that he was carrying out tests which were 'ongoing'. He said he had sent 'at a guess 50 items' to the laboratory 'to analyse, to carry out DNA profiling, to look at some of the [blood] staining in a little more detail.'

He went on: 'I have provided a spreadsheet with a kind of a snapshot of where we are today about what items have been examined, what has been found on them, which items were profiled, the results of those profile tests, although I have not put my evidence down in a statement form as yet.' James Dingemans, who examined him, then said: 'I think when all that is concluded Assistant Chief Constable Page is going to come back and tell us the results.'

When Page, some of whose evidence has proved extremely hard to understand because of its contradictory nature, subsequently returned to the Hutton Inquiry almost three weeks later, on 23 September, he was not asked and did not utter a word about the tests on Dr Kelly's clothing. He concluded his evidence by saying:

> I still have a few lines of inquiry to complete, although I should stress that I do not anticipate that those lines of inquiry will reveal anything of an earth-shattering nature; and I can say that based upon the inquiries we have made at the moment, further to my statement, that I do not believe that there was any third party involvement at the scene of Dr Kelly's death. I am reasonably satisfied that there was no third party involvement or criminal dimension to Dr Kelly's death in the wider dimension.

It is difficult to resist wondering why he was allowed to leave the High Court that day not only without having spoken about the promised test results but also ending his testimony on such a seemingly casual note. Who would have thought that a senior police officer saying he was only 'reasonably satisfied' there was no third party involvement in a suspicious death would be deemed acceptable to a senior law lord like Lord Hutton? No coroner, surely, would have stood for this.

One man who had a less straightforward time than ACC Page at the Hutton Inquiry and who, arguably, did not emerge from Hutton's report with his reputation enhanced was David Broucher. A professional diplomat who joined the diplomatic corps in 1966 and served as British Ambassador to Prague between 1997 and 2001, Broucher gave evidence to the inquiry as a result of having drawn to the attention of Foreign Office colleagues an extraordinary remark Dr Kelly made to him shortly before he died. Chillingly, Dr Kelly told him he thought he would be 'found dead in the woods' if Iraq was ever invaded.

When Iraq was occupied in March 2003, and Dr Kelly was then found dead in a wood in July 2003, Broucher decided he had no choice but to reveal his hitherto private conversation with Dr Kelly to Foreign Office officials. He did so just over two weeks after Dr Kelly's body was found. The police were immediately informed and it was hastily agreed Broucher would appear as a witness at the Hutton Inquiry.

Until now, there has always been confusion about whether Dr Kelly's and Broucher's encounter took place in 2002 or 2003. While this matter should have been resolved easily, it now appears very much as though Hutton had an interest in maintaining that confusion. I have not had cause to mention Broucher previously in this book but, when I was working on this new chapter for the paperback edition in the autumn of 2018, he was prepared to meet me to discuss his contact with Dr Kelly. His contribution has been illuminating.

Firstly, it is important to return to those aspects of

the Hutton Inquiry which relate to Broucher. At the time
Broucher gave evidence, on 21 August 2003, he was the
UK's Permanent Representative to the Conference on Dis-
armament in Geneva. He told Dingemans, who examined
him, that he had met Dr Kelly just once and that he
'thought' this meeting had taken place six months earlier,
on 27 February, in Geneva. The purpose of the meeting,
arranged at short notice, was to discuss Iraqi weapons
capability. As well as providing testimony about Kelly's
'dead in the woods' prophesy, which Broucher said he
probably took at the time to be a 'throwaway' remark, he
noted during his evidence that he 'thought he might have
meant that he was at risk of being attacked by the Iraqis
in some way.' He said he understood from Dr Kelly that
he 'might be concerned that he would be thought to have
lied to some of his contacts in Iraq' if the country were ever
invaded. Broucher also said during his evidence: 'He [Dr
Kelly] said to me that there had been a lot of pressure to
make the [WMD] dossier as robust as possible; that every
judgment in it had been closely fought over.' This last point
by Broucher was made with characteristic restraint.

Despite Broucher's evidence clearly placing his contact
with Dr Kelly in 2003, Dingeman surprisingly continued
to press Broucher as to the date of the meeting. Broucher
had to admit no minute of it was made and he did
not record it in his own diary either. Although he had
effectively volunteered himself as a witness to the inquiry,

his potentially explosive revelation about Dr Kelly being 'found dead in the woods' apparently seemed of less significance to the Hutton Inquiry than did the year in which he and Dr Kelly had met.

Confirmation of the Hutton Inquiry's desire to establish that this meeting occurred in 2002, and not 2003, is provided by the approach taken by Dingemans when Dr Kelly's daughter, Rachel, subsequently gave evidence to the inquiry on 1 September, some eleven days after Broucher. The first point Dingemans addressed when examining her related to Dr Kelly's diary.

Dingemans said to Rachel: 'Can I ask you to look at a diary entry for 2002? Before I ask you to look at that, can you just tell me where you found the diary?'

She replied: 'Yes. The diary was in my father's study.'

Of this 2002 diary, she went on to say without any prompting by Dingemans regarding the month he wished to consider: 'It mentions specifically a meeting with David Broucher on 18th February 2002, and the interesting thing with my father's diaries is he tended to write entries in them after the event and this would have been a meeting that he actually had because it is in his diary.'

Dingemans read to the court the relevant diary entry. It stated Dr Kelly had met Broucher at 9.30 a.m on 18 February 2002 (as opposed to 2003) at the US Mission in Geneva. His flight details into Geneva on 17 February and out of Geneva on 20 February were also logged.

Dingemans then put Dr Kelly's diary for 2003 up on the courtroom screen and said to Rachel: 'Finally, just to show the diary entry for February 2003. You will remember Mr Broucher thought the meeting was in February 2003. Does the 2003 diary show any entry for Mr Broucher in 2003?'

She replied: 'No, and in fact it does not record any trip to Geneva either. The only trip I have noticed is the February trip the previous year.' In her evidence Rachel said she was adamant that her father was in New York, and not in Geneva, in February 2003.

From this it can be concluded that it was important to the Hutton Inquiry to prove that Broucher was wrong in thinking he met Dr Kelly in February 2003. Indeed, with the intention of settling that matter unambiguously, Hutton wrote in his final report:

> Mr Broucher was clear in his evidence that he had only met Dr Kelly on one occasion. After he had given evidence, Dr Kelly's daughter, Miss Rachel Kelly, looked at her father's diary and found that it contained an entry that he had met Mr Broucher in Geneva on 18 February 2002… Therefore it appears to be clear that Dr Kelly's one meeting with Mr Broucher was in February 2002 and not in February 2003.

To this end, it is hard to escape the conclusion that

Rachel Kelly was unwittingly used to discredit Broucher through her surprisingly deep understanding of her father's diaries and diary-keeping habits – which she had apparently pored over in the six weeks between his death and her appearance at the Hutton Inquiry.

Even as matters stood at the point of delivery of the Hutton Report, this was a superficial and counterintuitive conclusion to have reached, given Broucher's testimony. Yet if Hutton and his lead counsel had stopped to think about this more closely, they would have realized that Broucher's evidence was sound. Apart from anything else, the WMD dossier about which he and Dr Kelly spoke had not even been written in February 2002. Neither were Western forces on the brink of invading Iraq at that time.

Believing that Lord Hutton's comments about him in the Inquiry Report represented him in a negative light, Broucher decided he must prove the veracity of his testimony. He has pieced together the jigsaw of his contact with Dr Kelly and has, he thinks, worked out what happened.

When Broucher and I met, he admitted to me that he was incorrect to tell the Hutton Inquiry that he met Dr Kelly only once. The speed with which his appearance was arranged meant he had overlooked that they had in fact met on two occasions. The first time they met was very briefly in 2002, after Dr Kelly gave a talk in Switzerland. Broucher chatted to him after this event, which is perhaps why their encounter was logged in Dr Kelly's 2002 diary. Broucher's reason for wanting to engage with Dr Kelly was that he sought an official meeting with him. Dr Kelly, however, was too busy at that time for a proper meeting. He did promise, though, that he would meet Broucher at some future point.

A year later, in February 2003, Dr Kelly rang Broucher unexpectedly at his office asking to see him. Broucher told me he believes Dr Kelly called him from Geneva Airport, having just stepped off a flight from America. He was apparently in Geneva to see a German colleague, whose identity Broucher refused to disclose to me but which he has established independently.

Broucher's secretary was on holiday, which explains why no minute of the meeting was taken and why it wasn't noted in his own diary. Broucher told me he and Dr Kelly spoke for about an hour face-to-face. He said Dr Kelly volunteered that he was particularly concerned about the British government's forty-five-minute WMD claim because he knew it was not true. And, crucially, Broucher told me that during their meeting Dr Kelly named Alastair Campbell as one of those exerting pressure to make the report as strong as possible on Iraq's possession of WMD. Broucher did not mention Campbell in his Hutton testimony, or indeed anywhere else before telling me this. But it is surely of the highest relevance that Dr Kelly apparently shared his concerns about Campbell with Broucher a full three months before he did the same with Andrew Gilligan. For this would mean that Dr Kelly tried to warn at least one other person in an influential position of his doubts about the British government's activities. Clearly, Campbell was at the front of Dr Kelly's mind as a person who Dr Kelly believed was at the heart of the policy to take Britain into war in Iraq – an idea that Campbell has always denied vigorously.

An obvious question to ask is why Dr Kelly's 2003 diary did not record his meeting with Broucher on 27 February. Broucher told me he was actually shown the diary by police after he had first contacted the Foreign Office to reveal to them Dr Kelly's 'dead in the woods' comment. Instead of recording Dr Kelly's intended presence in Geneva, the diary mentioned his visit around that time to New York. Given his meticulous nature, as described by his daughter Rachel, it looks very much as though Dr Kelly wanted to cover his tracks in order, discreetly and for his own reasons, to travel to Switzerland. It was Dr Kelly's misleading diary entry for February 2003 that led to Broucher's evidence being implied by Hutton to be unreliable.

My further analysis of all this is as follows. When, on 5 August 2003, Broucher first reported to the Foreign Office that Dr Kelly had told him he might be 'found dead in the woods', the explicitness of the prophetic wording took all interested parties by surprise. And yet what could have been construed as potentially useful evidence to the Hutton Inquiry in furthering the thesis that Dr Kelly had taken his own life – a thesis which it is clear at other times was important to Hutton and Dingemans to promote – apparently became less important to them than discrediting Broucher.

Why would this be? One explanation that cannot be discounted is that Hutton might have feared the only other plausible conclusion to be drawn from Dr Kelly's choice of words could gain currency – namely that in February 2003 when Dr Kelly met Broucher, Dr Kelly might have been anticipating his own assassination. Broucher gave testimony to this effect to the inquiry.

Preventing this interpretation gaining credence was, seemingly, of greater concern to Hutton than was capitalising on the opportunity to show that Dr Kelly might have been having suicidal thoughts as early as February 2003.

It has been suggested by some that Dr Kelly's 'dead in the woods' remark points to the idea that, long before his demise, he had already worked out the location of his death. For holders of this view this in turn somehow 'proves' that he was planning his suicide. Professor Keith Hawton, the Professor of Psychiatry at Oxford University who gave evidence to Hutton about Dr Kelly's mental state, gave no credence to this theory, describing the 'dead in the woods' remark as a 'pure coincidence'. His opinion was taken on board by Hutton.

Broucher told me it is impossible for him personally to

judge the final significance of Dr Kelly's bizarre prediction in the light of what happened to him. He did make it clear that he liked Dr Kelly, and found him to be a well-informed professional who was interested in the truth. Nonetheless, and for understandable reasons, Broucher feels he was 'discredited' by the way his evidence was portrayed at the inquiry. Dr Kelly's 2003 diary is not reliable, and Broucher's vindication, to which this account has hopefully been able to contribute, is well earned.

October 2018

ACKNOWLEDGEMENTS

Writing this book was made significantly easier thanks to the following people, each of whom helped in different ways: Camilla Alban Davies, Norman Baker, the late Martin Birnstingl, the late Dr Chris Burns-Cox, Margaret Crick, Neil Darbyshire, Dr Stephen Frost, Hilary Gibson, Margaret Goslett, Matthew Goslett, Peter Goslett, David Halpin, Sue Halpin, Margaret Hindle, Mary Hollingsworth, Anne-Marie Ingram, John Laird, Mark Lawson, David Leeming, Frank Pile, Dr Michael Powers QC, Professor Colin Pritchard, Dr Andrew Rouse, the late Brian Spencer, Peter Straker, Tom Teodorczuk, Rowena Thursby, Hugh Venables, Jayne Venables, Dr Andrew Watt and Wendy Wearmouth.

The 830 donors who in 2010 responded so quickly and generously to the call to raise the £40,000 which enabled David Halpin to bring his case to the High Court also deserve special praise. Their collective role in trying to settle a matter so clearly in the public interest is proof that some people are still determined to stop things from falling away.

My agent, Peter Robinson, provided valuable advice and assistance whenever it was needed. His commitment to this venture from the outset ensured I kept going and I am very grateful to him.

I would also like to thank everyone at Head of Zeus – in particular Neil Belton, Helen Francis and Christian Duck – for their unflagging enthusiasm, kindness and professionalism. Any factual errors in the text are my responsibility.

The well-organised mind and unfailing support of my father, Roland, were vital to the completion of this project. To him, I owe an incalculable debt.

Finally, I thank my wife, Priscilla. Without her constant encouragement, good ideas and extraordinary patience, this book might never have been written at all. I dedicate it to her and to Penelope and Humphrey.

INDEX